Alternative Policies for America

AMERICA'S HOUSING CRISIS

WHAT IS TO BE DONE?

Edited by
CHESTER HARTMAN

The Institute for Policy Studies

Routledge & Kegan Paul
Boston, London, Melbourne and Henley

The Institute for Policy Studies, founded in 1963, is a transnational center for research, education, and social invention. IPS sponsors critical study of U.S. policy, and proposes alternative strategies and visions. Programs focus on national security, foreign policy, human rights, the international economic order, domestic affairs, and knowledge and politics.

The Institute for Policy Studies is a non-partisan research institute. The views expressed in this study are those of the authors.

First published in 1983
by Routledge & Kegan Paul plc
9 Park Street, Boston, Mass. 02108, USA,
39 Store Street, London WC1E 7DD,
464 St Kilda Road, Melbourne,
Victoria 3004, Australia and
Broadway House, Newtown Road,
Henley-on-Thames, Oxon RG9 1EN
Phototypeset in Linotron Times by
Input Typesetting Ltd, London
and printed in the United States of America
Copyright © Institute for Policy Studies 1983
1901 Que Street N.W., Washington, D.C., 20009, USA
No part of this book may be reproduced in
any form without permission from the publisher,
except for the quotation of brief passages in criticism

Library of Congress Cataloging in Publication Data

America's housing crisis.
(Alternative policies for America)
Includes bibliographical references.
1. Housing policy—United States—Addresses, essays,
lectures.   I. Hartman, Chester W.   II. Institute for
Policy Studies.   III. Series.
HD7293.A6877   1983   363.5'8'0973   83-11228

ISBN 0-7102-0039-0
ISBN 0-7102-0041-2 (pbk)

Contents

Contributors

EMILY PARADISE ACHTENBERG is a housing consultant working with community groups in Boston and a member of the Planners Network Steering Committee. She recently co-directed the technical assistance and evaluation components of a HUD-funded demonstration involving the management and disposition of HUD-foreclosed multi-family housing. She is the author of numerous technical reports, studies, and community-oriented publications on subsidized housing, rent control, and resident-controlled ownership. She is a former president and staff member of Urban Planning Aid, Inc., an advocacy planning organization.

JOHN ATLAS, a lawyer specializing in landlord-tenant law, is an editor and publisher of *Shelterforce*, a national housing publication; a founder of the National Tenants Union; and Vice-President of the New Jersey Tenants Organization. He is the author of several articles on housing, politics, and law and has appeared on numerous television shows. He recently produced a videotape on the housing crisis in New Jersey.

PAUL DAVIDOFF, a planner and lawyer, is Professor of Urban Studies at Queens College, City University of New York. He also is Director of the Queens College Center for Metropolitan Action (formerly titled Metropolitan Action Institute and Suburban Action Institute). He has been active in promoting advocacy planning and is concerned with democratizing the planning process.

CUSHING N. DOLBEARE is President of the National Low Income Housing Coalition, established in 1974, the principal national lobbying group for low-income housing programs. She is also Executive Secretary of the Low Income Housing Information Service. She was formerly Executive Secretary of the National Rural Housing Coalition and Managing Director of the Housing Association of Delaware Valley (formerly the Philadelphia Housing Association). She is a board member of Americans for Democratic Action and the American Friends Service Committee and in 1977–8 chaired HUD's Task Force on Tenant Participation in Public Housing Management.

PETER DREIER is Assistant Professor of Sociology at Tufts University. He has written widely on housing policy and tenants' rights and is currently co-authoring (with John Atlas) a book, *The Renters' Revolt*, to be published by Temple University Press. He works closely with a number of community organizations, including Massachusetts Fair Share and the Massachusetts Tenants Organization, and was a National Science Foundation Public Service Science Resident in 1981–2 to provide technical assistance to grassroots groups. His writings have appeared in *Working Papers, The Nation, In These Times, The Progressive, Social Policy, Shelterforce*, and other publications. He recently coordinated a research project on the Boston power structure called "Who Rules Boston?" He is on the National Executive Committee of the Democratic Socialists of America.

CHESTER HARTMAN is a Visiting Fellow at the Institute for Policy Studies in Washington, D.C. He has taught urban planning at Harvard, Cornell, Yale, the University of North Carolina, and the University of California (Berkeley) and chairs the Planners Network, a national organization of progressive urban and rural planners. He has been active in community-based housing struggles in Boston and San Francisco and is the author of *Housing Urban America* (Aldine, 1980), *Yerba Buena: Land Grab and Community Resistance in San Francisco* (Glide, 1974; revised edition in preparation), *Housing and Social Policy* (Prentice-Hall, 1975), and *Displacement: How to Fight It* (National Housing Law Project, 1982).

PETER MARCUSE, a lawyer and planner, is active on housing and related issues in New York City, where he chairs the Housing Committee of Manhattan's Community Board 9. He is Professor of Urban Planning at Columbia University and a member of the Planners Network. He was formerly president of the Los Angeles Planning Commission, on the faculty of the University of California at Los Angeles, and Majority Leader of the Waterbury (Connecticut) Board of Aldermen. His articles have appeared in *The Nation, Social Policy*, the *International Journal of Urban and Regional Research*, and many other publications.

FLORENCE WAGMAN ROISMAN has, since 1971, been counsel to the National Housing Law Project, a Legal Services back-up center. From 1967 to 1970, she was a staff attorney, specializing in housing law, with the Neighborhood Legal Services Program of the District of Columbia. She has taught at the University of Maryland Law School, Catholic University Law School, Antioch School of Law, and Georgetown University Law Center. She holds a B.A. from the University of Connecticut and an LL.B. from Harvard. She is a partner in the Washington, D.C. law firm of Roisman, Reno and Cavanaugh.

MICHAEL E. STONE is Associate Professor and Head of the Center for Community Planning at the College of Public and Community Service, University of Massachusetts in Boston. He is the author of *People Before Property: A Real Estate Primer and Research Guide* and *Research: A Manual for Arson Analysis and Property Research*; he is co-author of *Tenants First: A Research and Organizing Guide to FHA Housing* and *Hostage: Housing and the Massachusetts Fiscal Crisis*; and is completing work on *Shelter Poverty: New Ideas on Housing Affordability*.

1 Introduction: A radical perspective on housing reform

Chester Hartman

This editor's introduction is being written just as President Reagan has submitted his 1984 budget to Congress. For the third year in a row, housing is taking it on the chin. This administration seems intent on reversing, to the maximum possible extent, the federal government's fifty-year-old role in providing housing aid for those the market cannot adequately serve.[1] And that category continues to grow, perceptibly and relentlessly.

The government's move on housing

Specifically, the Reagan Administration's goals (to a large extent already achieved) are:

(1) To virtually end all programs that directly add, through construction and substantial rehabilitation, to the stock of housing available to lower-income households. The 1984 budget proposes a 94 per cent cut in the level of new budget authority for housing (distinct from ongoing contractual housing payments for housing which HUD already assists). New budget authority for HUD's low-income housing programs is about 2 per cent of what it was when President Reagan took office and 2 per cent of the budget President Ford proposed in 1977, just before leaving office (Low Income Housing Information Service, 1983).* Con-

* References for all chapters are given beginning on p. 237.

struction of new public housing, new or substantially rehabilitated Section 8 housing, new Section 202 housing for the
elderly and handicapped – these programs are totally ended
or all but ended.

(2) To reduce housing subsidy requirements, by forcing
recipients to devote higher proportions of their own inadequate incomes to housing. Rather than paying 25 per cent
of their incomes in order to qualify for a subsidy, lower-
income households must now pay 30 per cent – a change
that over a five-year period extracts nearly $6 billion from
the pockets of the poor to get the government off the hook
by a similar amount. And the new budget reintroduces a
proposal made in 1982, but rejected by the Senate Agriculture Committee, to count the value of food stamps (which
half of all public housing and Section 8 residents receive) in
determining rent levels and eligibility for housing subsidy
programs – in effect taxing 30 per cent of these benefits,
with the lowest income households, who receive the largest
food stamp allotments, being taxed most severely. Other
similar changes in housing subsidy calculations are proposed
to extract more out of those who can least afford it, but the
food stamp gambit is perhaps the most obscene.

(3) To reduce the existing stock of subsidized housing,
through demolition, conversion, sale, and planned deterioration. HUD's plans are that 100,000 public housing units
– 8 per cent of the current stock – will be sold or demolished
over the next five years (Bureau of National Affairs, 1983,
p. 882), and similar efforts are underway to reduce the stock
of units subsidized under HUD and Farmers Home Administration programs (National Housing Law Project, 1981,
1982).

(4) To rely exclusively on the existing housing supply to
meet low-income housing needs, via introduction of a limited, direct cash housing payment designed to cover the gap
between existing rent levels and what lower-income households can afford. The model for such an approach – tested
since 1970 via HUD's Experimental Housing Allowance
Program – revealed that the program was least successful in

aiding minority, very poor and large households, and those living in poor quality dwelling units; that only one-fourth of the housing payment was used to obtain better housing; that little mobility was triggered by the program; and that little renovation work other than minor patchup tasks resulted from use of housing allowances. The approach assumes the existence of large numbers of moderately-priced vacancies in decent or easily and cheaply repairable condition, and a housing market that does not discriminate against applicants because of race, household size and composition, source of income, or life-style – a world of fantasy and wishes rather than what the real housing market looks like (see Hartman 1983a; Abrams, 1983; Hartman, 1983b). And in any event, only a tiny fraction of those who need such assistance will get it under the administration's version of this approach; it is to be a very limited program, not an entitlement.

All this is being done partly out of "political philosophy" – less federal involvement and intervention (at least when it comes to traditional welfare programs that aid the poor; in other instances, such as seeking to notify the parents of teenage girls who request contraceptives or withholding federal housing and community development aid from cities that enact effective rent controls, the hands-off policy of the Reagan Administration yields to more fundamental biases and class interests). And these goals are being pursued partly to save money, because housing aid is so expensive. The good itself is costly, the gap between housing costs and what people can afford keeps growing, and our housing programs have generally involved long-term (5- to 40-year) commitments. The per-household assistance level proposed for the voucher program level will be about 20 per cent below what the Section 8 existing housing program makes available. (For a more detailed discussion of these four thrusts – which amount to what Emily Achtenberg and Peter Marcuse term an "ideological attack on housing standards" – see Hartman, 1982a.)

Challenging the current housing system

Whereas the Reaganites are acting punitively and parsimoniously with respect to housing programs, they have a real point in claiming that housing programs are expensive – a point that progressive analysts and activists ought not to deny, and should use aggressively and creatively. The fact is that our housing programs are so expensive because they make virtually no attempt to influence the cost structure of our market-dominated housing system. Rather, they accept as givens the enormous profitability of the housing system for a wide variety of actors – lenders, land and real estate speculators, brokers, landlords, materials manufacturers, and others – and simply try to shoehorn a relatively small number of needy households into that system. And if the total bill gets too high (relative to the existing tax system or budgetary priorities), then regulations are tightened, aggregate and per-recipient subsidy amounts are decreased, and whole programs are eliminated. No effort is made to structure housing subsidies and the housing system more generally to reduce profit-taking from housing and to bring costs down to the level where more people can afford it without subsidies or with smaller subsidies.

By contrast, our view is that if the nation really is in an economic crisis – whether it be due to lower productivity, the political decisions made on how to allocate existing revenues and resources, or the overall unequal distribution of wealth and income – we can no longer allow the extensive profit-taking, or perhaps any profit-taking, on so basic a human need as housing. And that means increasingly turning to the public and non- and limited-profit sectors to meet the nation's housing needs. The profit-oriented housing industry is not interested in cost containment or social goals. Its drive to maximize profits from every aspect of housing production, ownership, operation, and transfer must be sharply reined, if the majority of Americans are to get decent, affordable housing. Serious efforts to do this are likely to cause the various actors in the private housing sector to withdraw to other enterprises – lenders to shift their money to other types of loans, real estate developers and landlords to turn to non-residential properties, etc. For these reasons, and because there is a strong case in and of itself to be made for public and private non-profit housing enterprise, this is the direction in which we must turn, and is the central theme of the essays in this book.

It now is irrefutable, except to those who simply do not wish to acknowledge the fact, that the housing system is not performing in a way that produces, for the vast majority of Americans, satisfaction of the economic, social, and personal need for a decent place to live, in a decent and suitable environment, at an affordable cost.

The conservatives/reactionaries respond to the growing housing crisis by saying (to some people), "Tighten your belts, we're in tough times – accept lower wages and benefits, higher unemployment levels, a reduced living standard." The traditional liberal response is to propose 1960s-type programs of greater government spending and involvement, but without any basic structural changes in how the system operates. Many of their programs – urban renewal, the federal highway system, FHA/VA mortgages – in fact created serious housing problems for some even as they were helping others solve theirs, and also helped create the illusions and structural flaws that characterize the current housing system. In the housing area, as in so many others, it is obvious that traditional liberal responses are no longer sufficient, if ever they were.

This is the time for people to take a deep and honest look at what is wrong with our housing system – why it can't meet the society's needs – and to propose alternatives that really are capable of providing everyone in our society with what Congress, way back in its preamble to the 1949 Housing Act, said we ought to have – "a decent home and suitable living environment for every American family." That condition of course cannot be met if people are paying more than they can afford for housing and therefore leaving themselves with inadequate amounts for life's other necessities. (And here Michael Stone's research on "shelter poverty" – the concept that no single housing cost/income ratio should be promulgated; that what people can afford for housing, if they are to have sufficient income left over for other necessities of life, is a function of income level and household size; and that for truly low-income large households the "proper" proportion of income that public policy should demand is 0 per cent – is a major contribution to housing analysis and program formulation.)

What we believe

The six contributions in this volume – all responding to the question of what should be done about America's housing crisis – represent a variety of approaches, some more comprehensive than others, some more radical than others.

Cushing Dolbeare puts forward the eight-point program the National Low Income Housing Coalition has developed: an income-based housing payment entitlement; expanded production and preservation programs for needs not met by housing payments; guaranteed fair access to housing; more progressive tax and spending policies; greater reliance on community-based non-profit entities; retention of the existing subsidized housing stock; cheaper and more available housing credit; and reduction of displacement. In an Appendix to her chapter, Dolbeare offers a detailed critique of the tax expenditure system for homeowners.

Florence Roisman concentrates primarily on the considerable portion of the nation's housing stock characterized by direct or indirect involvement by one level of government or another, as owner, subsidizer, insurer, or mortgage provider. Maximizing the leverage inherent in this involvement, through legislation, litigation, and community and national political action, can prevent loss of this stock to the unregulated private sector, and also can be the core of a significant alternative housing system in the U.S. that can then be expanded as it proves its superiority to the unregulated, commodified housing stock in meeting people's needs.

Michael Stone proposes three short-term steps: cutting the federal deficit and redistributing income downward (through cuts in military spending, repeal of recent tax cuts – which primarily aided the wealthy – closing tax loopholes, eliminating the income tax for low-income people, and targeting housing and economic development subsidies to non-speculative owners and developers); federal credit controls; and federal price controls. His longer-range proposals involve massive income redistribution, vastly reduced dependence on credit for the provision of housing, and creating alternative ownership and investment vehicles that operate for society's overall well-being rather than for speculation and profit maximization. He also offers some immediate applications of his shelter poverty concept to the rent-setting formulas used for public housing tenants.

John Atlas and Peter Dreier concentrate more on the political mobilization process that will engender radical housing reform. They see the nation's renters – a little over one-third of all households at present – as "the sleeping giant." The housing crisis is making it harder for people, even middle-class people, to own their own homes, and is leading to an identity of interests between tenants and homeowners. Growing tenant organization and sophistication have led to considerable gains in legal protections for tenants over the past two decades, and Atlas and Dreier see the potential for alliances and coalitions that can produce basic reforms in the housing system, by tying tenants' interests to those of other groups and by politicizing their common struggle.

Paul Davidoff delves more deeply into the meaning of a housing entitlement program. He develops a two-faceted location right, based on both the right to housing mobility and the right to housing stability. And he links housing with economic development, so that housing programs can help bring jobs, decent incomes, and a solid economic base to all communities. To the extent that jobs and incomes poli-

cies can provide more people with adequate resources, housing subsidies per se (but not housing market controls) will
be less needed.

Finally, Emily Achtenberg and Peter Marcuse outline in
broad strokes a criticism of how and why the housing system
functions as it does in the U.S. today, and why it is not
meeting housing needs. Based on their analysis, they spell
out the general principles and strategic implications of a
comprehensive program to "decommodify" housing, through
social rather than profit-oriented ownership and production
of housing, public financing, land-use and cost controls,
socially determined allocation of resources, resident control
of neighborhoods, and guarantees of housing choice.

There is thus substantial agreement among most or all of
us on a number of basics, as laid out below. And this reflects
in part the degree to which we have more or less drawn on
each other's work in recent years and deepened our common
understanding of the nature of the housing problem and
what must be done to meet it. A process of circulating
chapter drafts among us also helped to solidify some common positions.

The understanding we try to impart is of the structural
nature of the housing crisis: that it is rooted in the failure
of incomes to keep up with housing costs, in the over-
reliance on credit for building and buying housing, and in
the workings of the profit system as it manifests itself in all
phases of housing development, ownership, trading, and
management.

We also try to understand and explain the housing crisis
not in isolation but as a central and emblematic part of a
broader crisis of the U.S. economy and social system, in
turn now part of an international economic crisis. Just as
the current system cannot house its people decently, it cannot feed them adequately, or provide them with decent
health care, education, environmental protections, and bod-
ily security (either in the international sphere or in the
neighborhood). The same insights, goals, and programmatic
directions necessary to solve our housing crisis have applica-

bility to these other spheres as well. Or, as Michael Stone so well expresses it, "there really can be no solution to the housing affordability problem without a solution to the broader political and economic crisis, but at the same time there can be no solution to the broader problems that does not deal with the roots of the housing crisis."

Part of that education role involves describing how housing is treated in other countries where the goal of decent housing for all is taken more seriously and where social justice criteria are given precedence over profitability imperatives. Much more description and analysis is needed of the housing systems of Western industrialized democracies such as Sweden and Great Britain, Third World socialist states like China and Cuba, radical urban reform programs such as existed in Bologna in the 1970s, and fascinating historical case studies such as Vienna of the 1920s.[2] At a minimum, it is important for Americans to learn how extensive and successful the non-profit and public housing sectors have been in countries like West Germany, England, and Sweden, and the ways in which many countries have surpassed the United States in solving the affordability problem.

At their most generalizable level, the alternatives we put forth lie in the direction of "decommodification": removing as much of the housing system as possible from the profit-maximization drive, and basing it instead on development of institutions and actors, financing, development, and management mechanisms that have as their central motor provision of decent, affordable housing service rather than the extraction of profits. Our central theme is that decent, affordable housing is a *right*, an *entitlement* (not merely a goal), and that the country unquestionably has the resources to make this available to all its people.

Other common themes through the book are:

> That the government must make a quantum leap in the amount of resources it directly devotes to housing. Data in the Achtenberg-Marcuse and Stone

chapters show how little our nation spends on housing, compared with other advanced economies, our own economic capacities, and what is now spent in socially wasteful areas. A recent study by Jobs With Peace (nd [1983]) spells out the implications of shifting $20 billion a year for five years from the military budget to housing. Using direct construction, weatherization, and public housing renovation grants, a revolving loan fund for buyers of new homes and recovery of abandoned buildings, and grants to state home mortgage finance agencies to subsidize private homebuyers, the annual $20 billion shift over a five-year period would create 1.9 million new housing units (nearly two-fifths in the public sector, the remainder with a public "handle" permitting profit restrictions), rehabilitate and weatherize 2.3 million others, and in the process create 1.5 million construction and related jobs (23 per cent more than are created by an equivalent military hardware expenditure). Applying the principles of "decommod-ification" most explicitly set forth in the Achtenberg-Marcuse and Stone chapters provides the most efficient and effective way to expend those additional resources.

That wholesale revision is needed in the income tax system as it affects housing. "Tax expenditures" resulting from the deductibility of mortgage interest and property tax payments by homeowners have gotten totally out of hand, rising by over $10 billion annually, primarily as a result of rising house prices, interest rates, and extraction of value increases by homeowners via refinancing. The system is notoriously regressive, as is pointed out in elaborate detail by Cushing Dolbeare, who also makes the remarkable observation that these regressive tax expenditures in 1981 alone exceeded HUD's (and predecessor agencies') cumulative direct federal outlays for lower-income housing programs since their inception in 1937![3] The ways in which the tax system's treatment of capital gains from housing sales adds to inflationary pressures, a speculative mentality, and dangerous over-reliance on housing credit are suggested in Michael Stone's chapter.

That, as Florence Roisman details, immediate protection is needed for the existing stock of government-aided housing, some 4.5 million units that are virtually irreplaceable and are under severe attack by the Reagan Administration. To attack these direct expenditure programs, aimed primarily at renters, at the same time the indirect tax expenditures for middle- and upper-income homeowners are rising at astronomical rates, is outrageous.

That there is, or should be, a "right to stay put," as Paul Davidoff and Florence Roisman detail, a tenure or property right that protects tenants against forcible removal from their homes and neighborhoods simply because the non-resident property owner wishes to increase his or her profit from ownership of that property (see Hartman, forthcoming; Hartman, Keating, and LeGates, 1982).

That radical housing reform will come about only through political mobilization equal to or more powerful than the organized housing interests in the for-profit sector. Those who control and benefit from the current housing system will not allow fundamental change without real struggle.

The making of housing policy

Housing policy has always been made in Washington, through the interaction of the Administration and Congress on the one hand, and the various nationally organized interest groups on the other. Business interests like the National Association of Realtors, the National Association of Home Builders, the U.S. League of Savings Institutions, the American Bankers Association, the Mortgage Bankers Association, and the Associated General Contractors are well represented and highly influential in the process of developing policies, laws, and regulations. (For a good description of the political activities and influence of the National Association of Home Builders, see Lilley, 1980.) The American Bankers Association alone has a staff of 400 in its headquarters Washington office. These groups, through their Political Action Committees (PACs), are major financial contributors to the campaigns of members of the key Congressional committees that deal with housing legislation. Realtors PAC, for example, led all other PACs in contributions to the 1982 Congressional races, contributing over $2 million, $400,000 more than its closest competitor, American Medical PAC (Clymer, 1983). Such contributions may take the indirect form of speakers' fees as well: Jake Garn, the Republican Chair of the Senate Committee on Banking, Housing and Urban Affairs, reported $78,000 in speaking fees in 1981, "most of [which] were paid by groups with interests in banking, housing, and urban affairs"; of the $48,000 he kept for himself ($30,000 was given to charity), at least $19,500 was from such clearly identified housing industry interest groups as the National Association of Home Builders, Citibank, the National Lumber and Building Material Dealers Association, National Savings and Loan League, and Oregon Bankers Association (*Washington Post*, 1983b). For a description of the American Bankers Association's extraordinary clout in bullying Congress – *over* the objections of the administration and the Republican Chair of the Senate Finance Committee – to repeal the 1982 tax law amendment requiring savings institutions to withhold 10 per cent of all interest and dividends, see Shribman (1983).

At the local and state levels, these interest groups have perhaps even greater clout. The National Association of Realtors has over 600,000 members and 1,800 local boards. They strongly influence state and local legislation and administrative actions through political contributions, lobbying efforts, and, most effectively, through the fact that state and local legislators, whose official work usually is not full-time, often double as realtors, insurance brokers, attorneys, landlords, and other occupations in whose interest past and current housing policies and programs have been molded.

The two-way flow of personnel between the public and private sectors has gone a long way toward ensuring the complementarity of public actions and private interests. Much like the relationship between the Department of Defense and the defense industry, key HUD officials and staff of Congressional committees that deal with housing issues regularly leave government service to take high-level positions in trade associations of the housing industry and with individual corporations and financial institutions. In the other direction, HUD assistant secretaries, deputy assistant secretaries, and other political appointees, as well as key Congressional staff members, are drawn from the housing industry (see Lilley, 1980, for examples).

One of the more recent and egregious manifestations of this interlock phenomenon and captive public policy was President Reagan's Commission on Housing, appointed in June, 1981, nineteen of whose thirty members were from the banking, real estate, and construction business worlds, another seven of whom were lawyers (and twenty-five of whom were white males). Predictably, the Commission's recommendations centered primarily around getting the government off industry's back, removing all barriers to private construction (see Hartman, 1983a). "The genius of the market economy, freed of the distortions forced by government housing policies and regulations that swung erratically from loving to hostile, can provide for housing far better than Federal programs," intoned the Commission (U.S. President's Commission on Housing, 1982, p. xvii).

Housing consumers, particularly lower-income consumers, are hardly represented at all in this process. The National Association of Housing and Redevelopment Officials, representing state and local program administrators

– who often are at odds with housing consumers – has minor influence; and the National Low Income Housing Coalition, while an effective force in "damage control" and occasionally in generating progressive new national housing legislation, is, with its staff of two, hardly a match for its far better-heeled and better-connected sister lobbying organizations. Local and national consumer-oriented housing groups have little funding or staff, and the more solidly based community organizations – still minuscule compared with the private sector trade associations – can focus only a limited portion of their resources on housing issues. (See the Appendix "Housing Action Resources" for a list of twenty-one such groups, whose combined staffs doubtless could fit comfortably into some corner of the National Association of Home Builders' Washington headquarters building.)

Part of the problem is that the power individual consumers have over housing issues is tiny compared with the stakes held by big lending institutions, building materials manufacturers, homebuilders, and realty firms. Another aspect of the problem is the perception of many housing consumers that they benefit enormously from the present housing system, in particular the idea that ownership of a home provides the possibility of acquiring huge capital gains, which the income tax system treats most protectively (by allowing homeowners to defer taxes on capital gains from the sale of their principal residence, without limit, if they reinvest that gain in another residence within two years, and by allowing a one-time permanent exemption of capital gains up to $125,000 for homeowners 55 years and older). Homeownership has thus been for many Americans a terrific form of tax-free profit with which to cushion old age. Since two-thirds of Americans own their homes, the reality or dream of this kind of profit from homeownership (combined with the other financial and non-financial benefits the system creates, compared with renting) has been a powerful narcotic. But as extreme housing inflation decreases the possibility of homeownership for ever larger numbers of

American households and as homeownership itself becomes an increasingly tenuous proposition, the potential for organizing housing consumers – both owners and renters – into an effective political force opens up dramatically.

Our housing system will not change in any fundamental way unless and until organized housing consumers force those changes to occur. How that organization can come about, then, is a fundamental political question. Basically, we believe that, unless there is a vast expansion and radical redistribution of government housing assistance and effective controls over the private sector, the inadequacies and limitations of the present housing system will manifest themselves in increasingly severe ways for greater and greater numbers of Americans: that the housing cost/income squeeze will result in more mortgage defaults and foreclosures and increasing vulnerability of the economy to these credit failures; in increasing property tax delinquency and utility shutoffs; in more evictions, displacement, and homelessness; in increasing numbers of people unable to afford a decent standard of living because housing is consuming so large a portion of their incomes; in deterioration of neighborhoods and neighborhood services; in greater overcrowding; in ever higher levels of construction industry unemployment and business failure; in increasing losses and failures among lending institutions. The "affordability squeeze," as Michael Stone puts it, contains the seed of real social unrest and political instability. The increasing resistance to tenant displacement (see Hartman, Keating, and LeGates, 1982, for a cataloguing of these efforts); the rising number of squatting actions all around the country (Borgos, forthcoming); and the grassroots rebellions against farm foreclosures, involving organized farmers who prevent such sales as well as the remarkable spectacle of sheriffs refusing to carry out and judges halting these sales (Robbins, 1983; *Washington Post*, 1983a; *New York Times*, 1983a, 1983c) – all portend both the need for and the possibility of the radical restructuring of the housing system most of us envision and work for.

Exacerbation of these many and related problems may not take a straight-line form – there may be temporary upsurges and relief here and there – but the general and inexorable trend will be for the housing system to fail more and more people. In this context, we see our role as twofold: to enable people to understand the true reasons for these failings, and to put forth workable, credible, humane alternatives.

We believe that the formulation and popularization of credible alternatives to the present housing system can serve as a powerful political mobilizer; and that low-, moderate-, and middle-income housing consumers (owners and renters) can become one of the most powerful political forces, at all levels of government, behind the creation of a society that treats housing as a human right for everyone, a society that ensures sound, safe, and healthy neighborhoods and communities.[4] It is time to go on the offensive with our analyses and solutions.

The housing crisis in brief

By most physical criteria – notably, quantity and quality of living space – Americans are among the best-housed people in the world. The three decades following the end of World War II showed a marked reduction in most indices of housing distress – overcrowding, lack of adequate sanitary facilities, and structural dilapidation.[5] During the same period, there was an increase in homeownership, principally of single-family detached suburban homes with some private outdoor space.

But since the early 1970s, severe problems have appeared at an alarming rate, which throw into serious question the system's ability to house its people decently, and highlight the nation's persistent gap between the living conditions of its rich and its poor. These often-overlapping problems are:

(1) An ever-higher proportion of housing consumers – renters and owners alike – are being forced to spend percentages of their income that exceed what they should be paying, if they are not to be vulnerable to mortgage default or eviction and have enough cash remaining for other necessary items. Slightly more than half (53 per cent) of all renters – who comprise more than a third of the nation's households – now pay 25 per cent or more of their income for housing, and over a third (34 per cent) pay 35 per cent or more. By comparison, in 1970, only two-fifths of all renter households were paying 25 per cent or more of their income for housing, and only one-fourth were paying 35 per cent or more (U.S. Bureau of the Census, 1982b, Table A–2).[6] Broken down by income class (see Cushing Dolbeare's chapter), the data reveal the extent to which those with lowest incomes must devote the highest proportions of income to shelter. Between 1970 and 1979, the median gross rent rose 101 per cent, whereas the median income for renter households rose only 59 per cent (U.S. President's Commission on Housing, 1982, p. 10). (It should be noted that housing quality also rose during this period.)

The failure of renters' incomes to keep pace with housing costs, the decreasing supply of rental housing because of inadequate construction levels, conversion of apartments to condominiums, and abandonment of rental units in some central city neighborhoods are all factors in this squeeze on renters.[7]

Data on housing expenditures relative to income are less

well-developed for homeowners and inherently more difficult to standardize. This results from the ways in which different mortgage positions – whether one has a mortgage, and what portion of the house price is mortgage as opposed to down payment – affect current expenditures. But the Annual Housing Survey now computes, for homeowners, monthly housing costs (real estate taxes, insurance, utilities, fuel, water, garbage/trash collection, and mortgage payments) separately for those who do and do not have mortgages on their homes. Among those with mortgages, nearly one-third (31 per cent) pay 25 per cent or more of their income for housing, and slightly more than one-fifth (21 per cent) pay 35 per cent or more. The high and rising cost of non-mortgage-related housing expenditures is revealed in the fact that even among those without mortgages on their homes (over one-third of all homeowners – elderly householders with lower incomes for the most part), nearly one-fifth (19 per cent) pay 25 per cent or more of their income for housing, and one-seventh pay 35 per cent or more (U.S. Bureau of the Census, 1981a, Table A–1).[8]

(2) Shelter costs inflated enormously during the 1970s. While the Consumer Price Index for all items rose from 116.3 in 1970 to 269.0 in May, 1981, the Shelter Index (rent, home purchase, mortgage interest rates, property taxes, maintenance and repairs) went, during that same period, from 123.6 to 308.4 (U.S. Bureau of the Census, 1981c, p. 468). The combined impact of rapidly escalating prices and rapidly escalating mortgage interest rates can be shown in the following comparison:

> In 1975, the average-priced new single-family home cost $44,600, and the contract interest rate for a conventional first mortgage averaged 8.75 per cent. With an 80 per cent mortgage and housing costs at 25 per cent of income, a family in 1975 would have needed a down payment of $8,920 – 65 per cent of median family income that year – and, on a thirty-year mortgage, would have had a monthly mortgage payment of $280.69, which in turn required a minimum annual income of $13,473 – 2 per cent below the nation's median family income that year.

> In 1981, the average-priced new single-family home cost $94,100, and the contract interest rate for a conventional first mortgage averaged 14.1 per cent. With an 80 per cent mortgage and housing costs at 25 per cent of income, a

family in 1981 would have needed a down payment of $18,820 – 84 per cent of median family income that year – and, on a thirty-year mortgage, would have had a monthly mortgage payment of $897.93, which in turn required a minimum annual income of $43,101 – nearly double the nation's median family income that year (calculated from ibid., p. 772, and U.S. Bureau of the Census, 1981b, Table 2).

(For taxpayers who itemize, these out-of-pocket payments are offset by end-of-the-year tax deductions, albeit in a highly regressive fashion, as detailed in the Appendix to Cushing Dolbeare's chapter.)

As a result of low levels of new construction, high rates of new household formation, and increased investment and speculation in housing as a hedge against inflation, the median price of existing homes is now only slightly lower than that of new homes – a situation that did not exist in previous decades when one could satisfy homeowning inclinations at a much lower price by purchasing a used home.

(3) Mortgage interest rates are double what they were a decade ago, and triple what they were in the 1950s and early 1960s.

(4) Residential mortgage credit is in short supply, as stronger borrowers – principally governments and corporations – compete for a lower level of savings. As a proportion of disposable personal income, personal savings have dropped sharply over the last decade, from the 8 to 8.5 per cent range in the first half of the 1970s to the 5 to 5.5 per cent range beginning in 1977 (U.S. Bureau of the Census, 1981c, p. 427).

(5) A variety of new inflation-sensitive mortgage instruments are being introduced, which rapidly are replacing traditional level-payment mortgages, as lenders seek to shift the burdens of inflation to borrowers. The result is more tenuous home-ownership status, as owners who use such instruments (either because no other mortgages are available or because super-ficially attractive temporary advantages are offered as a marketing device) no longer have the security of predictable fixed payments for the life of the mortgage.

(6) Homeowner mortgage delinquency rates are increasing and, with that, the likelihood of default and foreclosure. For the third quarter of 1981, 5.33 per cent of all mortgage loans in the nation were thirty days or more past due, the highest

rate the Mortgage Bankers Association has recorded since 1953, when it began its quarterly surveys. In high unemployment areas, such as the Midwest, the delinquency rate was 7.78 per cent. By comparison, in the last half of the 1970s, the delinquency rate was in the 4.5 per cent range (Winston Williams, 1981; Teeley, 1981). Data collected by the Federal Home Loan Bank Board on mortgage loans sixty days or more overdue show that the trend continues: in February, 1983, 2.36 per cent of mortgages held by savings and loan institutions were at least two months overdue, a substantial rise over the .83 per cent rate of December, 1981; and in the first half of 1982 alone, foreclosure – a step lenders generally resort to most reluctantly – took away the homes of one out of every 400 mortgage-holders in the U.S. (Gulino, 1983; Mariano, 1983).

(7) The major prop to the construction industry and home-ownership – the savings and loan industry – is in deep trouble. A 1982 Brookings Institution study asserts that more than 400 savings and loans and mutual savings banks "must find merger partners to avoid potentially irreversible losses of net worth," that 200–600 others "will require financial assistance from depository insurance agencies to arrange mergers," and that some closings and liquidations may occur in any case (Carron, 1982). The problem of the thrifts inheres in their inability to withstand prolonged inflation: they "borrow short, lend long."

(8) A new class of lenders is being created: homeowners forced to take back purchase-money mortgages as the only way to sell their homes. This reduced liquidity of home-as-asset decreases mobility and "trading up" possibilities, as well as reducing options regarding use of capital. It also makes many more people highly vulnerable to economic distress, which results in a higher incidence of defaults and foreclosures.

One financing device being introduced to attract residential mortgage lending is "equity participation," whereby as a condition for getting a mortgage loan, the lender shares in the value appreciation upon sale. While making it possible for some people who otherwise might not have been able to secure financing to purchase homes, this device also reduces the attractiveness of homeownership as a long-term investment and a means of producing a nest egg.

(9) Construction levels are extraordinarily low. In 1982 and in 1981 total housing starts for the nation were 1.1 million

(and these rounded figures actually conceal a drop of 28,000 starts from 1981 to 1982), compared with 1.3 million units in 1980, 1.8 million units in 1979, and slightly over 2 million units in 1978 (U.S. Bureau of the Census, 1983a, Table 1). While, incredibly, no data are collected on the number of construction firms that fail, by firm size, membership in the National Association of Home Builders has dropped from 127,000 to 107,000 between 1980 and 1982, and it is estimated that one-half of all homebuilders were not actually building homes in late 1982.[9]

Unemployment in the construction industry is at a post-Depression high: between 1979 and 1980 the official unemployment rate in the construction industry rose from 10.2 per cent to 14.2 per cent (U.S. Bureau of the Census, 1981c, p., 393). By November 1982, it was an astounding 21.9 per cent (U.S. Department of Labor, 1982).

(10) Displacement of residents from their homes and communities is occurring at disturbingly high rates. The U.S. Department of Housing and Urban Development, in a 1981 report to Congress, estimates that approximately 2.5 million persons – more than 1 per cent of the population – are forced to leave their homes each year, for various reasons, including: gentrification, undermaintenance, eviction, arson, rent increases, mortgage foreclosures, property tax delinquency, speculation in land and buildings, conversions, demolition, "planned shrinkage," and historic preservation (U.S. Department of Housing and Urban Development, 1981a.) The financial and psycho-social costs of forced moving often are truly severe for the households affected, and the community instability associated with such a high rate of forced displacement is detrimental to society.

(11) Utility costs for lighting, cooking, heating, and air conditioning have been rising in recent years at an extraordinary rate. Costs for these services, particularly in the Northeast and Midwest, now are averaging in the hundreds of dollars monthly for a great many households. The Consumer Price Index for fuel oil, coal, and bottled gas rose from 110.1 in 1970 to 685.8 in mid-1981; in that same 11-year period electricity prices rose by 175.7 points, compared with a 152.7 rise in the CPI for all items (U.S. Bureau of the Census, 1981c, p. 468). Permanently high oil and electricity prices, probable deregulation of natural gas, and aggressive rate increase campaigns

by utility companies all indicate that these costs will continue to consume gargantuan proportions of the family budget.

(12) Local property taxes also are increasing dramatically as local and state governments experience severe fiscal crises and the federal government continues to cut back traditional aid programs. In some jurisdictions, such as California and Massachusetts, property tax reform measures have put a ceiling on these increases, but over the long run the cure may be as bad as the disease. Cutbacks in vital public services, such as fire protection and education, have characterized Massachusetts' Proposition 2½, leading to militant actions and voter counter-rebellions. The benefits of California's Proposition 13 property tax measure went primarily to owners of commercial rather than residential properties; renters got no benefits at all (although they pay the landlord's property taxes as part of their rent bill). Proposition 13's provision that properties must be reassessed at current market value with each change of title means that tax bills will steadily increase and will keep pace with current inflationary levels over time. It also means that residential properties will bear an ever-increasing percentage of total property taxes, because these properties change hands more frequently than office buildings, factories, and other commercial structures.

(13) Severe shelter problems are increasingly concentrated among identifiable sub-populations, some of which are not so small: racial minorities, female-headed households, large households, public assistance recipients, the elderly, farm-workers. Although these groups generally have lower-than-average incomes, their problems with securing decent housing go beyond affordability. Those problems result from institutional discrimination in all segments of the housing market, and from the fact that the housing stock, in terms of unit size and location, is inadequate to match people's needs.

(14) In recent decades, housing-related problems had not been a major public health concern, but there is now increasing awareness of dangers to health and safety that are clearly and causally related to housing conditions. These are the modern-day analogues to tuberculosis, respiratory ailments, and other infectious diseases that in the nineteenth century and earlier were caused by substandard housing conditions:

- The neurological damage to children by lead poisoning from ingestion of lead-based paint, the cumulative effect of which is heightened by increasing levels of lead in the air and dirt children play in.

● Carcinogenic properties of widely used asbestos-based building materials.

● Fires and asphyxiation caused by improperly installed and vented heating devices used to cope with cold weather and high heating bills.

● Hypothermia caused by absence of adequate heating, in turn attributable to inability to pay heating bills and subsequent shut-off of utilities.

● Pollution and allergenic effects of air trapped within the house because of improper air circulation and excessive insulation.

● Possible carcinogenic effects of the pesticide chlordane, pumped into and around concrete slab foundations to kill termites, which then leaks into the home ventilation system.

● Death and injury from fires set to collect insurance awards or to eliminate from potential development sites buildings protected by historic preservation ordinances and other protective measures.

(15) Although no data have as yet appeared that show an increase in overcrowding, several housing consumption trends seem to indicate that space standards are being lowered in the United States. In response to increasing land and construction costs, the homebuilding industry has been turning to the "basic house," one which not only has fewer amenities but also less square footage than homes built in the 1960s and 1970s. The median size of new single-family homes sold has dropped steadily from 1979, when it was 1,650 square feet, to 1,560 square feet in 1981, to 1,530 square feet in 1982 (U.S. Bureau of the Census, 1983b, Table 21). The increasing use of condominium apartments rather than free-standing homes to satisfy homeownership inclinations means considerably less square footage of living space on the average. The increase in "accessory" or "in-law" apartments – adjuncts to existing dwellings, sometimes in a garage or basement – is further evidence of this trend. To an extent, creation of such units (often, if not usually, done without permits) represents an adjustment of the housing stock to changing household sizes. But many of these units are just at the margin of, or below, building and health codes regarding ceiling height, room size, and other space and amenity standards, and they

generally reflect a lowering of housing standards. Estimates by the Census Bureau and Urban Land Institute put the number of such conversions/additions at 2–3 million during the 1970–1980 decade.[10] The "shared housing" movement is another response to increased housing costs (as well as to the need for companionship and security for older people).[11] Anecdotal evidence from several cities where housing costs have really gotten out of hand – Washington, San Francisco, New York, etc. – suggests that one way lower-income people have responded to increased housing costs has been to "double up." As many as 17,000 families in New York City's public housing projects, 10 per cent of all such households, are illegally doubling up, a "problem that is growing geometrically," according to the Housing Authority chair (Rule, 1983c). And the phenomenon of married and unmarried adult children returning to their parents' empty nests is getting increasing attention (Winerip, 1983).

(16) "Homelessness" – among young people and the elderly, whites and blacks, families and individuals – appears to be increasing in reality and in the society's consciousness. Shortages and high costs of rental housing, the elimination of centrally located rooming houses and low-priced hotels from downtown redevelopment areas, the trend toward deinstitutionalizing persons with mental disabilities, and inadequate provision for the maintenance and continued operation of publicly subsidized housing – all have been important forces that have contributed to the creation of a large group of men and women who sleep in parks, store and church entranceways, shelters, bus and train stations, packing cases, abandoned autos and buildings, steam tunnels, atop warm streetgrates, and in other quasi-shelters. The recent spate of books, articles, photo essays, and protective lawsuits relating to people without regular places to live has highlighted this issue and society's failure to take care of this basic need (Hombs and Snyder, 1982; Rousseau, 1981; U.S. House of Representatives, 1982).[12] The contradiction revealed by this growing army of the dispossessed is particularly striking here in the nation's capital, where they are to be found, in large numbers, sleeping on grates within a few dozen yards of such monumental edifices as the State Department and Treasury Department, and demonstrating – complete with soup kitchen, a tent city, and crosses memorializing those who have died of

hypothermia in the past year – right in Lafayette Park, across Pennsylvania Avenue from the White House.

(17) Many urban neighborhoods continue to deteriorate. Despite well-publicized instances of gentrification in San Francisco, New York, Washington, Cincinnati, Baltimore, and many other cities, there are massive levels of dissatisfaction with municipal services, community facilities, and general livability qualities in many, if not most, urban neighborhoods. Nearly one-third of all renters and one-seventh of all homeowners – in the latter case a slight increase over 1975 – gave "poor" or "fair" as their overall opinion of their neighborhood in the 1980 Annual Housing Survey. High levels of dissatisfaction were reported with recreational facilities, hospitals and health clinics, and police services, as well as with street/highway noise, state of street repairs, and trash/litter (U.S. Bureau of the Census, 1982a, Table A–3). In some areas, policies of "planned shrinkage" and "triage" – in which the city government decides to cut back on services drastically in order to encourage the emptying of the area so it can be redeveloped for other uses – threaten entire sections of cities (Hartman, Keating, and LeGates, 1982, pp. 72–78).

Notes

1 See also the conclusions drawn by the Urban Institute's Raymond Struyk, John Tuccillo, and James Zais (1982, p. 406): "In 1981, as the administration looked at some $250 billion in unspent but appropriated budget authority to be spent over the next thirty years, it decided that housing assistance already had received its slice of the shrinking domestic pie. This position is at sharp variance with the actions of Republican and Democratic administrations dating back at least twenty-five years."

2 A forthcoming collection of progressive housing readings, being compiled by Rachel Bratt, Chester Hartman, and Ann Meyerson, will contain original essays on these six examples by, respectively, Richard Appelbaum, Stephen Schifferes, Judy Kossy, Jill Hamberg, Thomas Angotti/Bruce Dale, and Peter Marcuse.

In its April, 1982 Final Report, the President's Commission on Housing offered fully eighty-seven recommendations, covering details as small as the composition of membership of model code organizations and adoption of accounting guidelines in the financial futures market. But with respect to what is by far the nation's largest housing program – and, as Cushing Dolbeare points out, its only housing entitlement program – the homeowner tax deductions, the Commission had only this to say:

> The Commission . . . recommends that there be no changes in the current system at this time. The Commission also recognizes the broad scope of this issue and recommends that any further analysis of this topic be considered only within the context of a thorough review of the U.S. tax system (U.S. President's Commission on Housing, 1982, p. 75).

4 An Institute for Policy Studies working group that includes most of the authors in this volume is currently refining and integrating these alternatives into an omnibus national housing bill, with state and local variations as well.

5 It is important to note that the decennial Housing Census has been measuring only a small and decreasing number of items. Local and state housing codes are far more detailed and comprehensive, and were housing conditions nationally, or even locally, to be measured against these standards, the picture would be far less rosy. Cf. the following:

> It is readily apparent that even the most conscientious user of Census data . . . would arrive at a total "substandard" housing figure which grossly underestimated the number of dwelling units having serious housing code violations. To use a total thus arrived at as a figure for substandard housing is grossly inaccurate and misleading, because it flies in the face of extensive consideration given by health experts, building officials, model code drafting organizations, and the local, state and federal court system to what have become over a period of many years, the socially, politically, and legally-accepted minimum standard for housing of human beings in the United States. . . . Even if public and private efforts eliminate all housing which is substandard under most current federal definitions, there will still be millions of dwelling units below code standard (National Commission on Urban Problems, 1969, pp. 83, 102).

6 Not included in these calculations are units for which no cash rent was paid and units occupied by families and primary individuals who report no income or a net loss, since rent/income ratios are incalculable for such households. Of the 1,583,000 renter households in the "not computed" category, 270,000 had no income or an income

loss, and 1,313,000 had no cash rent (an unknown number of whom also might have no income or an income loss). As expressed in the text, the data thus slightly overstate the extent of rent burdens. (Phone interview with Paul Harple, Housing Division, u.S. Census Bureau, November 5, 1982.)

7 A recent General Accounting Office study (U.S. Comptroller General, 1979) referred to rental housing as "an endangered species."

8 Not included in these calculations are units occupied by families or private individuals who reported no income or a net loss and households who did not report the amount of their mortgage or similar debt, as no ratio can be computed for such households. The exclusion of the former group, by far the smaller of the two, means that the data as expressed in the text slightly understate the extent of housing cost burdens, while no conclusions can be drawn about exclusion of the latter group. (Phone interviews with Kathryn Nelson, U.S. Department of Housing and Urban Development, November 4, 1982, and Paul Harple, Housing Division, U.S. Census Bureau, November 5, 1982. It should be noted that, according to Mr. Harple, the larger, "not reported" category has apparently been incorrectly defined in the Annual Housing Survey publication cited above; while the definition describes this category as "households that did not report the amount of or did not pay mortgage or similar debts and/or real estate taxes," it should only have embraced the first half of that group – those that did not report the amount of their mortgage or similar debt.)

9 Phone interview with Robert Sheehan, Director of Economic Research, National Association of Home Builders, December 22, 1982.

10 Phone interview with Patrick Hare of Patrick Hare Associates (2027 Que Street N.W., Washington, D.C. 20009), which serves as an informal clearinghouse for information on accessory apartments. Data are only sketchy at this time, due to the recency of the phenomenon and the lack of clear definitions.

11 The Shared Housing Resource Center (6344 Greene Street, Philadelphia, PA 19144) was established in 1981 as an information and technical assistance clearinghouse.

12 A national Coalition for the Homeless (see Appendix, "Housing Action Resources") was begun in 1981 to act as an advocacy group in persuading local governments to take responsibility for providing adequate shelter facilities. The major legal victory and precedent won to date resulted from a class action suit brought against the City and State of New York on behalf of men without shelter, which led to a court-ordered consent judgment in August, 1981, under which the City guarantees to provide shelter, meeting minimum standards, for any homeless man requesting it. (see *New York Times*, 1981.)

A subsequent class action suit won parallel rights for homeless women (*New York Times*, 1983b). And in March, 1983, the Legal Aid Society filed a class action to extend such protections and rights to homeless families (Rule, 1983a, 1983b).

2 The low-income housing crisis

Cushing N. Dolbeare

The focus of this paper is on the problems of low-income people. Even though others have growing housing difficulties, for most of the last three decades housing *problems* have generally been confined to low-income and minority people. Others had housing *inconveniences* – about which they were sometimes very vocal. Basically, however, white families with steady jobs at reasonable pay didn't have to worry about having roofs over their heads or keeping warm. They might pay more than they wanted, or not be in the kind of neighborhood they wanted, or be forced to rent when they wanted to own, or forced to own when they wanted to rent. But they really didn't experience true housing problems – if by these we mean that the unit was so substandard as to present either a health or safety hazard, or the household paid so much that it couldn't afford the other essentials of life.

We are now heading into a decade or so where middle-income people with political clout are having some real housing problems too – far less severe and widespread than the housing problems of lower-income people, to be sure – but middle-income people perceive themselves to have housing problems, and are so perceived by others.

This expansion of the problem creates both a danger and an opportunity. The danger is that so much attention will be focused on these new housing problems that those of low-income people will continue not to be dealt with or be dealt with less and less. The opportunity, since we will have people feeling housing problems who have never felt them before, is to link that perception to the perception that there are also others with more critical housing problems. We need a national housing policy that helps everybody who has a real problem, not just the people who have newly arrived on the scene with their problems.

The housing situation of low-income people

The housing problems faced by low-income people are multiple and varied. Historically, a major focus of housing concern has been on quality. Indeed, as recently as 1940, 45 per cent of all occupied units in the United States were either dilapidated or lacked basic plumbing facilities. That figure has now fallen to well below 10 per cent, with those units almost exclusively occupied by poor people.

As the incidence of substandard housing has declined, so another major housing problem has arisen for low-income people: affordability. Housing costs include not only the mortgage or rent, but also utilities, taxes, insurance, and maintenance (although some or all of the latter are typically included in rents). These operating costs, particularly utilities, have skyrocketed in recent years. All of us have felt the pinch of rising energy costs, but the impact has been worst for the poor.

The final, major housing problem faced by low-income people to a far greater degree than others is availability. Availability may be a problem either because supply is inadequate or because of discrimination on the basis of race, income source, family composition, or for other reasons. People with special housing needs, such as the handicapped or the frail elderly, large renter households, and migrant farmworkers, face special problems of availability. So do blacks and other minorities, families with children – especially if there is only a single parent – and households with irregular or very low incomes.

Since 1949, when Congress adopted the national goal of "a decent home and a suitable living environment for every American family," there has been bipartisan support for efforts to deal with the acute housing problems of low-income people. Meanwhile, several decades of economic prosperity have created very high housing expectations for most Americans.

Between 1970 and 1979, according to Annual Housing Survey data, the number of occupied housing units increased by almost one-quarter (24.9 per cent). In 1979, almost two-thirds (65.4 per cent) of all households owned or were buying their own homes. The number of units lacking plumbing facilities, a traditional measure of housing quality, dropped by 46 per cent. While average household size fell sharply (from 3.0 to 2.6 persons for owner-occupied units and from 2.3 to 2.0 persons for renter-occupied units), housing units increased slightly in size. The number of units with three or more bedrooms increased by one-third. There were sharp increases in the number of elderly households, single-parent households (both male and female heads), and single-person households.

Unfortunately, the cost of housing has increased far more rapidly than household incomes. According to data in the 1980 and 1979 Annual Housing Surveys, between 1970 and 1980, median income for owners rose 104 per cent (from $9,700 to $19,800), while median home value tripled (from $17,100 to $51,300); median renter income rose 66 per cent (from $6,400 to $10,600), while median monthly rents increased by 123 per cent (from $108 to $241).

The income gap between owners and renters continued to grow. In 1970, median renter income was 65 per cent of median owner income; by 1979, it had dropped to 55 per cent. As Table 2.1 shows, there were more renters than owners at the very lowest income levels (below $7,000), while owners outnumbered renters by more than 10:1 in the top income brackets (above $50,000).

The very rapid recent rise in housing costs, particularly for low-income renters, is shown in Table 2.2. While median

TABLE 2.1   *Income distribution for owners and renters, by race, 1980 (households in thousands)*

Income	Owners	Renters		
		All	Black	Hispanic
$ 3,000 or less	2,155	2,748	788	232
$ 3,000–6,999	5,750	6,479	1,483	616
$ 7,000–9,999	4,367	3,862	697	422
$10,000–14,999	7,217	5,553	841	519
$15,000–19,999	6,977	3,672	477	264
$20,000–24,999	6,707	2,263	264	156
$25,000–34,999	9,814	1,984	203	101
$35,000–49,999	6,002	699	61	29
$50,000–74,999	2,445	207	13	4
$75,000 +	1,082	88	–	6
Total	52,516	27,555	4,827	2,349
Median	$19,800	$10,600	$7,600	$9,300

Source: 1980 Annual Housing Survey, Part C, Financial Characteristics of the Inventory.

TABLE 2.2   *Changes in median rents and median rent/income ratios, 1978–80*

Income	Median Rent			Median rent/income ratio*		
	1980	1979	1978	1980	1979	1978
$ 3,000 or less	$179	$147	$130	72+%	60+%	60+%
$ 3,000–6,999	187	172	165	47	44	42
$ 7,000–9,999	222	205	193	32	31	29
$10,000–14,999	249	232	214	25	24	22
$15,000–19,999	274	252	233	20	18	17
$20,000–24,999	296	277	256	17	16	14
$25,000–34,999	327	303	284	14	13	13
$35,000–49,999	362	337	326	12	11	11
$50,000–74,999	393	401	347	9–	10–	8–
$75,000 +	423	359	283	7–	6–	5–
All renters	241	217	200	27	26	25

* Ratios above 60% or below 10% are NLIHC estimates.
Source: Estimated by National Low Income Housing Coalition from data in Annual Housing Survey, Part C, Financial Characteristics of the Inventory.

rents for all renters rose by 21 per cent in the three years from 1978 through 1980, median rents for very, very low-income renters (below $3,000) rose by 38 per cent. Moreover, at all income levels, the proportion of income spent for shelter was rising, although the median was 25 per cent or more *only* for households with incomes below $15,000.

While housing costs rose generally, both the amount and the impact of the increase were greatest for low-income households. For example, while the number of renter households with incomes below $3,000 per year dropped by slightly more than half, from 5.8 million to 2.7 million, between 1970 and 1980, the number of units in the stock at rents which those in this income group could afford (paying 30 per cent of their income) dropped by 70 per cent, from about 5 million to 1.5 million.

TABLE 2.3 *Monthly shelter cost at 25% and 30% of income for selected income levels*

Income	25%	30%
$ 3,000	$62	$75
$ 7,000	146	175
$10,000	208	250
$15,000	312	375
$20,000	417	500
$25,000	521	625
$35,000	729	875
$50,000	1042	1250
$75,000	1562	1875

Thus, there is a wide and growing "housing gap" for very low-income people. Even if all other things were perfect – which we know they are not – there are more than twice as many renter households with incomes below $3,000 as there are rental units available at 25 per cent of their incomes. Even using a 30 per cent rent/income ratio, there is a gap of more than 1.2 million units at the very bottom of the income scale (see Tables 2.3, 2.4, and 2.5). The impact of these changes in housing costs has been traumatic for renters at the bottom of the income scale. In 1970, the 5.8 million renter households (24 per cent of all renters) with household incomes below $3,000 per year had a median rent of less than $85 per month. By 1980, while the number of renter households in this bottom bracket had dropped to 2.7 million (10 per cent of all renters), their median rent was $179 per month.

TABLE 2.4 *Renter households and affordable units at 25% rent/ income ratio, 1980*

Income	Households	Units	Gap/surplus	
			In income range	Cumulative
$3,000 or less	2,748	1,301	−1,447	−1,447
$3,000–6,999	6,479	3,807	−2,672	−4,119
$7,000–9,999	3,862	5,415	+1,553	−2,566
$10,000–14,999	5,553	9,920	+4,367	+1,801
$15,000–19,999	3,672	4,576	+904	+2,705
$20,000–24,999	2,263	1,503	−760	+1,945
$25,000–34,999	1,984	814	−1,170	+775
$35,000 +	990	215	−775	0
Total	27,551	27,551	−	−

Source: Estimated by National Low Income Housing Coalition from data in Annual Housing Survey, Part C, Financial Characteristics of the Inventory.

In 1970, a family with an income of $3,000 who paid the median rent for households of that income class of $85 spent 34 per cent of its income for shelter, and had $165 monthly left over for all other needs.

In 1980, a family with an income of $3,000 who p
the median rent for households of that income cla
of $179 spent 72 per cent of its income for shelter, and
had only $71 monthly left over for all other needs.

TABLE 2.5 *Renter households and affordable units at 30% rent/
income ratio, 1980*

Income	Households	Units	Gap/Surplus	
			In income range	*Cumulative*
$ 3,000 or less	2,748	1,513	−1,235	−1,235
$ 3,000–6,999	6,479	5,694	−785	−2,020
$ 7,000–9,999	3,862	7,496	+3,634	+1,614
$10,000–14,999	5,553	9,012	+3,459	+5,073
$15,000–19,999	3,672	2,545	−1,127	+3,946
$20,000–24,999	2,263	791	−1,472	+2,474
$25,000 or more	2,974	500	−2,474	0
Total	27,551	27,551	–	–

Source: Estimated by National Low Income Housing Coalition
from data in Annual Housing Survey, Part C, Financial
Characteristics of the Inventory.

What are the characteristics of these 2.7 million renter
households with such very low incomes?

- Forty-nine per cent were single individuals, but 51 per
cent were in households with two or more people, and
6 per cent had five or more.
- Fourteen per cent were married couples; 7 per cent
were male-headed single-parent households; and 29 per
cent were female-headed single-parent households.
Twenty-seven per cent had children of their own under
18, and 4 per cent had three or more children under 18.
- Nineteen per cent were single, elderly people; but 30
per cent were single, non-elderly individuals.
- Fifty-two per cent had moved within the last year and
92 per cent had moved within the last ten years.

- Only 19 per cent lived in subsidized housing.
- Fifty-eight per cent paid 60 per cent or more of their income for rent. Only 4 per cent paid less than 25 per cent.
- Forty-six per cent lived in housing built before 1939.
- Ten per cent lived in units lacking plumbing facilities. Five per cent were overcrowded.
- Twenty-nine per cent were black; 8 per cent were of Hispanic origin.
- Twenty per cent lived in the Northeast; 27 per cent in North Central states; 37 per cent in the South; and 16 per cent in the West.
- Forty-six per cent lived in central cities; 31 per cent lived in non-metropolitan areas.
- All had incomes below 75 per cent of the poverty level.

These households are the poorest of the poor, but in 1980 they were fewer than one-third of all households with incomes below the poverty level. There were also another 3.3 million renter households with incomes above $3,000, but still below the poverty level, and 4.9 million owner-occupants below the poverty level.

In other words, low-income housing needs affect *millions* of people: 29 million in all, including more than 11 million children (4 million of them under six) and 4 million elderly persons.

Some accomplishments of low-income housing programs

1982 marks the forty-fifth anniversary of the adoption of the U.S. Housing Act of 1937, which established the public housing program. In the ensuing decades, our subsidized housing inventory has risen to about 4.5 million units: 3.4 million through programs of the Department of Housing and Urban Development (HUD) and the rest in rural areas and small towns through the Farmers Home Administration (FmHA) of the Department of Agriculture. (A substantial portion of these units is not in the permanently subsidized inventory, however: 1.4 million are in homeownership subsidy programs in which the existing occupant, but no successor occupant, is subsidized; and about 0.8 million units are in the Section 8 Existing housing program, where the subsidy runs with the household rather than with the unit.)

In contrast, as President Reagan's Commission on Housing has pointed out, there are approximately 20 million households with incomes below 50 per cent of median and more than 30 million households with incomes below 80 per cent of median. Small wonder, then, that fewer than one-quarter of all households with incomes below the poverty level are living in federally assisted housing.

Most subsidized housing assistance has been given to renters, particularly through HUD programs. The Farmers Home Administration has placed more emphasis on homeownership programs. Table 2.6 gives current estimates on the number of occupied subsidized units provided under all programs of HUD and FmHA. Yet, despite their inadequate

TABLE 2.6   *Estimated federally subsidized units as of September 30, 1981*

Agency Program	Units
HUD Public housing	1,204,000
Section 202 housing for elderly and handicapped	
Original program	44,392
Revised program (post-1974)	55,994
Rent supplements	157,779
Section 236 rental housing assistance	537,206
Section 8 housing assistance payments	1,318,927
Subtotal, rental housing	3,318,298
Less Section 202 units also receiving Section 8	−55,994
Less estimated Section 236 units also receiving Section 8 assistance	−95,000
Less estimated Section 236 units also receiving rent supplement assistance	−66,000

TABLE 2.6 *continued*

Agency Program	Units
Net rental units	3,101,304*
Section 235 home ownership assistance	
Old program (pre–1974)	158,226
Revised program	82,313
Net home ownership units	240,539
Total HUD-subsidized units	3,341,843
FmHA Section 515 rental housing (estimated units)	210,000
Section 502 homeownership loans	1,639,309
Section 504 very low-income repair grants	39,269
Subtotal, homeownership	1,678,578
Less estimated unsubsidized Section 502	−540,000
Net FmHA homeownership units	1,138,578
Rural rental assistance (with Section 515)	1,517
Farm labor housing loans (Section 514)	1,395
Farm labor housing grants (Section 516)	188
Site loans (Section 524)	165
Self-help housing grants	348
Supervisory/technical assistance (Section 525)	57
Total FmHA	1,151,000†
GRAND TOTAL	4,493,000

* Total subsidized rental housing units higher than (1980) figure given in Table 2.7 due to inclusion of vacant units, addition of units to subsidized housing stock in 1981, and possible sampling errors in Current Population Reports.
† Includes rough estimate of net units provided through project loans and grants (primarily farm labor housing, since other project loans listed here are coupled with Section 515 or Section 502 assistance).

Source: Estimated from Department of Housing and Urban Development, Farmers Home Administration, and Congressional Research Service sources.

scale, our low-income housing efforts *have* made a critical difference to millions of low-income households. While only 11 per cent of all rental units are subsidized, almost three-fifths (57 per cent) of the units renting for less than $100 monthly are subsidized, as are one-fifth (22 per cent) of the units renting for $100–49. Perhaps more important, as Table 2.7 shows, subsidized housing provides shelter for almost one-quarter of all very poor renter households (incomes below the poverty level). Almost one-third (32.7 per cent) of all very poor elderly renters live in assisted housing, as do comparable proportions of very poor black renters (33.1 per cent) and female-headed renter households (31.2 per cent). Very poor Hispanic households and white households are less well served: 17.7 per cent of very poor Hispanic renters and 20.0 per cent of very poor white renters are in subsidized housing. Finally, it should be noted that public housing serves poor renters living in cities better than those elsewhere: 29.4 per cent of very poor renters in central cities live in subsidized housing, compared with 19.4 per cent outside of metropolitan areas.

TABLE 2.7 *Households served by federally assisted rental housing programs, 1980 (in thousands)*

	Total	Below poverty levels	
		Below 100%	*Below 125%*
All households	82,368	10,968	15,557
All renter households	26,487	6,063	8,153
All renter households living in subsidized housing	2,777*	1,430	1,866
Per cent of renter households living in subsidized housing	10.4%	23.6%	22.9%
Households with children under 18 years			
Total	34,329	4,928	6,607
Renter households	10,036	3,126	3,949

TABLE 2.7 *continued*

	Total	Below poverty levels	
		Below 100%	*Below 125%*
Renter households living in subsidized housing	1,297	787	917
Per cent of renter households living in subsidized housing	12.9%	25.2%	23.2%
Householder 65 or over			
Total households	16,912	3,188	5,137
Renter households	4,128	1,237	1,931
Renter households living in subsidized housing	956	405	652
Per cent of renter households living in subsidized housing	23.2%	32.7%	33.8%
White householder			
Total households	71,872	7,828	11,593
Renter households	21,135	3,934	5,549
Renter households living in subsidized housing	1,612	745	1,029
Per cent of renter households living in subsidized housing	7.6%	20.0%	18.5%
Black householder			
Total households	8,847	2,864	3,588
Renter households	4,618	1,941	2,383
Renter households living in subsidized housing	1,075	643	771
Per cent of renter households living in subsidized housing	23.6%	33.1%	32.8%
Spanish-origin householder			
Total households	3,906	956	1,317
Renter households	2,085	685	908
Renter households living in subsidized housing	223	121	155
Per cent of renter households living in subsidized housing	10.7%	17.7%	17.1%

TABLE 2.7   *continued*

	Total	Below poverty levels	
		Below 100%	Below 125%
Inside central cities			
Total households	24,473	4,106	5,743
Renter households	11,343	2,878	3,895
Renter households living in subsidized housing	1,534	846	1,091
Per cent of renter households living in subsidized housing	13.5%	29.4%	28.0%
Outside metropolitan areas			
Total households	26,296	4,224	5,935
Renter households	6,526	1,801	2,357
Renter households living in subsidized housing	688	349	459
Per cent of renter households living in subsidized housing	10.5%	19.4%	19.4%
Female-headed household			
Total households	9,082	2,972	3,666
Renter households	4,529	2,112	2,492
Renter households living in subsidized housing	1,029	674	771
Per cent of renter households living in subsidized housing	22.7%	31.2%	30.9%

* See footnote to Table 2.6 for explanation of discrepant figures for total subsidized rental units in Table 2.6 and 2.7.

Source: Current Population Reports, "Characteristics of Households Receiving Noncash Benefits, 1980," CPR P–60, no. 128.

Perhaps the most reliable, relatively recent data on characteristics of households living in federally assisted housing appear in a 1980 Census Bureau report containing data from the March 1980 Current Population Survey. The data, which include rental housing assisted under all programs, are summarized in Tables 2.8 and 2.9. The information belies some widely held assumptions about the occupants of federally subsidized housing:

TABLE 2.8   Characteristics of households living in subsidized rental housing, 1980 (households in thousands)

Characteristics	Total	Median income $	Below 100% poverty No.	%	Below 125% poverty No.	%
All households	2511	4978	1170	46.5	1573	62.6
Inside metro areas	1858	4959	867	46.6	1176	63.2
Inside central cities	1373	4880	692	50.4	921	67.0
Outside central cities	485	5386	175	36.0	256	52.7
Outside metro areas	653	5078	302	46.2	397	60.7
Northeast	794	6172	279	35.1	415	52.2
North Central	538	4696	276	51.3	349	64.8
South	809	4617	476	58.8	583	72.0
West	370	4651	139	37.5	227	61.3
White	1473	4822	592	40.1	863	58.5
Black	967	5367	549	56.7	671	69.3
Spanish origin	202	6146	99	49.0	126	62.3
Family households	1491	6812	718	48.1	894	59.9
Married couples	596	9507	151	25.3	230	38.5
Male householder	28	–	8	28.5	15	53.5
Female householder	867	5325	558	64.3	650	74.9
Non-family households	1020	3955	452	44.3	680	66.6
Male householder	28	–	8	28.5	15	53.5
Female householder	792	3845	363	45.8	542	68.4
Householder aged 15–24	289	6227	143	49.4	174	60.2
aged 25–34	543	6708		49.5	337	62.0
aged 35–44	339	7100	180	53.0	210	61.9
aged 45–54	221	6286	104	47.0	136	61.5
aged 55–64	256	4720	125	48.8	164	64.0
65 or over	863	4087	349	40.4	552	63.9
Single persons	980	3892	443	45.2	662	67.5
Two persons	494	6425	171	34.6	235	47.5
Three persons	436	6758	186	42.6	241	55.2
Four persons	277	7054	147	53.0	178	64.2
Five persons	159	6861	107	67.2	124	77.9
Six persons	83	4245	54	65.0	63	75.9
Seven or more	82	8895	62	75.6	71	86.5
Households with member(s) under 19	1173	6475	659	56.1	797	67.9
Total people in households with member(s) under 19	2680	6516	1711	63.8	2007	74.8
Households with member(s) who worked in 1979	989	8283	312	31.5	434	43.8
Households with member(s) who did not work in 1979	1456	3981	854	58.6	1128	77.4

Source: "Characteristics of Households and Persons Receiving Noncash Benefits, 1979 (Preliminary data from the March 1980 Current Population Survey)," Table 5. Bureau of the Census, Current Population Reports, Series P–23, no. 110.

- Almost three-fifths of the households are white.
- Over one-third are 65 years or older.
- About two-fifths of the households have at least one member who works at least part of the time.
- Almost half have incomes below the poverty level and over three-fifths have incomes below 125 per cent of the poverty level.
- While only 16 per cent of assisted households consist of five or more persons, they are among the poorest. Two-thirds of the five- and six-person households and three-quarters of the households with seven or more persons have incomes below the poverty level.

TABLE 2.9 *Characteristics of households living in subsidized rental housing, 1980 (% distribution)*

Characteristics	Total	Median income	Below 100% poverty	Below 125% poverty
All households	100%	100%	100%	100%
Inside metro areas	73.9	99.6	74.1	74.7
Inside central cities	54.6	98.0	59.1	58.5
Outside central cities	19.3	108.1	14.9	16.2
Outside metro areas	26.0	102.0	25.8	25.2
Northeast	31.6	123.9	23.8	26.3
North Central	21.4	94.3	23.5	22.1
South	32.2	92.7	40.6	37.0
West	14.7	93.4	11.8	14.4
White	58.6	96.8	50.5	54.8
Black	38.5	107.8	46.9	42.6
Spanish origin	8.0	123.4	8.4	8.0
Family households	59.3	136.8	61.3	56.8
Married couples	23.7	190.9	12.9	14.6
Male householder	1.1	–	.6	.9
Female householder	34.5	106.9	47.6	41.3
Non-family households	40.6	79.4	38.6	43.2
Male householder	1.1	–	.6	.9
Female householder	31.5	77.2	31.0	34.4

TABLE 2.9 *continued*

Characteristics	Total	Median income	Below 100% poverty	Below 125% poverty
Householder aged 15–24	11.5	125.0	12.2	11.0
aged 25–34	21.6	134.7	22.9	21.4
aged 35–44	13.5	142.6	15.3	13.3
aged 45–54	8.8	126.2	8.8	8.6
aged 55–64	10.1	94.8	10.6	10.4
65 or over	34.3	82.1	29.8	35.0
Single persons	39.0	78.1	37.8	42.0
Two persons	19.6	129.0	14.6	14.9
Three persons	17.3	135.7	15.8	15.3
Four persons	11.0	141.7	12.5	11.3
Five persons	6.3	137.8	9.1	7.8
Six persons	3.3	85.2	4.6	4.0
Seven or more	3.2	178.6	5.2	4.5
Households with member(s) under 19	46.7	130.0	56.3	50.6
Households with member(s) who worked in 1979	39.3	166.3	26.6	27.5
Households with member(s) who did not work in 1979	57.9	79.9	72.9	71.7

Source: "Characteristics of Households and Persons Receiving Noncash Benefits, 1979 (Preliminary data from the March 1980 Current Population Survey)," Table 5. Bureau of the Census, Current Population Reports, Series P–23, no. 110.

The cost of federal low-income housing programs

While there is a great variety of federal housing programs, there are several patterns to the way they are subsidized. It is useful to analyze housing subsidies in terms of three principal components of housing costs: (1) the capital cost of the structure or unit (including site acquisition, site preparation, and the cost of designing and building the housing); (2) financing, since subsidized housing is financed exclusively through long-term loans; and (3) operating costs, including management, utilities, maintenance, and taxes.

Briefly, all of the HUD and FmHA lower-income housing programs provide (construction or purchase) financing subsidies. This is done through tax-exempt bonds (public housing and some Section 8), through payment of part of the interest on privately financed loans (Section 235 home-ownership, Section 236 rental housing, and the "new" Section 202 housing for elderly and handicapped); or through direct loans (Farmers Home and the "old" Section 202 program). (For reasons too complex to discuss here, FmHA loans are sometimes referred to as "insured," but the money is borrowed from and repaid to FmHA.)

It has never been possible to provide affordable housing for very low-income people (incomes below the poverty level or 50 per cent of median) with financing subsidies alone. Hence, programs which receive only financing subsidies either do not serve very low-income people or, if they attempt to, run into serious financial problems. (This has been notably true of the Section 236 rental housing program.)

The primary capital subsidy programs are public housing and Section 8. Under the public housing program, the federal government signs an "annual contributions contract" and agrees to pay the principal and interest to retire the bonds floated by a local housing authority financing the projects. Under the Section 8 new construction and substantial rehabilitation programs, the fair market rents on which the subsidy is based reflect the cost of paying off the financing for the project. The cost differential between the Section 8 new construction and the Section 8 existing housing programs can be regarded as a capital subsidy. The Farmers Home Administration has two very small programs which pay partial capital subsidies: the very low-income repair grant program (Section 504) and the farm labor housing grant program (Section 516).

The rent supplement program – now being phased out – is similar to Section 8 in that part of the subsidy offsets the cost of retiring the loans to finance the project.

For two decades, operating costs alone have been more than most very low-income people can afford at a reasonable percentage of their income. Moreover, operating costs have been rising far more rapidly than incomes. This has forced the provision of operating subsidies for programs serving poor people.

In public housing, operating subsidies are provided in a separate, line-item appropriation calculated according to a formula which few claim to understand. The designers of the Section 8 program recognized the need to subsidize operating costs, but relied on market discipline to limit these costs. Thus, Section 8 contracts are limited by "fair market rents" for comparable unsubsidized housing. (One major problem with this concept is that "comparables" have been hard to find as unassisted rental housing construction has dried up.) Annual adjustments are made to reflect rising costs in the market area.

Other programs which provide funds to cover operating costs are the FmHA rural rental assistance program and HUD's rent supplement program. Rural rental assistance is used together with the Section 515 1 per cent-interest-rate program; rent supplements have been widely used with the similar HUD Section 236 program. Section 8 subsidies have also been linked with Section 236 and Section 515 projects to make them viable for very low-income people.

Not only is housing subsidized in a variety of ways, but federal budget figures do not give a true picture of subsidized housing costs. The three major elements of "the low-income housing budget" are (1) outlays for housing payments; (2) budget authority for additional housing assistance; and (3) authorization of credit for subsidized, unsubsidized, and federally insured loans.

> (1) The level of housing payments is largely uncontrollable: it is the cumulative cost of all of the contracts for housing assistance ever signed under all of the various subsidy programs which provide long-term assistance. Basically, these payments cover capital and financing costs for already occupied units, along with some operating assistance. In addition, annually appropriated operating subsidies for public housing and some lesser operating subsidies under

other programs are reflected in these housing payments. They can be reduced only by jeopardizing the viability of housing projects or by raising rents to unaffordable levels.

(2) Budget authority for incremental assistance is the figure around which low-income housing funding decisions focus. This figure is easily misunderstood. Because assistance is provided under long-term contracts (fifteen to thirty years), budget authority is the maximum annual assistance multiplied by the term of the contract. In other words, the maximum annual cost is multiplied by the number of years that the contract runs. This is equivalent, for an individual, to purchasing a house with a twenty-year mortgage and estimating its costs by including *all* the principal, interest, taxes, maintenance, utilities and other expenses for the twenty-year period. Few houses would cost less than $500,000 if calculated that way! For example, the 1982 appropriation initially approved by Congress (before later rescissions) to provide for an estimated 140,000 units was over $17 billion. Most members of Congress (and others outside of Congress) divide the $17 billion by 140,000 units and get an average cost of over $120,000. Then they ask why we're spending so much on housing for low-income people when other people pay only half as much.

If we ran out costs that way for tax expenditures, we could put things in a better framework. One of the concerns about low-income housing constantly raised by the Reagan Administration is that, if we never provide another dollar for additional assistance, we still have over $250 billion in budgeted expenditures already contracted for. Some of these contracts run into the next century. That looks like a lot of money. But if we run out the cost of homeowner deductions for mortgage interest and property tax payments over the rest of the century, we find that they will cost over $5 trillion! (See Appendix, p. 60).

(3) The housing budget category "credit," primarily for FmHA loans, is a separate appropriation each year to reimburse the Rural Housing Insurance Fund for the cost of subsidizing FmHA interest rates and the small losses incurred under FmHA programs. In computing the credit budget, there are also limits on HUD mortgage insurance and other housing credit programs not serving low-income people.

This review of housing subsidy approaches is essential to an understanding of both the complexity of housing assistance programs and the manifold HUD and FmHA programs which have been adopted and refined over the years in an effort to find satisfactory approaches to the dilemma of how best to provide adequate housing assistance while avoiding either waste or windfalls.

There has been much rhetoric, particularly in these times of concern over the federal deficit, about the cost of low-income housing programs. A threefold problem exists here: (1) to provide adequate levels of assistance; (2) to identify what low-income housing really costs; and (3) to avoid waste and unnecessary costs.

There would be no need for low-income housing programs if providing shelter did not cost more than low-income people can pay. This truism is worth underscoring; ignoring it leads to efforts to save money either by serving a higher income group – bypassing the poorest households – or by cutting back on assistance levels so that projects become unviable. Our present inventory of assisted housing is a valuable national resource which would cost many times as much to replace as it would to maintain adequately.

Instead of focusing on the high cost of budget authority for low-income housing – a quirk of the budget process which seriously jeopardizes our capacity to expand housing assistance – let us consider how little, after forty-five years, we are spending for this major human need.

- Outlays for low-income housing assistance have never, in any year, been even 1 per cent of total federal outlays.
- The cost of housing-related tax expenditures to the Treasury in 1981 alone exceeded *the cumulative outlays* for low-income housing assistance under all of the programs of HUD and its predecessor agencies from the adoption of the U.S. Public Housing Act of 1937 through 1981.
- Compared to the anticipated cost of housing-related tax expenditures, primarily homeowner deductions, the budget authority committed to long-term contracts for federal housing assistance is almost trivial. Unless constrained, and neither Congress nor the Reagan Administration appears inclined to address this issue, foregone revenues from homeowner deductions for the rest of this century will be many trillions of dollars (see Appendix and U.S. Congressional Budget Office, 1981).

There are ways of reducing the cost of housing assistance for low-income people. One of the most effective approaches would be to focus the provision of housing assistance on individual households and on public, non-profit, and limited equity housing owners.

Elements of a comprehensive housing policy

No single approach can deal with low-income housing needs. National housing policy must start with the principle that access to affordable housing is a basic human right. This right must be firmly established as the basis for federal housing policy and programs. Society has a fundamental responsibility to assure that everyone living in this country is able to obtain decent housing at affordable costs. The federal resources necessary to make this right a reality for low-income people can and should be provided.

The National Low Income Housing Coalition has identified eight major components of a comprehensive housing policy. These components are interdependent and inter-related. An adequate housing policy requires:

1 Adoption of an adequately funded entitlement, income-based housing assistance program to enable low-income people to obtain decent housing at costs they can afford.
2 Expansion of production and preservation programs to meet those low-income housing needs which cannot be met by an income-support program alone.
3 A strong reaffirmation of the federal government's role in guaranteeing fair access to housing by all citizens, including strengthening of the federal fair housing law and its enforcement.
4 Restructuring tax and spending policy to shift federal resources from those who have to those who do not.
5 A strong role for community-based, non-profit organizations, in the implementation of housing programs, along with the availability of federal assistance to meet a broad range of housing needs at the neighborhood and community level.
6 A strong reaffirmation of the federal government's continuing commitment to retaining the current stock of federally assisted and insured housing, now occupied by low- and moderate-income people, for their use. This includes all present public housing, HUD-assisted, HUD-insured, and HUD-held units, as well as units assisted by the Farmers Home Administration. The necessary funds should be provided to maintain this housing in viable condition.
7 Modification of monetary and credit policies to counteract the high financing costs for housing and the credit-related sharp fluctuations in residential construction, which increase the costs, prices, and rents of all housing.
8 A strong reaffirmation of the responsibility of the federal government to bring its resources to bear to prevent

displacement of low-income people from their homes and neighborhoods by either public or private action.

Several of these components are elaborated elsewhere in this volume (see in particular Florence Roisman's proposals for protecting the existing stock of government-aided housing and Paul Davidoff's discussion of anti-displacement strategies). A key and perhaps still controversial element which is absolutely fundamental is an entitlement, income-based housing assistance program – call it "housing allowances," "housing vouchers," "an entitlement to Section 8 existing housing," or by any other name. (I will use "housing allowance" or "housing assistance" to avoid the political connotations of "vouchers.")

The need for an entitlement program

Entitlement means that housing assistance for low-income people will be provided for everybody who needs it. In other words, *all* low-income households needing housing assistance would receive a payment to cover the difference between what they can afford and what housing of the size they need costs in the area where they live. These payments ought at least to be the same kind of entitlement as food stamps or Medicaid. With all of the program's faults, if a person is eligible for food stamps and applies for them, but is turned down, there is an appeals procedure; if eligibility is established, the food stamps are provided. The same is true of Medicaid.

Before Medicare and Medicaid, there really was no perceived crisis in health care delivery. Making health care affordable for millions of people who had never been able to get it was what led to the perception of a crisis in this area. The enactment of Medicaid and Medicare placed demands on the system and forced some responses, even though these were inadequate.

The health care experience is relevant because one of the

objections raised to housing allowances is that the housing is not available to make the program work. That is true. But an entitlement to housing assistance would dramatize how much more housing we have to build or rehabilitate for occupancy by low-income people. This would, in turn, strengthen the political constituency for housing and make it far easier to obtain action on production and rehabilitation programs. On the other hand, conditioning advocacy of vouchers as an entitlement on the prior availability of the housing would be comparable to postponing Medicaid until health care services were adequate.

This discussion of the fundamental need for an entitlement to housing allowances is necessarily incomplete. Considerations of eligibility, payment standards, and how an entitlement program should be phased in (assuming that this will be necessary) are beyond the purview of this chapter. However, the dimensions of the housing affordability problem are so compelling that an income-based program is essential, along with greatly expanded construction and rehabilitation programs. In 1980, according to the Annual Housing Survey:

> There were seven million households in this country who were paying more than 50 per cent of their income for housing. Almost 70 per cent of those households were renters and their median household income was between $4,000 and $5,000 a year.

> There were also six million households paying between one-third and one-half of their income for shelter. Almost 60 per cent of those households were renters and their median income was around $7,400 a year.

> There were an additional ten million households paying between one-quarter and one-third of their incomes for shelter. Roughly half were renters and their median income was $10,700 per year.

Low-income people have the highest shelter/income ratios. This is often overlooked by those concerned with the

problems of the first-time homebuyer or the plight of families with incomes of $20,000 spending 50 per cent to 60 per
cent of their income to buy their homes. Of the five million
owners paying over one-third of their incomes for total
housing costs (including taxes and utilities), only 333,000
(7 per cent) had incomes over $20,000. With so grave a
problem of housing affordability, we need to have a system
of assistance which will pay the difference between what
housing costs in the market area where people live and what
they can afford to pay for it.

There are many people who agree that an entitlement
housing allowance program is absolutely necessary to deal
with the housing problems of those on low incomes but
hesitate to support one because of its cost. They forget that
there is already a housing entitlement program: the homeowner deductions of mortgage interest and property tax
payments which people take if their incomes are high
enough. During the past few years, while Congress debated
whether we could afford another 400,000 units – or 600,000
or a million, or whatever – we were having *increases* in the
entitlement program which goes to people who are de-
monstrably the least needy – and the less need you have,
the more you get – and which were more than our *entire
expenditures* for low-income housing assistance.

The federal cost of housing-related income tax expenditures now tops $40 billion annually – more than five times
the cost of housing assistance presently provided for low-
income people. The bulk of these tax expenditures benefit
people in the top quarter of the income distribution. The
top 2 per cent of the population get more indirectly in
federal housing-related expenditures through the tax system
than the bottom 20 per cent of the population get directly
(see Appendix for further discussion).

How we got into this situation and some ideas for how
we can move toward where we should be are explored
below.

Roots of the present crisis

The present crisis in low-income housing has several roots. First is the generation-long lack of organized consumer and public interest-based advocacy for low-income housing programs. The major national housing legislation adopted in 1937 and 1949 was passed in large part because of the work of a coalition of labor, church, civil rights, and other groups, with the help in both instances of an administration in office that was pushing it. That coalition then fell apart. There was a perception in 1949 that we had passed a housing act and it was going to give everybody housing within ten years, and so other things came on to the agenda. The public interest groups that had been behind that push for low-income housing drifted away. That left a hiatus. Moreover, during these years, the conventional wisdom was that the only way to get low-income housing legislation approved at all was to bury it in omnibus housing bills and hope that Congress wouldn't really notice it. Any direct advocacy that called attention to low-income housing needs and legislation would be counterproductive.

In 1974 we were in the depths of the Nixon Administration's housing moratorium. A low-income housing effort could not be counterproductive because things could not get much worse. So a group of organizations met to see what they could do to raise low-income housing as an issue as Congress considered the 1974 Housing Act. We weren't intending to start a new organization. We just started meeting and working together. The Ad Hoc Low Income Housing Coalition which resulted from this effort became the National Low Income Housing Coalition in 1978. The National Low Income Housing Coalition has begun to provide some organized advocacy. In certain respects it does very well and in others, for reasons that have to do with its very slender resources, it has only begun to tap the potential.

One thing that became absolutely clear very soon after that first meeting in 1974 was that there *is* a constituency for low-income housing. There are organizations that care about this issue. Unfortunately, most of them do not have the staff to follow housing issues, let alone housing legislation. For example, there are many churches and religious organizations deeply concerned with low-income housing as a social issue. Some may even operate housing programs, but they have no staff responsible for following housing legislation from the perspective of what would be needed to achieve the objective of providing adequate housing for low-income people. The same thing is true of civil rights groups, most labor unions, and practically every kind of constituent organization that would care about low-income housing either from a consumer perspective or from that of concern about social issues and social justice. The constituency was there, but what it needed more than anything else was to be serviced.

One of the things the National Low Income Housing Coalition and its sister organization, the Low Income Housing Information Service, have been able to do is to service that constituency by providing information on housing needs, housing issues, and housing programs, and by mobilizing action on low-income housing.

A second root of the present crisis is the poor image of federal low-income housing programs. When the Coalition first started trying to organize support for them, many people expressed reservations about the quality of the programs and wondered whether they were worth supporting. There has been a perception, based on the failure of some housing projects, that the housing programs we have had have been so poor that they were not worth fighting for, and that we should be developing new approaches instead.

In housing, unlike any other program, mistakes are permanent and visible, and successes disappear. I am sure that just as many mistakes were made in the 1950s and 1960s in education, in employment, in health, and in all the other initiatives of the Great Society. But those things are now in the history books, while the housing projects still stand. For example, fewer than 10 per cent of the units in the public housing program are in the monster, high-rise projects that so many think of as public housing. There are some other projects that people can identify as public housing, but the successful ones are not known as public housing because they look like everybody else's housing. They are not "projects." The successes are invisible, so it is often hard to persuade people that there really are so many. The failures, unfortunately, are all too visible.

A third problem has been reluctance to face up to the cost of an adequate low-income housing program. If we had spent as much time, or even half as much time, explaining why it is that housing assistance for low-income people costs a substantial amount of money as we've spent in the last forty-five years trying to hide the cost of housing programs, we would have much better housing programs. They do cost a lot of money, and a major constraint is simply that there is – and always has been – a general unwillingness to spend a lot of money on low-income housing, particularly since the cost is high and the impact is low. We need to remind people that we have accomplished a lot with low-income housing programs. For example, almost one-third of all the female-headed renter households with incomes below 125 per cent of the poverty level live in subsidized housing (see Table 2.7). We would only have to provide another 1.7 million units or so for all of them to live in subsidized housing. Now, providing 1.7 million units is something that people can understand.

It is very hard to persuade people that we should spend a great deal of money for an effort that might take care of 1 per cent of the problem. If we could persuade them that for the same amount of money the problem would be solved in a reasonable time, there would be a greater willingness to make the commitment.

Arousing the constituency for housing

The key to obtaining an adequate national housing policy is a broad-based, articulate constituency for housing. It has been hard to arouse this constituency, because so many of the federal programs have not been perceived as responsive to neighborhood and community needs. There are reasons why most neighborhoods, regardless of their composition, do not want subsidized housing projects. While the basic one is often prejudice against low-income or minority people, there are also reasons that have to do with the way projects are designed and administered.

The usual reaction of neighborhoods when a low-income housing project is proposed is, "Don't put it here, put it somewhere else." We are never going to arouse the constituency for low-income housing as long as that is the reaction neighborhood people have to low-income housing. We must work at the problem both by trying to build neighborhood support and by developing housing programs which neighborhood people see as responsive to their needs, not as threats to their community.

Another difficulty in constituency building is that one cannot really promise people very much. Our housing need is on the order of 16 million units, just counting households now living in substandard housing or paying more than a third of their income for shelter. In the forty-five years since we began subsidizing housing for poor people, all of the low- and moderate-income housing programs we have had, with all of their numbers and all of their shapes and varieties and the range from bottom- to moderate-income groups that have been served – all of those programs together, rural and urban, have provided roughly 4.5 million subsidized housing units. That is what the private building industry provides in two good years, back-to-back. Moreover, almost a million of the currently subsidized units were not built as low-income housing. They are existing units occupied by families with Section 8 existing certificates.

Another barrier to grassroots mobilization is the confusing nature of existing low-income housing programs. Not only are the multiple approaches and programs difficult to understand, but they often divide low-income people into different constituencies for the individual programs.

Community groups must become the source of strength for housing support. But what happens when you say to a community group, "Look, we really need you to meet with your member of Congress and talk about the importance of supporting the low-income housing budget, and not cutting it in half or cutting another 100,000 units off of it" – which is what the issue comes down to very quickly – or, "We want you to write a letter to the President telling him to reject OMB's proposal to cut the housing budget and go back up to 600,000 units." What is that going to mean in a low-income community? One more unit; perhaps two; maybe five; perhaps an additional development. You cannot honestly ask people to undertake the kind of political action necessary on the housing issue if, at the same time, you have to tell them that whatever they do is not going to make much difference in solving their immediate problem. They have other things on their minds: there is daycare; there are food stamps; there is public assistance. There are a lot of things that people have to work on. It is very hard to build a constituency for housing programs under these circumstances; it is even hard to organize waiting lists.

One of the most worthwhile steps to take would be to organize people on waiting lists for subsidized housing. The problem here is that organizing raises expectations. If expectations were not raised, however, it would be difficult to motivate people to organize. Yet one should not create expectations that cannot be fulfilled.

And so, at least so far, we have not asked people to do too much. In the first place, if anybody does anything, it is so much more than has ever been done before that it seems a great deal. We have discovered, for example, that it is really quite easy to get people to sign letters to the President; it is probably quite easy to get organizations to sign letters to members of Congress – even a handful of letters has an impact.

There are probably some issues that can be organized around. For example, when President Carter was working on his urban policy, the National Low Income Housing

Coalition took a very simple-minded approach. It was basically that the premise of the national urban policy ought to be to avoid displacement. The central thrust of urban policy should be to enable people to stay in the neighborhoods where they live and to locate jobs convenient to them. That would provide a theme and a coherence and would also be a focus for organizing.

Many groups are now organizing effectively against displacement at the local level. But there needs to be a second step – taking a local activity and translating it into national advocacy. (John Atlas and Peter Dreier, in their contribution to this volume, outline some important ways of linking local, single-issue struggles with broader, multi-issue organizing.)

If individuals and organizations would take 10 per cent or even 1 per cent of the time and energy they are spending on local housing matters and put it into what is happening nationally on federal housing programs, then there would be a chance of making some major change. This urgently needs to be done, because federal housing programs – like them or not – form the base for neighborhood and community activity. These are the tools we have to use. Moreover, the amount which can be done to improve housing and neighborhood conditions for low-income people basically rests upon the quality, level, and responsiveness of federal programs.

Thus, it is vital for people working in low-income housing neighborhoods to pay attention to national legislation. Members of Congress must be approached and asked to help. The community, its needs, and its aims must be described and members asked directly to pass a law providing the required assistance. Very few members of Congress hear such requests in any detail. They need to, and if enough of them do, they will respond.

One thing to keep in mind is that only a minority of the members of Congress represent districts with substantial numbers of minority or poor people. It is very hard, therefore, to get Congressional majorities for low-income programs. Yet we must generate some sense of support for the programs in the Congressional districts of these members. That can be done in two ways: by political organizing in the districts (because there are very few that do not have some low-income enclaves or neighborhoods), or by using institutions which cut across the urban/suburban boundaries. There *are* institutions which bridge that inner-city/suburban gap. Churches are the primary institutions; labor unions are also significant in this area. Similarly, we need to make some alliances between those in the inner cities and rural people. For years, there have been far fewer differences between inner-city and rural housing needs than between inner-city and suburban problems and needs. They have common problems of lack of financing, of poverty, of poor delivery systems, and of general neglect. Therefore, both rural and inner-city advocates who are concerned about poor people should join forces and work on common or mutually supporting approaches and strategies.

Above all, we must remember that housing is more than bricks and mortar. Our housing shapes our lives, our families, and our communities. The importance we give to housing reflects our values as a society. Do we care that millions of children must live in homes and neighborhoods that violate basic standards of safety and decency? Do we care that millions of old people must end their lives without dignity or the assurance of a sound roof over their heads and heat in their homes? Do we still believe that the federal government must play a role in ending injustice, and in providing resources and assistance where no one else can do so? The answer to these questions can and must be "Yes."

Appendix: The need to limit homeowner deductions

Statement of Cushing N. Dolbeare, President, National Low Income Housing Coalition, before Committee on Finance, United States Senate, May 18, 1981.

The National Low Income Housing Coalition urges immediate action to limit homeowner deductions and convert them to tax credits. Doing this will reduce their costs, curb their most pernicious aspects, and benefit the majority of homeowners (who now do not take these deductions). . . .

Tax expenditures are far more important than direct expenditures in dealing with housing. The primary focus of attention in limiting federal housing expenditures has been placed on programs serving people who can least afford housing: low- and moderate-income people living in housing subsidized through programs of the Department of Housing and Urban Development or the Farmers Home Administration. These programs have been declining: each year since 1976, fewer assisted units have been provided. Even President Carter's budget request for 1982 called for fewer than half the units actually funded in 1976. A primary reason for this decline, in the face of rising need, is cost. Yet the cost of these programs is dwarfed by federal tax expenditures for housing, primarily homeowner deductions.

Measured in dollar outlays, the Treasury Department has estimated that tax expenditures related to housing account for more than 80 per cent of total housing costs. Moreover, tax expenditures are rising dramatically. The Treasury estimates them at $28.8 billion in 1980, $35.3 billion in 1981, and $44.1 billion in 1982. Meanwhile, direct outlays for housing assistance were estimated at only $6.1 billion in 1980, $7.4 billion in 1981, and $9.0 billion in 1982. Over 99 per cent of housing expenditures for homeowners are tax expenditures. For rental housing, however – the place where both direct and tax expenditures are being cut in the Reagan Administration's Economic Recovery Program – tax expenditures are between one-quarter and one-fifth of total outlays (Table 2.10). Table 2.11 shows the amount and cost of the various housing-related tax expenditures for 1980–2. (These figures are lower than those just cited: they use the conventional definition of tax expenditure rather than "outlay equivalent," which is an adjusted figure.)

TABLE 2.10   *Housing tax expenditures and budget outlays ($ millions)*

Description	Fiscal year		
	1980	*1981*	*1982*
Owner-occupied housing:			
Tax expenditures (outlay equivalent)	26,840	33,170	41,655
Outlays	115	150	310
Total	26,955	33,320	41,965
Tax expenditures as a per cent of total	99.6	99.6	99.3
Rental housing:			
Tax expenditures (outlay equivalent)	1,965	2,155	2,410
Outlays	6,025	7,280	8,680
Total	7,990	9,435	11,090
Tax expenditures as a per cent of total	24.6	22.8	21.7
All Housing:			
Tax expenditures (outlay equivalent)	28,805	35,325	44,065
Outlays	6,140	7,430	8,990
Total	34,945	42,755	53,055
Tax expenditures as a per cent of total	82.4	82.6	83.1

Source: Budget of the United States Government for Fiscal Year 1982: Special Analysis G: Tax Expenditures.

Homeowner deductions constitute over 90 per cent of all housing-related tax deductions. And by far the largest homeowner deductions are those for mortgage interest and property taxes. The contrast between the growth of these deductions and outlays for housing assistance is shown in

TABLE 2.11 *Housing-related tax expenditures,*[1] *1980, 1981, 1982 ($ millions)*

	1980	1981	1982	Change 1981–2	%change
Homeowner deductions					
Mortgage interest on owner-occupied homes	$15,615	$19,805	$25,295	+$5,490	+21.7%
Property tax on owner-occupied homes	7,310	8,915	10,920	+2,005	+22.5%
Subtotal (gross)	(22,925)	(28,720)	(36,215)	(+7,495)	(+26.1%)
Subtotal (net)	22,170	28,065	35,465	+7,400	+26.4%
Residential energy credits	485	540	615	+75	+13.9%
Deferral of capital gains on home sales	1,010	1,100	1,220	+120	+10.9%
Exclusion of capital gains on home sales	535	590	650	+60	+10.2%
Total	$24,200	$30,295	$37,950	+7,665	+20.2%
Investor deductions					
Expensing of construction period interest and taxes	$659	$745	$775	+30	+4.0%
Depreciation on rental housing in excess of straight line	385	410	430	+20	+4.9%
Five-year amortization for rental housing rehabilitation	15	25	35	+10	+40%
Exclusion of interest on state and local housing bonds	447	840	1,220	+380	+45.2%
Total	$1,506	$2,020	$2,460	+$440	+21.8%
Grand total	$25,706	$32,315	$40,410	+$8,095	+25.0%

[1] Tax expenditures are defined in the budget as "losses of tax revenue attributable to provisions of the federal income tax laws that allow a special exclusion, exemption, or deduction from gross income or provide a special credit, preferential rate of tax, or a deferral of tax liability affecting individual or corporate income tax liabilities."

Source: Compiled by Low Income Housing Information Service from *Special Analyses, Budget of the United States Government, 1982.*

Figure 2.1. Moreover, these are conservative estimates. The rate of increase beyond 1982 is 18 per cent annually. The Congressional Budget Office projects a much higher rate of increase, about 25 per cent for mortgage interest deductions between 1980 and 1982.

Costing less, but still significant, are provisions for deferral or exclusion of capital gains on home sales. Not estimated is a major tax benefit for homeowners, the imputed income for rent on owner-occupied homes.

Homeowner tax preferences create inequities in the tax system and are inefficient as a subsidy mechanism. William F. Hellmuth, in a paper prepared for a Brookings Institution conference, has commented on the effects of homeowner tax preferences on the tax system and the economy, as follows:

> They create horizontal inequities in the income tax system in that they provide tax savings for homeowners over tenants with comparable incomes, and differential savings between different homeowners with comparable incomes.

> They cause vertical inequities in the tax system. Since homeownership rises with income, the values of homes purchased increase as a proportion of income as incomes rise (that is, are income elastic), and the value of homeowner preferences is directly related to the marginal tax rate of the homeowner; high-income recipients benefit more from these preferences than do low-income recipients.

> They interfere with the allocation of resources between residential construction and other uses of resources. The tax expenditures favoring homeowners lower the cost of housing services and increase the after-tax rate of return on investment in homes, relative to other choices that consumers and individual investors have for the use of their funds. Tax incentives thus draw more resources into housing than would occur in the absence of such preferences.

They also distort the housing market choices in favor of residential construction suitable for homeowners, creating a demand for more single-family homes and apartments for purchase than for rental units.

Further, these homeowner tax preferences are relatively inefficient and expensive if they are considered as incentives to promote homeownership and the construction of more homes. The incentives are most valuable to those with higher marginal tax rates, the income class that would find it easiest to buy homes in the absence of tax incentives. And the incentives for homeownership are much weaker for families in the lower tax brackets whose income levels also make homeownership more difficult. Tax incentives are, of course, of no value to those whose income is so low that they pay no federal income tax. And to the extent that the tax preferences increase the demand for owner-occupied homes, the price of such dwelling units rises and puts them further beyond the reach of low- and modest-income persons. The greater value of these preferences for persons with high incomes and high marginal tax rates is likely to draw more resources into the construction of large and expensive homes; on the other hand, income-neutral incentives would be likely to result in more dwelling units to meet the housing needs of more people (Hellmuth, 1977).

Homeowner tax preferences were not planned, they just grew. It might be assumed that the homeowner preferences were a conscious policy decision, made after careful consideration of their impact and resting on the advantages of encouraging home ownership. This, however, is not the case. According to George Peterson of the Urban Institute:

The laws establishing mortgage interest and property tax payments as allowable deductions from

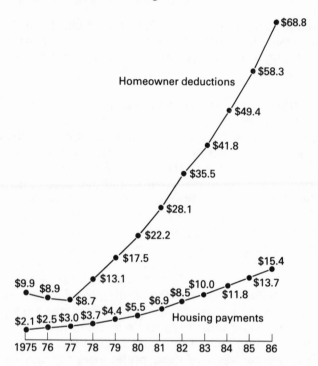

FIGURE 2.1 Homeowner deductions and housing payments, 1975 through 1986. Amount of assisted housing payments (in $ billions), compared with estimated cost of homeowner mortgage interest and property tax deduction (also in $ billions).

Source: Relevant volumes of *Budget of the United States* and Special Analyses (with homeowner deductions projected beyond 1982 at rate of 18% per year).

homeowner incomes were adopted by Congress during the Civil War, when the treatment of housing costs was debated briefly before passage of the emergency tax act which helped to finance the North's war effort. Since that time, the country has merely applied old definitions of taxable income in its successive income tax laws, despite a total transformation in the personal income tax system. The longstanding homeowner deductions did not take on true significance until World War II, when the marginal federal tax rate paid by most Americans was suddenly jumped from 4 per cent to 25 per cent, making the deductibility of homeowner expenses far more valuable than it previously had been and in the process creating an important after-tax gap between homeownership and rental costs (George Peterson, 1977).

Most homeowners do not benefit from the deductions. Peterson finds the growing importance of homeowner preferences a major cause of the increased rate of homeownership since 1950, particularly for middle- and upper-income families. But changes in tax laws have led to a "bracket creep" for homeowner deductions: they are concentrated increasingly at the upper end of the income distribution:

Without much fanfare, however, recent tax changes have worked to diminish the tax benefits of owner occupancy by making it more attractive for taxpayers to claim the standard deduction. The proportion of taxpayers itemizing their returns – and thus gaining the full benefits of the tax advantages for homeownership – fell from 58 per cent in 1969 to 31 per cent in 1975. After the recent tax revision of 1977, further increasing the standard deduction, it is estimated that only 20–25 per cent of taxpayers will itemize their returns in 1978. Ironically, the tax code then will be restricted primarily to subsidizing the housing costs of the affluent, encouraging them to consume more expensive and larger housing without greatly affecting homeownership rates over the rest of the income distribution. This shift in the tax structure will also make it more difficult to apply federal tax benefits to any but the most lavish condominiums, since most households with earnings of less than $24,000 to $26,000 will find it to their advantage to claim the standard deduction (ibid.).

The federal government spends less on housing for low- and moderate-income households than for upper-income people. In 1979, the most recent year for which figures were available, mortgage interest or property taxes were deducted from 25.6 per cent of all returns filed. Peterson's prediction was correct: at least 95 per cent of the value of the deductions was received by taxpayers with incomes above the median, and almost 60 per cent went to taxpayers with incomes in the top 10 per cent of the income distribution.

Thus, the notion that the homeowner deductions go largely to middle-income families is wrong. Moreover, homeowner deductions are entitlements: they may be taken by all who qualify, regardless either of need or of the cost to the federal government. In contrast, only one household in ten who qualifies for and needs low-income housing assistance actually receives it.

TABLE 2.12   *Revenue cost of allowing homeowners' deductions for mortgage interest and real estate taxes (1979 law, 1979 levels)*

	Returns with tax savings		Average tax savings (returns with savings)	Total revenue cost	Revenue cost as per cent of total tax paid by members of class
Expanded income class	Number of returns	Per cent of all returns filed in class			
($000)	*(thousands)*		*($)*	*($ millions)*	
Under 5	83	0.4	$104	$9	*
5–10	1,083	5.8	172	187	2.8
10–15	2,553	17.6	254	649	3.7
15–20	3,955	33.3	331	1,310	5.4
20–30	8,153	51.7	536	4,369	8.3
30–50	5,924	73.9	1,023	6,058	11.9
50–100	1,658	82.9	2,048	3,395	11.0
100 +	375	85.6	3,320	1,245	4.2
Total	23,785	25.6%	$724	$17,221	8.1%

Note: Details may not add to totals because of rounding.
* Total tax paid by members of this class is a negative amount.

Source: Reproduced from U.S. Department of Housing and Urban Development, *1980 Housing Production Report,* Appendix A. Office of the Secretary of the Treasury, Office of Tax Analysis.

Indeed, the pattern of housing assistance provided by the federal government is so inequitable (see Table 2.12) that, were we to start with a clean slate in designing housing assistance programs, and propose a pattern of entitlements, benefits, and assistance that is equivalent to what is now in place, not only would it fail to pass the Congress, but it is doubtful if anyone could be found who would introduce it.

Benefits from federal housing programs are so skewed that *the total of all the assisted housing payments ever made under all HUD assisted housing programs, from the inception of public housing in 1937 through 1980, was less than the cost to the federal government of housing-related tax expenditures in 1980 alone.* Assuming that the beneficiaries of direct and tax expenditures are arrayed, by income group, as they were in 1977, the latest year for which such an analysis is available, we would find that, for 1980:

- $4.2 billion, or 14.1 per cent of all direct and indirect housing expenditures, went to people at the bottom of the income scale, those with household incomes below $5,000. Only one household in eight receives housing assistance, and the average monthly expenditure, per recipient, was $132.

- Only $1.2 billion, or 4.0 per cent of direct and indirect housing expenditures, went to households with incomes between $5,000 and $10,000. Fewer than one household in ten in this income range received housing benefits, and the average monthly amount, per recipient, was $60.

- $16.7 billion, or 56.4 per cent of all direct and indirect housing expenditures, went to people with incomes between $20,000 and $50,000. Two-fifths of all households in this range received housing benefits and the average amount per recipient was $67 per month.

- $7.5 billion, or 25.5 per cent of all direct and indirect housing expenditures, went to people with incomes above $50,000. More than four-fifths of all households in this income bracket received tax benefits, and the average monthly amount per recipient was $309.

Homeowner tax preferences contribute to inflation in the housing market. The tax system is a major factor in encouraging investment in housing. The tendency of people who are already adequately housed – indeed, generously housed by the standards that are applied to lower-income people – to purchase bigger and more expensive houses drives up prices. Indeed, the widespread tendency to purchase housing more as an investment than as a necessity has led George Sternlieb to coin the term "post-shelter" society.

In a curious symbiotic relationship, not only do homeowner tax preferences contribute to inflation in housing, but they also make it possible for homeowners to benefit from inflation. In the words of Anthony Downs of the Brookings Institution, "investment in housing has become far more than a strategy for 'keeping up' with inflation: it helps millions of households *gain positive benefits* from inflation" (Downs, 1980). Downs finds that the average house purchased with a 20 per cent downpayment in 1976 had shown a 67.5 per cent increase in initial equity by 1980. And, because the tax on capital gains from homeownership can be excluded or deferred, the profits are tax-free.

The contrast with return from other types of investment is striking. Downs calculates, for example, that a $10,000 bond purchased in 1970 would have declined in real value by 53 per cent by 1980. But, had the investment been made as a 20 per cent down payment for a house costing $50,000 which increased in value at the national average rate, the gain over the decade would have been 891 per cent. Small wonder that those who can afford to do so purchase their homes. In addition, the costs of carrying a mortgage – at least a conventional one – decline with inflation. Since debt service often accounts for at least half the cost of living in a home, this means that real costs decline. And the deductibility of mortgage interest means that after-tax rates of interest are considerably lower than nominal rates. Moreover, the reduction becomes larger as income rises. Thus, a purchaser with a 14 per cent mortgage and taxable income of $12,000 actually pays 11 per cent after taxes, but a purchaser with a $45,000 income pays 8 per cent and one with a $60,000 income pays only 7 per cent.

At these interest rates, there is a temptation to refinance and arbitrage the money by investing in other areas – or simply to trade up and use part of the profits for personal consumption. According to the U.S. League of Savings Associations, more than four-fifths of the people who sold their homes in 1979 did not use all their proceeds for reinvestment in another home. About one-third shifted more than half their equity out of housing. The average seller took out about one-third. Because of this, Downs suggests that we may be investing too much capital in financing housing and that "much of the increased flow of mortgage funds has gone into raising the prices of existing homes, or even into non-housing consumption, rather than into expanding the housing stock to meet valid social needs."

All of this, of course, makes it harder for households who are left behind: young families and low-income families, who need housing for shelter.

The impact on rental housing. The economic advantages of homeownership, fueled by tax preferences, are at the root of a crisis in rental housing production. With inflation, rents in unsubsidized new units have risen to unprecedented levels: $500 monthly or more. At $500, a rent-income ratio of 25 per cent would require an income of $24,000. Yet, only one renter household in twenty at that income level spends as much as 25 per cent of income for rent, including utilities. Assuming a marginal tax rate of 30 per cent, the renter would have to earn $650, before taxes, for each $500 rent check. Contrasting that with the advantages of homeownership means that, in fact, tenure choice is no more real at the upper end of the income scale than it is for lower-income people. Small wonder that very little rental housing is now being produced, except with federal subsidy.

Anthony Downs describes the impact of this situation as follows:

> One of the main reasons why so few new unsubsidized rental units are being built is the immense attraction of homeownership. Most households who can afford to pay a significant amount each month for housing prefer to own their own units rather than rent. This extremely widespread preference springs partly from the great financial advantages of investment in homeownership described earlier.
>
> In the past, the overall supply of unsubsidized rental housing was constantly supplemented through new construction of apartments by private developers. Most new apartments had monthly rents that the majority of renting households could not afford. But as these new units aged, many "trickled down" through the income distribution, eventually becoming available to less affluent households. Thus, the willingness of some households to pay relatively high rents for new apartments helped keep the total supply of rental units expanding. It also helped upgrade the rental inventory as these new units replaced the oldest, most deteriorated units removed through demolition and fires.
>
> But when rapid inflation greatly magnified the financial advantages of homeownership in the late 1970s, fewer relatively affluent households were willing to rent. Why should they, when they could enjoy the benefits of owning instead? Hence, production of new unsubsidized rental apartments fell drastically in the late 1970s. This reduced the high-quality inputs into the rental inventory that had kept raising its average quality level. There is now a sizable chance that this quality level will begin

deteriorating through overly-prolonged use of older units. . . .

Thus, the outstanding success of public policies designed to increase the attractiveness of homeownership, plus the impacts of inflation, have undermined the market for new rental housing. . . .

This process distorts the entire rental housing market by cutting down the supply of new rental units. That will in turn ultimately cause overly-intensive use of older existing units. This is one important way in which public policies that make homeownership "over-attractive" have negative impacts upon some groups in society, partly offsetting their positive impacts upon homeowners (Downs, 1980).

Rather than inventing new ways of stimulating and subsidizing rental housing production for middle-income families, would it not make more sense to curb the excessive and costly homeowner preferences which have so inhibited rental housing production?

Tax preferences create condominium conversions. A major factor in investment in rental housing is the availability of tax shelters. Indeed, for most investors these shelters, rather than anticipated cash flow, are key. The nature of the shelter, however, forces owners to sell after a holding period: the shelter diminishes; cash flow increases, but is not substantial enough to offset the shelter loss; and the recapture period ends. The process of investment and sale to another investor has been going on for years. But now, all too often, the sale is not to an investor in rental housing but to a condominium converter. The result: a diminution of rental housing, displacement, and rising housing costs.

The two sides of the Internal Revenue Code come together here: not only do the incentives to invest in rental housing force its sale, but the homeowner preferences mean that there is a strong demand for converted units. This demand has strengthened as the cost of new single-family houses has risen and household size has declined, so that over half the households in the U.S. now consist of only one or two people. (For further information on the manner in which tax provisions affect condominium conversions, see Bourdon, 1980.)

For all of the above reasons, the unrestrained growth of homeowner deductions cannot be allowed to continue. The National Low Income Housing Coalition does *not* advocate repeal of homeowner tax preferences. We do urge that the Congress act promptly, however, to impose some limits on them. The Congressional Budget Office has suggested that a $5,000 cap on the mortgage interest deduction would save $4.3 billion in 1982 and $35.6 billion by 1986. Moreover, this change would affect only one taxpayer in twenty. Converting the deduction to a 25 per cent tax credit would increase revenues by about $3.5 billion in 1982. Moreover, this approach would make the deduction less regressive.

If either of these steps were taken, the cuts imposed in lower-income housing assistance programs could be restored and the programs expanded to a more adequate level without adding to the federal budget deficit.

The Urban Institute recently studied the potential impact of converting homeowner deductions to a 25 per cent tax credit. The shift would cause highest-income owners to lose both the price and income subsidies they now receive. They would have no real incentive to consume more housing, since this would increase their taxes. But middle- and lower-middle income owners would have lower taxes and an incentive to consume more housing of higher value. New construction would be stimulated. This, in turn, would relieve some of the pressures on the lower end of the housing market, thus making the lot of low-income households easier (Andreassi et al., 1980).

Moreover, if a tax credit limited, say, to a maximum of $5,000 were introduced simultaneously with a cut in individual tax rates, it could be designed so as to have little or no adverse impact. It would increase the tax reductions given to low- and middle-income people, while the higher tax for a limited number of affluent people could be offset by the reduction in marginal tax rates. If necessary, a "hold harmless" provision could be introduced for the principal residence, until it is sold or the owner moves out.

The National Low Income Housing Coalition is convinced that justice and equity demand that low-income people not be asked to bear the brunt of reducing federal housing expenditures. Moreover, a limit on homeowner deductions can again make production of unsubsidized rental housing financially feasible. And, given the other advantages and attractions of homeownership and the high rate of household formation, converting homeowner deductions to a tax credit need not have a negative impact on construction of single-family housing for middle-income people and younger families.

The challenge is here. The time to act is now.

3 Legal strategies for protecting low-income housing

Florence Wagman Roisman

This chapter proposes actions that would ameliorate the housing crisis. The proposals are made from the peculiar point of view of a lawyer whose concerns are with enforcement of existing legal requirements and with "rounding out" these requirements so that in similar situations, similar standards are applied.

A lawyer's starting point is the national housing goal set by Congress in the 1949 Housing Act: "the realization as soon as feasible of the goal of a decent home and a suitable living environment for every American family."[1] That goal never has been achieved. In the 1968 Housing Act, Congress acknowledged this failure and stressed that "the highest priority and emphasis should be given to meeting the housing needs of those families for which the national goal has not become a reality." Congress set a ten-year housing production goal and directed that in each of the ten years HUD file a report on its progress in meeting the goals. At the end of the decade, neither the specific production goals nor the overall goal had been met. The government's response was to end the requirement that HUD file such reports.[2]

The national housing goal ought to be implemented now – not at some indefinite time in the future – for every person in the United States – not narrowly "every American family" – and we ought to assure that the first, fastest, broadest effort is expended on behalf of the neediest people.

Accepting this goal leaves many questions unanswered.

It does not determine what shall be the mix of ownership and rental, high- and low-rise, urban, suburban, exurban, and rural housing. It does not determine whether the siting, design, occupancy, and management decisions should be made by government officials (at any of several levels), by neighbors, or by occupants. It does not determine what housing arrangements will be made for people who sometimes are perceived as undesirable neighbors: minorities, single-parent (especially female-headed) households, farmworkers, deinstitutionalized mental patients, people whose behavior does not conform to middle-class expectations. It does not determine the way in which the necessary subsidies shall be provided: by government construction, direct government loans, tax expenditures, or otherwise.

We do not need to answer all these questions now. However, we do need now to provide housing for the hundreds of thousands – probably millions – of people who live in parks, on grates, in cardboard boxes, in cars, in unheated, dangerously substandard, excessively expensive mobile homes, apartments, and houses.[3] We need to re-unite the families where children are in foster care or institutions only because their parents cannot secure housing that will accommodate them. In the face of this immense, desperate need, we must provide as quickly as possible a very large number of housing units that are physically decent and are affordable by and genuinely available to poor people.

To meet that immediate need will require a large expenditure of federal dollars. Large sums are necessary because housing is very expensive and a great deal of housing is required. At least one-third of the households in the United States need financial help to secure decent housing. The poorer the household, the more help is required; for very poor people, expenditures on non-housing needs consume most of the household's income. The total amount of money needed to help house the low-income half of the population is enormous. Elsewhere in this volume, Michael Stone arrived at an estimate of $55–77 billion (in 1982 dollars) as the annual cost of providing all needy households with housing subsidies. For funding of that magnitude, we can look only to the federal government.

Why should the federal government spend this money to help house people? The short answer is: because it is right to do so. Most of these people could not possibly obtain the money necessary to secure decent housing on their own or with the help of their families: these are desperately needy people, children, handicapped persons, and other hard-pressed human beings. Their moral claim on the federal government is compelling, even for critics who distinguish between the "worthy" and the "unworthy" poor. Vast numbers of needy people are "worthy" by anyone's standards. We can keep busy for years, housing these people, before we reach any of the able-bodied whose ability to secure housing unaided might be debated.

Further, basic fairness requires that the federal government make a substantial contribution to subsidizing housing for poor people, since the federal government now expends approximately $39 billion a year on subsidizing primarily upper-income people simply by allowing income tax deductions for mortgage interest and property taxes (Congressional Budget Office, 1981, Table 1).

These homeowner deductions are highly regressive: they help only people with incomes high enough both to own homes and to justify itemizing deductions; the advantage of the homeowner deduction increases as the amount of the mortgage and the amount of income increase; the "homeowner" deduction is available for as many "homes" as a person – or partnership or corporation – owns; and the deduction is available even when the person (or the entity) taking the deduction does not occupy the "home" at all, but is in the business of renting it to others.

The homeowner deduction has survived politically because of the notion that it serves "the average person" (Joan Williams, 1981). As people look more carefully at the deduction, however, they will see its regressive nature, and that examination should lead to some reforms: limiting it to only one, owner-occupied house; transforming it into a tax credit; and "capping" it, to allow credit for only a specific amount of mortgage interest payment. (For further discussion of homeowner deductions, see the Appendix to Cushing Dolbeare's chapter, p. 60.)

The homeowner deduction ought to be reformed, but low-income housing needs should be met regardless of what happens to it. The only pertinence of the deduction for our purposes is that fairness requires that if the federal government spends nearly $30 billion yearly to subsidize housing for the richest 20 per cent of households (U.S. Congressional Budget Office, 1981, Table 2.5), the federal government ought to spend at least that much to subsidize the poorest 20 per cent of households. If we cannot make both sets of expenditures, we ought to choose to spend the money on people who need it, not on people who can help themselves. There are, moreover, practical reasons for providing housing help to the poorest people: if we provide people with decent housing, we are likely to need to spend less money on juvenile and criminal justice systems and institutions, on health care, on foster care, and many other social services.

Morality, fairness, and practicality aside, respect for the law requires that the federal government take effective action to house poor people. Congress's declarations with respect to housing have been taken seriously by the courts. The United States Court of Appeals for the District of Columbia Circuit held, with respect to the 1949 Act's establishment of the national housing goal: "This statute is not precatory; HUD is obliged to follow these policies. Action taken without consideration of them, or in conflict with them, will not stand . . ., although there is, of course, broad discretion in the agency 'to choose between alternative methods of achieving the national housing objectives.' "[4] Other courts have agreed that these Congressional enactments have real substance. In a 1975 case, federal judge Gerhard Gesell enforced "the [HUD] Secretary's statutory mandate to seek to better housing conditions for low-income groups. . . ." Judge Gesell held that HUD "must . . . act in an appropriate manner and for a rational reason related to the achievement of the statutory objectives."[5] And the requirement unquestionably applies to the Farmers Home Administration (FmHA) and to the Veterans Administration (VA) as well as to HUD; all federal agencies dealing with housing "shall exercise their powers, functions and duties . . . consistently with the national housing policy . . . and in such manner as will facilitate sustained progress in attaining [this] . . . national housing objective. . . ."[6]

Thus, there is strong authority for the proposition that where HUD, FmHA, and the VA act with respect to housing, their actions must be consistent with the national housing goal set by Congress. The next step is for courts to order HUD, FmHA, and the VA to act affirmatively to achieve that goal. A suggestive analogue to the law with respect to achieving the housing goal is the law with respect to achieving school desegregation. In 1954, the Supreme Court directed that school desegregation be accomplished "with all deliberate speed."[7] By 1969, the Supreme Court had directed compliance "now."[8] Applicants for public housing have been held to have a constitutionally protected property interest with respect to their prospective tenancy.[9] Delay in satisfying a property claim can be an unconstitutional taking of the property interest.[10] Using these lines of reasoning, courts could well compel HUD to act affirmatively to achieve the goal set in the 1949 Housing Act.

And if, for whatever reason, the government chose to perform its housing obligations, it could do so without dramatic legislative changes. With adequate funding, we could ameliorate the housing crisis substantially. Common wisdom teaches that our current housing programs are designed to fail, and that "throwing money at problems" cannot produce solutions – to housing problems, at least. Neither of these propositions is true. We do have housing programs that are effective and efficient; adequate funding for these programs would swiftly effect dramatic improvement in the housing situation. What we need to do is largely to enforce existing law, adhering to three principles:

1   preserve the existing stock of housing available to poor
    people;
2   increase the stock of housing available to poor people;
3   prohibit displacement.

1   Preserve the existing stock of housing available to poor people

This country has a large stock of housing that is available
for use as decent, affordable housing for poor people. Since
existing housing is almost invariably far less expensive than
new housing, it makes great financial sense to make the
most of what we have. Some of this housing is "available"
to poor people because of some form of government involvement: (A) government ownership; (B) government
subsidization of privately owned housing; or (C) government mortgage insurance or financing of privately owned
housing (commonly but inaccurately described as "unsubsidized" housing programs). The bulk of this existing housing is (D) "private market" housing, created and maintained
without direct government involvement. The discussion that
follows considers each form of housing, and identifies ways
in which we can maintain that housing for low-income use.
The same general principles apply to each form of housing:
all units should be well-maintained and made available at
affordable cost with the neediest people being accorded
priority. In general, the greater the government involvement
in the housing, the easier it is to impose these principles,
for the most compelling justification for government involvement in housing at all is that the government is helping
those who cannot help themselves. Thus, the case for dedication to low-income use is easiest to make for
government-owned and -subsidized housing.

(A) Government-owned housing

This comes in at least three varieties: (1) housing owned by the federal government; (2) conventional public housing, owned by local public housing authorities; and (3) other housing owned or financed by state or local governments.

(1) Federally owned housing. Hundreds of thousands of units of single- and multi-family housing are owned now by HUD, the Farmers Home Administration, and the Veterans Administration, or are effectively owned by these agencies as mortgagee-in-possession. Usually, these units are acquired by the government after default by the borrower and foreclosure. In general, the law now requires that those units that had a low-income character before they came into the agency's hands must continue to serve low-income people while under government ownership and after disposition. The heart of this rule is in the 1978 amendments to the Housing Act, which provide that formerly subsidized units must continue to serve low-income people after acquisition and disposition by HUD; HUD's regulations extend similar requirements to formerly unsubsidized HUD-financed units that were in fact occupied by low-income people.[11] This general principle is a sound and important one; it needs to be enforced and expanded to apply to situations similar to those identified in the statute.

Enforcement is necessary because the Reagan Administration has evidenced a willingness to ignore the legal requirements: in at least one instance, HUD attempted to sell formerly subsidized projects without regard to these requirements.[12] Tenants, would-be tenants, and others concerned with low-income housing must exercise vigilant oversight of units that enter the HUD inventory, to be sure that HUD maintains the units' low-income character. Concerned persons also must beware that HUD not frustrate the protective principle by indirection: by tolerating vacant units or inadequate maintenance or by making disposition arrangements that substitute a shallow or short-term subsidy (such as certificates under the Section 8 Existing program) for long-term subsidies. The statute is not satisfied if a project that was deeply subsidized for a long term passes into HUD's hands and emerges with Section 8 Existing certificates for the tenants and no provision for their security after the term of the certificate expires.

In addition to enforcing the directions of the 1978 amendments, low-income occupants, would-be occupants, and their advocates need to round out the principle. With respect to HUD, ideally this means securing an express Congressional prohibition of vacancies (for at least one court has evidenced hostility to the suggestion that the existing legislation requires full occupancy[13]). This also means extending to all "FUP" (formerly unsubsidized project) units the requirement that now applies only to units occupied by low-income people; and that all these requirements be applied to single-family as well as multi-family units. The requirements also should be strengthened, for the statute now permits HUD some unnecessary leeway. "Rounding out" these principles further requires that they be applied to FmHA-and VA-owned housing, formerly subsidized and formerly unsubsidized, single-family and multi-family.[14] HUD, FmHA, and the VA should be required to assure that for every unit that comes into their control, the agency will:

- put the unit and building into the best possible condition, including rehabilitation and retrofitting for energy conservation;
- assure that shelter costs are affordable by even the poorest people;
- give priority to the neediest people in filling vacancies (as vacancies occur – not compelling existing tenants to leave); and
- in appropriate cases, transfer ownership to residents, accompanied by financing that assures decent conditions, low-income occupancy, resident control, affordable cost, and no private profit.

To implement these requirements, every HUD, FmHA, and VA office ought to maintain a waiting list of people in need of housing, keeping the list by unit size and according priority to the lowest-income applicants.

There are many other housing units, and land suitable for housing, owned by other federal agencies, notably the General Services Administration. When dealing with property that has been declared to be surplus to the needs of the United States, the government already has the authority to dedicate the property for use as low-income housing.[15] In one case, litigation produced a settlement agreement that dedicated surplus property to that use.[16] With or without the prod of litigation, the federal agencies should implement a policy of putting surplus property to this use.

(2) Public housing. The federally financed low-rent public housing program was created by the United States Housing Act of 1937, 50 Stat. 888 as amended, 42 U.S.C. Sec. 1401 et seq. It is the oldest, largest, and most successful low-rent housing program in the United States, accommodating about 3.4 million people in about 1.2 million units. Although a popular perception of "public housing" is of high-rise buildings, in fact, as Cushing Dolbeare points out elsewhere in this volume, only 10 per cent of all such housing units are in high-rise structures. What is distinctive about the conventional public housing program is its funding mechanism: the federal government pays all of the capital costs and much of the operating cost; and the occupant gets a deep subsidy, based on what the government's formula says the occupant can afford. In addition, while the program also benefits high-income taxpayers who buy the public housing authority's tax-exempt bonds, that indirect expenditure by the Treasury is really the only "payoff" to the real estate/financing interests, making conventional public housing the least expensive of the housing programs, that which inserts the least pork into the subsidy barrel. The financing mechanism works; the administration of the program is de-centralized; and every other aspect of the program is amenable

to variation: the units can be single-family or multi-family, high- or low-rise, attached or detached; the units can be managed by the public housing authority, a private firm, or the tenants; even cooperatives and homeownership are available as part of the conventional public housing program.

To release this program's great potential for ameliorating the housing crisis, we need to address at least these crucial problems:

- thousands of units are vacant;
- many occupied units need repair or rehabilitation work;
- rents are too high for many residents;
- much public housing still is racially segregated;
- communities often oppose public housing;
- management sometimes is oppressive and ineffective.

Many of these problems can be solved simply by increased funding. The money would be very well invested: these are, after all, housing units that are owned by local public agencies. The federal government and the local communities already have an enormous investment in this housing. It makes eminent good sense – fiscal as well as social – to invest in the public housing program the relatively modest amount of money required to put substandard units into good condition, so that they are decent, energy-efficient, and genuinely affordable by poor people. This means increased funding for modernization, full and prompt payment of operating subsidies, and elimination of the 30-per-cent-of-income formula for rent in favor of a formula that charges for rent no more than the household can afford – taking into account not only income and the number of dependents, but also a realistic assessment of the household's other essential expenses. (For elucidation of this concept, see Michael Stone's chapter in this volume.) That money could solve the vacancy, repair, and high-rent problems is self-evident.

Even the problem of racial segregation in existing housing

can be ameliorated by additional funding for new public housing. Frequently, a public housing authority operates several public housing projects, some virtually all-black in tenancy, some virtually all-white. To integrate those projects by requiring wholesale movement of people from one to another would be intolerably disruptive of people's lives. To integrate by attrition would be impermissibly slow – and painful for the first few pioneers in each project. Often, the best and fastest way to cure segregation in public housing will be to build new public housing, to require that it be integrated racially, and to permit tenants from existing projects to transfer to the new project, subject to the constraints imposed by the goal of integration. Then, as vacancies open up rather rapidly (assuming substantial numbers of tenants in existing projects will prefer to move to the newer developments), the older projects can be repopulated from the housing authority's waiting lists in a way that reflects a conscious attempt to achieve racial balance.

Additional funding also would go far toward reducing community opposition to public housing. That opposition has different roots: some objections are to the intrusion of housing that is architecturally inconsistent with the neighborhood; some objections are to the inadequate maintenance and the "run-down" appearance of public housing; some objections are to the failure of public housing to "pay its own way" for municipal services. These objections can be overcome by adequate funding for design, construction, maintenance, and the payments-in-lieu-of-taxes public housing authorities are required to make.

Of course, there is also opposition to public housing because of race and class discrimination. Additional funding for public housing cannot eliminate such prejudice, but if it eliminates all the other, "respectable" bases for opposing public housing, the race and class bias will be exposed, and its impact much more likely to be overcome by judicial decision, other government action, or community opposition to discrimination.

Money is not the solution to all the problems of public

housing. Oppressive management practices, for example, probably will endure as long as people who have power are disposed to use it oppressively. The best protection against oppressive management comes from giving some real power to the tenants of and applicants for public housing. This could be done in part by vastly increasing the supply of public housing and in part by giving to tenants and representatives of those on the waiting list the right and the means to monitor management. This is not a panacea, but a step toward assuring that management will be more responsive to the concerns of tenants and applicants.

Public housing, like federally owned housing, is under vigorous attack. The Reagan Administration has announced its determination that many units of public housing be demolished and has made clear its desire that as much public housing as possible be sold or otherwise converted to uses other than subsidized housing.[17] For the oldest public housing projects, the forty-year Annual Contributions Contracts with HUD are expiring, and public housing authorities may try to divert that housing from low-income use. Congress has authorized HUD to provide an extended operating subsidy in exchange for a commitment to keep the housing as low-rent public housing.[18] But that authority does not help where the public housing authority prefers to convert to another use. Locally, advocates must be alert to any threatened demolition, sale, or conversion of public housing units; Congress and state governments must be urged to act to preserve that housing for its original purpose and to provide the financing to make the preservation feasible.[19]

(3) Other housing units owned or financed by state or local government. Some state and local governments have undertaken to become owners of housing units, by purchasing projects from the federal government or from private parties or by direct construction of units. In other situations, state and local governments have become the owners of residential property involuntarily, because the owner defaulted in some obligation and a government agency took

title by foreclosure. This kind of title transfer could occur in one of the many states that have state housing finance agencies. Those agencies finance housing development and may end by having to make good a borrower's default in her/his repayment obligation. The same kind of transfer of title to a government agency also occurs because of tax foreclosures when the owner's failure to pay taxes leads the local government to foreclose and take title to the property. Another category of state- and local government-owned housing is property that government agencies long since have owned for other uses; for example, buildings that were once schools or other public institutions could now be used for housing people.

State- and city-owned properties are numerous; in some places conflict already has erupted over the proper use of this housing.[20] State- and locally-owned housing should be subjected to the same principles proposed for federally owned housing and conventional public housing. Current occupants should be protected. Whether the present occupants are homeowners who defaulted on their mortgages or taxes, or tenants of owners who left taxes or mortgages unpaid, the government should work out a way for the occupants to stay. This should be done to avoid the social as well as personal costs of displacement. The government can more easily afford a moratorium on shelter payments than otherwise provide for homeless children and abused spouses. When vacancies do exist, they should be filled promptly, with preference accorded the neediest people. The housing should be well maintained, and the shelter costs set at a level residents can afford.

State and local governments can use some of their own funding for these purposes; they also have access to federal block grant funds appropriate for this kind of use, certainly including Community Development Block Grant funds.

(B) Government-subsidized, privately owned housing

In addition to the units that federal agencies own or effectively own as mortgagee-in-possession, there are more than two million privately owned housing units over which federal agencies have substantial regulatory control. Some of these are the federally subsidized units built under the Section 221(d)(3), Section 236, Section 202, and Section 8 programs of HUD and the subsidized homeownership, rural rental, and farm labor programs of the Farmers Home Administration.[21] In general, these units are now serving lower-income people; certainly, the statutes and regulations were drawn up to achieve that result. What is needed with respect to these units is careful monitoring for law enforcement – to assure, for example, that ineligible people are not admitted to Section 8 projects. In addition, HUD and FmHA should be vigilant to assure that lowest-income people are preferred – or, at the least, are not discriminated against – when vacancies occur. HUD and FmHA ought to assure that all units in these buildings that can be subsidized are subsidized, and that they are subsidized as deeply as possible. Finally, the federal agencies ought to be vigilant to keep these units in the program permanently, and to encourage non-profit, cooperative, or resident-controlled ownership.

In fact, of course, the Reagan Administration's policy has been exactly the opposite of what it should be. This administration has encouraged the reduction of government involvement in the subsidized housing stock; has taken no steps to limit the ineligible population; has encouraged the substitution of shallower, shorter-term subsidies for deeper, longer-term subsidies; has permitted the termination of commitments by project sponsors; and has actively encouraged non-profit and cooperative owners to involve syndicators in refinancing their projects, thus producing at best only a small amount of money for the project and a very large amount for the syndicators, all at the expense of the federal taxpayers.

To some extent, these problems can be addressed by vigilance on the local level. Thus, for example, HUD recently agreed to permit the non-profit sponsor of a subsidized project for the elderly to prepay its mortgage in order to sell the property to a profit-motivated entity. The prepayment and sale would have converted the 150-unit building into housing for much wealthier people. (The HUD-regulated Section 202 rent for a one-bedroom apartment was $194 per month; the landlord's proposed increase was to $425 per month.) The tenants complained to Congress, prompting a hearing and investigations by the General Accounting Office and HUD's Inspector General. The tenants also sued HUD and the sponsor, and secured relief.[22] Local vigilance is essential, but so is national supervision. When federally subsidized housing is in danger of diversion to other uses, Congress must ride herd on HUD and FmHA. In the case of Section 202, existing law clearly prohibited HUD's conduct; similar principles can and should be applied to other programs.[23]

(C) Government mortgage insurance or financing of privately owned housing

There are millions of "unsubsidized" units that are subject to some control by HUD (or FmHA) because the agency made the original financing possible, even though it provided no direct subsidy. These agencies do have some power to assure decent conditions and regulate rents and management practices in such buildings, and to withhold permission to prepay mortgages, convert to condominium or other higher-income use, or demolish or sell the buildings. In general, the Reagan Administration has been trying to reduce its ability to regulate these projects.[24] The federal government should, instead, exercise all the control it can to make these units serve the national housing goal.

That control will not be asserted by the agencies voluntarily. Local vigilance and insistence on preservation of housing is essential. Litigation often has been unsuccessful, partly because courts have regarded these housing programs as intended to benefit the developers rather than lower-income (or indeed any) residents.[25] Congress could, of course, clarify the obligation to devote these units to lower-income use, and could provide supplemental funding to encourage that dedication (together with rehabilitation and retrofitting for energy conservation). Of course, the likelihood of Congressional action is tied to the magnitude of constituent complaints.

(D) "Private" housing

Most people in the United States – and most poor people in the United States – live in housing that is not owned, subsidized, or overtly financed by the federal government. Of course, all housing is substantially influenced by the government's tax, fiscal, and monetary policies, but the largest block of housing is what we call "private" market housing.

Governments can exercise substantial control over private housing to dedicate at least some significant portion of it to low-income use. Rent control is an important part of such an effort: at the least, landlords should not be permitted to raise rents unless they can justify doing so (Urban Planning Aid, 1973). Eviction control is a crucial part of rent control: tenants must be secure in their tenure unless the landlord can prove a particular good cause for eviction. Effective enforcement of housing, fire, plumbing, electrical, and related codes would help to maintain homes in decent condition.

Fifteen years ago, an authoritative study described various ways of securing code enforcement through civil penalties, injunctions, receiverships, and municipal repair programs. The study concluded that imposition of civil penalties has many advantages, "that injunctive relief can be an effective sanction in housing enforcement," that court-appointed receivership is "one of the most effective and massive remedies for dwellings with major violations," and that municipal repair programs "remain a reserve power on the statute books, a reserve power that should be more frequently used" (Grad, 1968, pp. 40–70).[26] State and local governments would do well to heed now the advice given in 1968.

2 Increase the stock of housing available to poor people

The limitation of relying solely on existing housing is that even if there is in theory enough housing to go around, the existing housing may be the wrong size, in the wrong place, or actually unavailable because of discrimination based on race, sex, or source of income. For large families, minorities, single-parent households, handicapped people, farmworkers and other residents of rural areas, unless new housing is created specifically for them, no decent housing will be available.[27]

New production can be accomplished with relative ease. The public housing program has served us well for forty years. If it were not starved for funds, and public housing authorities were able to offer communities an assurance that public housing would be maintained decently, much of the local opposition to public housing would disappear. Some neighborhoods, of course, will oppose even decently maintained, architecturally consistent public housing because the neighbors want to avoid the economic and racial integration that public housing may bring. Some of even this opposition could be overcome by money: if a neighborhood were provided with a playground, a park, a swimming pool, a library, or reduced property tax assessments in consequence of the placement of public housing, the opposition to public housing could be lessened, if not eliminated.

The Farmers Home Administration's subsidized housing programs also have met the test of time. A new deep subsidy homeownership program (the Home Ownership Assistance

Program – HOAP) was created by Congress in 1968 but never funded; it should be implemented.[28] A great distinction of the FmHA programs is direct government lending, which eliminates much of the wasted expense associated with HUD programs that benefit lenders and investors at least as much as residents. A further great distinction of the public housing programs and some parts of the FmHA and HUD programs is that the units that have been produced are owned by public or private non-profit agencies so that they may be dedicated perpetually to the common good. in general, we ought only to pursue housing programs that spend money on creating housing directly, and avoid tax expenditures and other devices to benefit upper-income investors, financiers, and industry interests. We ought not to pay for housing that can be diverted from the use for which it was created. Housing programs ought to be aimed at providing housing for people who need it, not at subsidizing participants in the housing process.

New housing programs will take years to design and implement. Certainly, we should make housing legislation as close to perfection as possible, which may well involve substantial restructuring of the economy. In the meantime, however, we can swiftly bring substantial amelioration of the current disastrous housing shortage if we will only provide funding for producing housing with the existing programs that have earned support.

3 Prohibit displacement

Part of the principle of protecting what we have is protecting housing for the people who have it now, even if they are not the poorest people. Forced displacement should be prohibited in virtually every situation, excepting only cases where public necessity (not convenience) absolutely requires displacement, and suitable comparable and acceptable replacement housing actually has been provided for every displacee in the immediate neighborhood or wherever else is the choice of the displacee. (Paul Davidoff, in his contribution to this volume, proposes an interesting Constitutional theory to support an individual's right not to be displaced.) One way of combining avoidance of displacement and increases in the stock of housing controlled by the government and therefore available for housing low-income people, is to create a program of foreclosure-avoidance on government-insured and conventionally-insured units.

In principle, when HUD or FmHA subsidizes and insures the mortgage on a single-family house, the agency undertakes not only to protect the lender but also to assure the borrower – the homeowner – that at least in some circumstances the agency will extend some assistance to prevent the homeowner's loss of the home. By statute, the Farmers Home Administration is authorized to provide moratorium relief, including cancellation of interest due, to a homebuyer who is unable to make mortgage payments "without unduly impairing his standard of living" (42 U.S.C. Sec. 1475).[29] HUD homeownership programs are subject to similar requirements under the HUD Mortgage Assignment Program (24 C.F.R. Sec. 203.650 et seq.), whereby defaulting borrowers can ask HUD to take over their mortgages and afford them more time or otherwise better terms. The HUD Mortgage Assignment Program has been supplemented by the TMAP (Temporary Mortgage Assistance Payment) program of loans to help defaulting mortgagors (12 U.S.C. Sec. 1715 u(a)).[30]

The foreclosure-avoidance principle is an idea whose time has come. As our economic situation worsens, more and more people are threatened with loss of their homes. At the end of 1981, over 5 per cent of all mortgage loans were at least thirty days past due, the highest rate the Mortgage Bankers Association has recorded since it began its quarterly surveys in 1953; in high unemployment areas, the delinquency rate is close to 8 per cent. The government can provide a double service now, by offering assistance to the homeowners, permitting them and their families to continue to live in their homes as long as they please, providing only that when the residents choose to leave, the government has control of the housing and uses it to house other needy people. The current occupants need not lose any of their equity. This could be done by applying to conventional mortgages principles applied in the HUD Mortgage Assignment Program and TMAP program.

This sort of program has been proposed by Chester Hartman and Michael Stone (Hartman and Stone, 1980). The program need not be compulsory, and need not be universal. If it were made available to homeowners at their option – to avoid mortgage foreclosure – homeowners and purchasers would benefit immediately, and poor people would benefit ultimately as the original occupants moved and the housing was dedicated to low-income use. In the current housing market, even the lenders might be amenable to such a program as this.[31] The same principle should be applied to rental housing, to save the housing for the tenants when a landlord defaults.

What, then, ought to be done? We ought to make a commitment to devote vast resources to providing a stock of decent housing affordable by and available to the poor. We ought to reject the argument that the federal government has no obligation to house poor people and the arguments of those who promote subsidies to financiers and providers without regard to the need to subsidize the poor people who need housing in which to live. We ought to recognize housing as a human right and satisfy that entitlement. If we did so, we would have no housing crisis.

Notes

1   42 U.S.C. Sec. 1441(a).
2   In its April 1982 final report, the President's Commission on Housing rejected altogether the notion of setting housing needs and goals figures, placing instead unbridled confidence in the ability of the private sector to meet those needs, whatever they be, if only bars to housing developers and investment are removed (U.S. President's

Commission on Housing, 1982, p. 69). For a review of the lack of progress in meeting the goals, see National Housing Law Project (1981), pp. 1.2.1–1.2.2.

3 See, e.g., U.S. House of Representatives, Subcommittee on Housing and Community Development, 1982; Cummings, 1982.

In November 1982, the Council of Large Public Housing Authorities surveyed thirty public housing authorities, ranging from the New York City Housing Authority (with 147,000 conventional public housing units) to the Harrisburg, Pennsylvania, Public Housing Authority with 1,500 units. The thirty authorities reported 268,550 households on their waiting lists.

4 *Commonwealth of Pennsylvania v. Lynn*, 501 F.2d 848, 855 (D.C. Cir. 1974).

5 *Cole v. Lynn*, 389 F. Supp. 99, 102 (D.D.C. 1975); accord, *United States v. Winthrop Towers*, 628 F.2d 1028, 1035 (7th Cir. 1980).

6 42 U.S.C. Sec. 1441; see, with respect to Farmers Home Administration, *Rocky Ford Housing Authority v. United States Department of Agriculture*, 427 F. Supp. 118 (D.D.C. 1977).

7 *Brown v. Board of Education of Topeka, Kan.*, 349 U.S. 294, 301 (1954).

8 *Alexander v. Holmes County Bd. of Educ.*, 396 U.S. 19 (1969).

9 *Holmes v. New York City Housing Authority*, 398 F.2d 262 (2d Cir. 1968).

10 *Evans v. City of Chicago*, 689 F.2d 1268 (7th Cir. 1982).

11 Section 203 of the Housing and Community Development Amendments of 1978, 12 U.S.C. Sec. 1701z–11; 24 C.F.R. Part 290.27. For a discussion of the issues, see National Housing Law Project (1981), Sec. 15.3.3.

12 "1982 Developments in Federal Housing Law," *Clearinghouse Review*, 16, pp. 794–6 (January 1983). The lawsuit is *Krupp Bros. v. Pierce*, D.D.C. Civil Action No. 82–2261.

13 *Daniels v. U.S. Dept. of Housing and Urban Development*, 518 F. Supp. 989 (S.D. Ohio 1981).

14 Arguments for applying these principles to the Farmers Home Administration are made in National Housing Law Project (1982), Sec. 22.1.

15 40 U.S.C. Sec. 484(b). See National Housing Law Project (1982), Sec. 15.4, and National Housing Law Project (1981), Sec. 15.5.

16 *Alabama Cooperative Association v. Joel Solomon*, D.D.C. Civil Action No. 78–1936.

17 HUD's proposed budget for fiscal year 1983 provides for the demolition of 5,000 public housing units; "thinning out" of public housing units was recommended by the President's Commission on

Housing ("1982 Developments in Federal Housing Law," *Clearinghouse Review,* 16, p. 794 (January 1983)).
18 42 U.S.C. Sec. 1437g(a)(2); 24 C.F.R. Sec. 869; 45 Fed. Reg. 52373 (August 7, 1980).
19 National Housing Law Project (1981), Sec. 15.2.
20 In Philadelphia, for example, squatters occupied single-family houses owned by the city as well as by HUD (*Philadelphia Daily News,* October 13, 1981). On New York's Lower East Side, the issue has been joined over the city's acquisition of title to homes by tax foreclosure, and the city's plan for disposition of that housing. Washington, D.C., and other cities have experienced disputes over whether public buildings should be used to house the homeless; in New York and other cities controversy has arisen over the need to improve some public buildings such as armories so as to make them suitable for use as housing (Herman, 1981).
21 At the end of 1980, there were 3,148,000 HUD-subsidized rental units, of which 1,956,000 were not public housing (Zais, et al., 1982, Table 3–2, p. 54).
22 *Gordon v. HUD*, C.A. No. 82–4362-RMT(Mcx) (———D.CA. August 27, 1982), discussed in *Housing Law Bulletin,* XII, pp. 11–13 (September–October 1982).
23 For further discussion and analysis, see National Housing Law Project (1982), Chapters 15, 19, 20.
24 HUD has proposed the effective deregulation of rents in "unsubsidized" projects. 47 Fed. Reg. 26852 (June 22, 1982); "1982 Developments in Federal Housing Law," *Clearinghouse Review*, 16, pp. 794–6 (January, 1983).
25 See, e.g., *Tenants Council of Tiber Island-Carrollsburg Square v. Lynn*, 497 F.2d 648 (D.C. Cir. 1973).
26 In at least one state, New York, the receivers' lien can be superior even to the lien of mortgagees; see *In re: Department of Buildings of the City of New York*, 14 N.Y.2d 291, 200 N.E. 2d 432 (1964).
27 In theory, all housing could be made available to poor people by giving them enough cash – or coupons, stamps, certificates or vouchers – to purchase or rent whatever housing they pleased. In practice, vouchers do not go very far toward solving the problem. The deficiencies of vouchers are discussed in Hartman (1982b).
28 National Housing Law Project, (1982b), Sec. 21.2..
29 This provision has been implemented by regulations (24 C.F.R. Sec. 1951.17) and has been enforced judicially. See, e.g., *United States v. Gomiller*, 545 F. Supp. 17 (N.D. Miss. 1981), where Chief Judge Keady invalidated an FmHA foreclosure even though FmHA had complied with the regulations' requirement that it give written notice to the borrower of the availability of moratorium relief. In *Gomiller*,

the Court held that because the borrower could not read or write, FmHA had an additional obligation to explain *orally* the availability of moratorium relief.

30 The Mortgage Assignment Program originated in the consent order that succeeded Judge Will's opinions in *Brown v. Lynn,* 385 F. Supp. 986 (N.D. Ill. 1974), and *Brown v. Lynn,* 392 F. Supp. 559 (N.D. Ill. 1975). The most recent decision in this case is *Ferrell v. Pierce,* 560 F. Supp. (N.D. Ill. 1983). The Veterans Administration's handbooks and other subregulatory material authorize (if indeed they do not require) similar relief for defaulting mortgagors, but litigation has not yet succeeded in enforcing that requirement. See, e.g., *Rank v. Nimmo,* 677 F.2d 692 (9th Cir. 1982), *cert. denied,* ——U.S. ——(1982).

31 Lenders undoubtedly would prefer this form of relief to court injunctions against foreclosure sales. Such injunctions were recently issued in Allegheny and Philadelphia Counties, Pennsylvania (see, respectively, *In re: Order of Court Staying execution of Sales of Dweller-Occupied Buildings,* Court of Common Pleas, Allegheny County, Memo Opinion to Adm. Order No. 2 of 1983, January 12, 1983, Papadakos, A.J.; and *In re: Order of Court Staying Sheriff Sales of Owner-Occupied Dwellings,* Court of Common Pleas, Philadelphia County, January Term, 1983, 34–14, Edward Bradley, A.J.).

4 Housing and the economic crisis: An analysis and emergency program

Michael E. Stone

The nature and extent of the housing problem

I want to argue that most housing problems can be traced logically or historically to the problem of affordability – to the squeeze between incomes on the one hand and housing costs on the other. To be sure, not all housing problems are simply reducible to the affordability squeeze. Discrimination in housing, for example, has a dynamic of its own; restricted housing opportunity for oppressed people and groups is in part an affordability problem resulting from lower incomes caused by discrimination in education and employment, but clearly there is housing discrimination that is not reducible to income differences. In addition, some problems associated with or growing out of the design of housing are the result of certain assumptions and conventions about household structure and composition, the role of household members – most particularly the role of women – and cannot be fully understood in terms of cost or affordability constraints. Nevertheless, most other familiar aspects of the housing problem – including problems of physical condition and space, security of tenure, community viability, the amount, type and location of new construction, and the allocation of public and private financial resources to housing – not just the obvious cost problems of rents, utilities, taxes, interest rates, and sales prices – are ultimately reducible to the interaction between incomes and housing costs.

Several aspects of the relationship between incomes and housing costs are important to understand. Most important, the relationship between incomes and housing costs is fundamentally different from that between incomes and the cost of any other necessity of life. Indeed, income on the one hand and housing cost on the other are the two most decisive determinants of the living standard of most households.

Why should this be so? First of all, housing is physically quite different from other consumption items: it is large, durable, tied to location, and generally must be purchased as a complete dwelling unit, not as a shopping basket of separately selected items (rooms, facilities, amenities, location) in the way that food and clothing are purchased. And because housing is not literally consumed as food is, and thus is not purchased anew on a regular and frequent basis, once a household begins to consume the services of a particular dwelling it is relatively hard to alter the amount and type of housing services consumed; that is, it is much harder to move than to, say, switch food stores or food items or defer buying new clothing. What this means is that the amount that we have to pay for housing tends to be rather rigid and inflexible. Housing costs thus tend to represent the first claim on the disposable income of a household. Everything else generally has to fit into what is left of the income after paying for housing. To be sure, in extreme emergencies people are going to buy food to stay alive, even if it means not meeting their housing expenses, but in general people adjust their other expenditures to fit the constraints of their housing costs and incomes rather than adjust their housing costs to fit their other expenses.

Furthermore, because of the bulkiness of housing, its immobility, its attachment to land, when one purchases housing s/he is not just obtaining the services of the dwelling, but the advantages and disadvantages of the location, in terms of social environment, physical environment, accessibility, municipal services, and so forth. The amount that a household can and does pay for housing thus determines the entire environment in which it lives – not just the quality of the dwelling unit – in a way that is unmatched by any other consumption expenditure, even food and medical care.

There are two branches I now want to take in thinking about the importance of housing costs in relation to income. First is a quantitative branch – thinking about an appropriate way of conceptualizing how much a household reasonably can afford to pay for shelter. While this is important, in the long run I believe that the more qualitative aspects of the relationship between incomes and housing costs are even more profound, and I will dwell more on this second branch.

The conventional view of the housing affordability problem is based upon a certain notion of how much people reasonably can be expected to pay – namely, the famous 25 per cent of income rule-of-thumb. Even this rule-of-thumb is subject to various adjustments and interpretations depending upon one's point of view and one's political position. For a time analysts and policy makers thought 20 per cent was appropriate, and now 30 per cent is becoming the arbitrary rule that is being applied.

What I would like to show is why any particular percentage, regardless of what it is, does not make sense, whether it be 10, 20, or 30, rather than 25 per cent. I do not mean to suggest, though, that it is impossible to arrive at a quantitative standard of affordability. Indeed, the above analysis of the distinctive nature of housing costs provides a logical basis for developing such a quantitative standard, and it is a sliding scale of affordability.[1]

Imagine two households of comparable disposable (i.e., after-tax) incomes. Suppose that they both have disposable incomes of about $10,000; one is a single person, while the other is a single parent with five children. What would be the difference in the cost of non-shelter necessities of life, based upon some specified level of adequacy for these necessities? Obviously, the large household would need substantially more for its non-shelter necessities than would the small household to achieve a comparable material quality of life. This implies that a larger household can afford to spend *less* for housing – if it is to meet its non-shelter needs at the given level of adequacy – than can the smaller household.

That is, the conception that there is a maximum amount which a household reasonably can be expected to pay for shelter is perfectly plausible, for it recognizes the special significance of housing costs. It says that because housing costs are large and inflexible, and because they generally make the first claim on income, if a household pays too much for shelter it will not have enough money left to pay for its other necessities. Once one begins to play out the logic of this concept, one can see fairly quickly that there simply cannot be any single percentage – that in general, for a given level of income, smaller households can afford to spend more money and hence a higher percentage of income for housing than can larger households.

Similarly, if one were to take two households of the same size, but with different after-tax incomes, say, one with $20,000 and the other with $10,000, then both would need to spend about the same amount to achieve the same standard of living in terms of their non-shelter items. The higher-income household thus could afford to spend more for housing, as a percentage of income as well as in dollars.

Playing out this logic without yet discussing the question of a standard of adequacy for non-shelter items: a small household with a given income can afford to spend more than a large household of the same income; while a household of a given size can afford to pay a higher proportion of income for shelter as its income rises. That is, an appropriate standard of affordability for housing is a sliding scale, with household size and income as the principal variables, factors, or parameters which determine where on the scale a household lies.

Any attempt to reduce affordability of housing to a single percentage of income – no matter how low or high – simply does not correspond to the reality of fundamental and obvious differences among households. Even attempts to establish a few prototypical groups and have a somewhat different percentage for each, or to set up narrow ranges in order to recognize some differences, fail to grapple in a logically sound way with the range of variation in what households really can afford to pay.

Most households do not, of course, pay what they realistically can afford: many pay more, while some pay less. In doing so, though, they are not simply choosing freely among limitless opportunities. Since housing is a necessity, is costly, and its cost is inflexible and generally represents the first claim on households' disposable income, after paying for their shelter many people simply cannot adequately meet their non-shelter needs. I have labelled such a state "shelter poverty," a situation which does not refer to inadequate housing, but rather to deprivation of non-shelter necessities resulting from the squeeze between incomes and housing costs.

How then can the sliding scale of affordability and the shelter poverty concept be operationalized? In order to do so, it is necessary to determine what constitutes a minimum level of adequacy for non-shelter items and what would be the cost of achieving this minimum level, recognizing that the cost will certainly be different for each size household and will change over time as prices change; it will also vary geographically with climate and price differences, although geographical averaging is possible.

I have used the Bureau of Labor Statistics Lower Budgets for determining the cost of non-shelter necessities at a minimum level of adequacy.[2] Utilizing the costs from the Lower Budgets, scaled for various size households, and taking into account income taxes and social security taxes, I have operationalized the sliding scale of affordability developed above. Figures 4.1 and 4.2 present the scale for 1980. They reveal, for example, that in 1980 on average a family of four with a gross income of under $17,500 could not have afforded as much as 25 per cent for shelter; indeed, if their

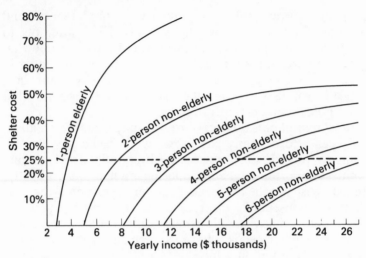

FIGURE 4.1   Maximum affordable shelter cost. U.S. 1980
(% of income)

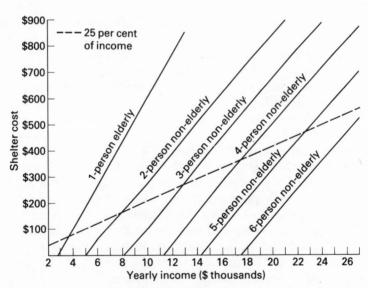

FIGURE 4.2   Maximum affordable shelter cost, U.S. 1980
($ per month)

income was under $11,000 they could not have afforded anything for shelter and still met their non-shelter necessities at the minimum level specified by the BLS Lower Budget. One-person households, on the other hand, could have afforded 25 per cent for shelter at an income of about $4,000 and a greater percentage at higher incomes, but six-person households needed incomes of nearly $30,000 to be able to afford 25 per cent of income.

Matching this affordability scale against the actual housing costs of households, we find that over 25 million households in the U.S. – 32 per cent of all households – were "shelter poor" in 1980. This total includes 11.6 million renter households and 13.6 million homeowners. However, two-thirds of all households are homeowners, so the relative incidence of shelter poverty among homeowners is only about 26 per cent while 43 per cent of renters are shelter poor. During the 1970s the number of shelter poor households increased by 6.4 million (34 per cent), with the rate of increase somewhat greater for renters than for homeowners.[3]

Shelter poverty is thus a pervasive and persistent problem. As a social indicator, the quantification of housing affordability in this way reveals the magnitude of squeeze between incomes and housing costs. Yet this measure cannot be said to exaggerate the scope of the problem, for comparing the incidence of shelter poverty with the extent of households paying 25 per cent or more of income, we find that 28 million households – 35 per cent of all households – were paying 25 per cent or more in 1980. The shelter poverty approach thus reveals a slightly less pervasive affordability problem than does the conventional standard.

More significant though than the comparison of aggregate figures on the extent of the affordability problem is the difference in distribution of the problem suggested by the shelter poverty approach. Shelter poverty reveals a far more serious and concentrated affordability problem among households of four or more persons and with incomes of under $15,000 than does the 25 per cent standard, since many such households are shelter poor even if they are paying less than 25 per cent of their incomes for shelter. Specifically, almost 95 per cent of all households (renters and homeowners) with four or more persons and incomes under $15,000 were shelter poor in 1980, while less than 30 per cent of such homeowners and less than 70 per cent of such renters were paying 25 per cent or more of their incomes for shelter. These differences amounted to nearly 2.4 million homeowners and over 800,000 renter households who were shelter poor though paying under 25 per cent of income for shelter.

On the other side, the shelter poverty approach suggests that smaller- and higher-income households have, in general, a less serious affordability problem than the 25 per cent standard shows, because many of these households can indeed afford to pay over 25 per cent without hardship. Thus, even though over 3.5 million households of one to three persons with incomes of $15,000 or more were paying at least 25 per cent of their incomes for shelter in 1980, nearly 3.3 million, or 93 per cent, of these households (2.5 million homeowners and 750,000 renters) were *not* shelter poor.

Responding to the quantitative affordability problem

The analysis so far has several major types of policy implications. First, it suggests the need for substantial changes in the formulas for determining eligibility and assistance levels for households in subsidized housing, so that whatever subsidy dollars are available are allocated more appropriately on the basis of true need. In principle, the full shelter poverty scale could be utilized: it could take into account local variations in living costs rather than just using national averages, and could be updated annually with changes in the cost of living, just as eligibility levels, fair market rents, and so forth, in subsidized housing are now computed with variations in space and time. In utilizing the approach with individual households who are applying for or being recertified for subsidies, the standard shelter poverty scale based on income and household size could even be adjusted to allow for such items as excess medical, childcare, and other so-called extraordinary expenses, as has been done in computing subsidized housing rents under the traditional formulas. Finally, since the shelter poverty formulas would have many of the largest and lowest-income households actually paying zero rent, the new approach might be easier to achieve politically in the short run if it were modified to require minimum rent payments of, say, 5 per cent of gross income, as was the policy in public housing until recently.[4]

The shelter poverty approach to housing subsidies is thus quite feasible administratively and could, in principle, be implemented independent of debates, struggles, and decisions about the overall need for and level of housing subsidy appropriations. However, since the shelter poverty approach does represent a sharp departure from the traditional formulas, it may be worth considering an administratively even simpler and perhaps politically more practical way of moving toward such a sliding rent scale in subsidized housing. The traditional rent subsidy formulas have required assisted households to pay 25 per cent (now moving in increments toward 30 per cent) of *net* income, where net income has been based on certain deductions, as mentioned above, such as standard deductions of $300 for each minor child.[5] The $300 deductions, though minimal in their impact, arose from the same concept as the shelter poverty approach, namely, that a certain dollar amount of income should be shielded from shelter costs in order to be available for other necessities and that larger households need more for non-shelter items than do smaller households. Permitting such standard deductions actually results in larger and lower-income households paying lower percentages of their gross incomes for shelter than smaller and higher-income households, even though all are paying the same percentage of *net* income. The deductions of $300 are too small and are not available for all members of a household, so in practice there has been only very slight skewing toward a sliding scale (see Table 4.2), but the principle has been established.

Thus, a strategy aimed at increasing substantially the standard dollar deductions and extending them to all household members might be more feasible than an attempt to eliminate and replace the existing formulas with the shelter poverty formulas. Furthermore, increasing the amount and extending the applicability of the dollar deductions, by shielding a larger amount of income for non-shelter expenses, would permit an increase in the percentage of net income which must be paid; lower-income and larger households would appropriately pay lower rents in subsidized housing, while the highest-income small households, who can afford to pay somewhat more, would be expected to pay higher rents. Indeed, the shelter poverty scale would be roughly approximated by defining net income as gross income minus $3,000 for each household member and then requiring the household to pay 70 per cent of net income for shelter.

Of course even this latter proposal, while quite simple conceptually and workable administratively, would be such a dramatic change that it is unreasonable to expect it could be achieved in one grand step. The new formula might be used, though, as a basis for political education around the inadequacy of the traditional approach and quite possibly could be achieved incrementally. That is, within the political context of attempts to raise the rents in subsidized housing by both raising the percentage of net income to be paid by tenants and reducing or eliminating deductions and counting other sources of income, an appropriate strategy would be to focus not on the percentage of income but on the definition of income. Increases in the required percentage of net income to be paid might be acceptable, but if and only if there are simultaneous and appropriate *increases in the deductions* allowed in computing net income.

I have done a series of calculations to determine what kind of changes in the definition of net income would be required to move toward more equitable subsidy formulas and thus mitigate the effects on the most needy of increases in the percentage of net income to be paid. With a 30 per cent of net income formula, increasing the deductions to $600 and allowing such a deduction for each and every household member in arriving at net income would raise rents by about $15–20 a month above the old 25 per cent formulas for the relatively higher-income families near the income limits, while reducing rents by as much as $30 a month for the lowest-income large households; the crossover between rent reductions and rent increases would occur at about 50 per cent of the income limits for small households and at about 80 per cent of the income limits for large households. If rents were raised to 35 per cent of net income, with deductions of $900 for each household member, the result would be about the same crossover between lower and higher rents and slightly greater rent reductions at the low-income end, along with somewhat greater increases at the higher-income end in comparison with the 30 per cent and $600 per person formula.

Tables 4.1 and 4.2 represent examples of the type of computations I have carried out, in this case for four person households with one adult, based on 30 per cent of net income and various possible definitions of net income.[6] These tables permit not only an examination of the changes I am suggesting, but also a determination of the impact of the changes being implemented and proposed by the Reagan Administration. Using Table 4.1, for example, a single parent with three children and with a cash income of $6,000 a year paid $100 a month in public housing under the old formula, assuming only the standard deductions. The recent changes, which will increase rents to 30 per cent of net income but keep the old deductions, will raise the rent to $120 a month. Increasing the ratio to 30 per cent and eliminating all deductions would make the rent $150 a month. By contrast, my approach of 30 per cent of net income with deductions of $600 per person would reduce the rent to $90 a month, while a 30 per cent ratio with $900 deductions would make the rent $60.

I recognize the political difficulty of achieving such increased magnitude and extended application of the income deductions, and the probable reluctance of some tenant groups to support a strategy which would reduce rents for some while tolerating increases for others. Nevertheless, if the initial demand were to increase and extend deductions to, say, $900 per person and also press for a return to 25 per cent of net income, with willingness to accept an outcome which would be a formula with 30 per cent of net income based on deductions of $600–900 per person, this would represent an important gain for most low-income tenants and progress toward a more equitable allocation of subsidies.

The attempts to tighten eligibility and reduce benefits in housing as well as for other assistance programs have obviously already met with some success even as resistance to further cuts grows. Within this context, though, the rhetoric about not hurting the "truly needy" and indeed about targeting benefits to those most truly in need should be seized upon and turned back to those who profess such concern. That is, simply raising the proportion of income of tenants in subsidized housing will hurt most the households of lowest income and largest size, who even now are shelter poor despite the subsidies. The approach I am advocating would at least allocate available subsidies in a way that is consistent with the professed philosophy of the Reagan Administration.

The changes I am suggesting in the housing subsidy formulas could, of course, occur in the context of increased appropriations as well as diminished or constant resources. Presently, about 3.4 million households receive housing subsidies under the various HUD programs, comprising only about 12–15 per cent of all households paying more than they can afford (the percentage depending upon which affordability approach is used), and costing the federal government about $8 billion in fiscal year 1982.[7] While tens of millions of households will continue to pay more for housing than they can afford – until, as I will argue below, there are fundamental changes in the way housing is owned and financed and until there is considerable income redistri-

TABLE 4.1 Subsidized housing rents under various rent formulas (non-elderly, 1-adult, 4-person households) ($ per month)

Gross annual income	Section 8 rent*		Public housing rent*		Alternative rent: 30% of net income‡ with deductions per person of				
	25–15†	30–10†	25–5†	30–10†	$0	$300	$600	$900	$1200
1000	13	8	4	8	25	4	4	4	4
2000	25	28	21	25	50	20	8	8	8
3000	44	53	41	49	75	45	15	13	13
4000	65	78	60	73	100	70	40	17	17
5000	85	103	80	96	125	95	65	35	21
6000	106	128	100	120	150	120	90	60	30
7000	127	153	120	144	175	145	115	85	55
8000	148	178	140	168	200	170	140	110	80
9000	169	203	159	191	225	195	165	135	105
10000	190	228	179	215	250	220	190	160	130
11000	210	253	199	239	275	245	215	185	155
12000	231	278	219	263	300	270	240	210	180
13000	252	303	239	286	325	295	265	235	205
14000	273	328	258	310	350	320	290	260	230
15000	294	353	278	334	375	345	315	285	255
16000	315	378	298	358	400	370	340	310	280
17000	335	403	318	381	425	395	365	335	305
18000	356	428	338	405	450	420	390	360	330
19000	377	453	357	429	475	445	415	385	355
20000	398	478	377	453	500	470	440	410	380

* Assuming no excess medical or other unusual expenses.

† 25–15 and 25–5 are the former formulas: 25% of net income, minimum of 15% or 5% of gross income; 30–10 is the mid-1983 formula with deductions as outlined in n.5: 30% of net income, minimum of 10% of gross income.

‡ Alternative rent assumes minimum rent of 5% of gross income.

TABLE 4.2 *Subsidized housing rents under various rent formulas (non-elderly 1-adult, 4-person households) (% of gross income)*

Gross annual income	Section 8 rent*		Public housing rent*		Alternative rent: 30% of net income‡ with deductions per person of				
	25–15†	30–10†	25–5†	30–10†	$ 0	$ 300	$ 600	$ 900	$ 1200
1000	15.0	10.0	5.0	10.0	30.0	5.0	5.0	5.0	5.0
2000	15.0	16.5	12.5	15.0	30.0	12.0	5.0	5.0	5.0
3000	17.5	21.0	16.3	19.5	30.0	18.0	6.0	5.0	5.0
4000	19.4	23.3	18.1	21.8	30.0	21.0	12.0	5.0	5.0
5000	20.5	24.6	19.3	23.1	30.0	22.8	15.6	8.4	5.0
6000	21.3	25.5	20.0	24.0	30.0	24.0	18.0	12.0	6.0
7000	21.8	26.1	20.5	24.6	30.0	24.9	19.7	14.6	9.4
8000	22.2	26.6	20.9	25.1	30.0	25.5	21.0	16.5	12.0
9000	22.5	27.0	21.3	25.5	30.0	26.0	22.0	18.0	14.0
10000	22.8	27.3	21.5	25.8	30.0	26.4	22.8	19.2	15.6
11000	23.0	27.5	21.7	26.0	30.0	26.7	23.5	20.2	16.9
12000	23.1	27.8	21.9	26.3	30.0	27.0	24.0	21.0	18.0
13000	23.3	27.9	22.0	26.4	30.0	27.2	24.5	21.7	18.9
14000	23.4	28.1	22.1	26.6	30.0	27.4	24.9	22.3	19.7
15000	23.5	28.2	22.3	26.7	30.0	27.6	25.2	22.8	20.4
16000	23.6	28.3	22.3	26.8	30.0	27.8	25.5	23.3	21.0
17000	23.7	28.4	22.4	26.9	30.0	27.9	25.8	23.6	21.5
18000	23.8	28.5	22.5	27.0	30.0	28.0	26.0	24.0	22.0
19000	23.8	28.6	22.6	27.1	30.0	28.1	26.2	24.3	22.4
20000	23.9	28.7	22.6	27.2	30.0	28.2	26.4	24.6	22.8

* Assuming no excess medical or other unusual expenses.

† 25–15 and 25–5 are the former formulas: 25% of net income, minimum of 15% or 5% of gross income; 30–10 is the mid-1983 formula with deductions as outlined in n.5: 30% of net income, minimum of 10% of gross income.

‡ Alternative rent assumes minimum rent of 5% of gross income.

bution, not just increases in housing subsidies – it is useful to finish playing out the subsidy implications of the quantitative housing affordability problem.

The cost of providing housing subsidies to all needy households would have been about $55–77 billion in 1982.[8] The cost of eliminating shelter poverty is greater than the cost of eliminating housing costs exceeding 25 per cent of income because even though there are fewer shelter poor households (as indicated above), each such household would require a much deeper subsidy to make its housing affordable. Apart from the somewhat different budgetary impact resulting from the two different definitions of housing need, though, there would be some significant differences in the eligible population. The shelter poverty approach would direct most of the subsidies to poor and working-class families, who can afford less than 25 per cent of their incomes for housing, and less of the subsidies to smaller, middle-class households, many of whom can afford to pay more than 25 per cent. The shelter poverty approach thus reveals the class nature of the affordability problem much more dramatically than does the conventional standard, suggesting important political and strategic differences depending on the definition of the affordability problem.

Furthermore, while it is apparent that in the political and budgetary climate of the early 1980s there is little likelihood of a new housing subsidy program of approximately $70 billion a year – especially one benefiting mostly the poorest families with the most children – it should be noted for comparison that $70 billion is only about 2 per cent of our $3 trillion gross national product, about one-quarter of the 1983 military budget, and, most interestingly, is in the same ballpark as the nearly $50 billion in housing subsidies provided to homeowners in fiscal year 1983, primarily through mortgage interest and property tax deductions, as well as deferral and exclusion of capital gains taxes on home sales.[9]

Finally, the shelter poverty affordability scale can also be a useful tool in local organizing. Helping people to calculate what they reasonably can afford to pay for their housing can, at the very least, be a practical starting point for political education, validating and quantifying the perception many poor people already have – namely, that 25 per cent of income is more than they can afford. In public and other subsidized housing developments the process of discussing affordability and having people compute appropriate rents may help in organizing to demand the kind of changes in the subsidy formulas suggested above. Indeed, this process may be valuable in overcoming the ideological and psychological message that people receiving housing subsidies are well off, i.e., have enough money after paying the rent to meet their other needs adequately and therefore have no cause to complain that the subsidies are not adequate.

In local private housing organizing around rent control, the shelter poverty concept could play an important part in moving beyond so-called "moderate" rent control, which guarantees "fair profit" for landlords rather than "fair rent" for tenants. The demand for rent control has obviously arisen directly out of the squeeze between incomes and housing costs, but when moderate rent control has been adopted it has not made much of a dent in the affordability problem, especially for lower-income, working-class tenants. Strict rent control, which would move toward a tenant affordability standard for rents rather than a landlord profitability standard, would certainly be harder to win politically, but might also be more successful in mobilizing low-income tenants and increasingly represents a necessary step for those hardest hit by the affordability squeeze. To be sure, such a demand would have to be presented as just the first step of a program moving first toward increasing social control of housing and ultimately toward social ownership, for such a rent control program would drive down profits and hence reduce property values and threaten the holders of mortgages on rental housing. That is, once the discussion and organizing moves beyond the realm of subsidies – outside the sphere of demanding subsidies to make up the difference between what households reasonably can afford to pay and what the private housing market requires in order to function – we are moving from the quantitative housing affordability problem to an examination of the deeper institutional bases and structural dynamics of the problem and to a recognition of the need for changes more fundamental than increased subsidies in order to solve the problem.

The roots of the housing affordability problem

When the housing affordability problem is expressed quantitatively in terms of the number and distribution of households paying more than they can afford according to one standard or another, not included are households who may not be paying too much, yet are unable to afford to alter their housing situations in ways that they need or want to. At the lower-income end of the income distribution such households are those who have relatively low housing costs but live in overcrowded conditions, in physically inadequate or dangerous units or buildings, or in physically or socially unsatisfactory locations. It is my contention, though, that while the 25 per cent standard reveals a large number of households not paying too much yet suffering from these forms of housing deprivation due to the affordability squeeze, the shelter poverty approach would show most such households to be paying more than they can afford as well as having unsatisfactory housing situations.

Thus, it seems to me that the principal segment of the population who are not objectively shelter poor, yet cannot afford to improve their housing situations in ways that they expected to be able to, are moderate-income, working-class families who are unable to become homeowners or who have lost their homes to foreclosure or had to sell their homes to avoid foreclosure. There has, of course, been a vast outpouring of popular, industry, and academic analyses of the crisis and future of homeownership. I do not intend to summarize or review this literature here, but do wish to note as relevant for this discussion that within some of this literature one can find fairly explicit acknowledgement of the role of homeownership in the myth of the U.S. as a middle-class society – the image of this country as a society with an insignificant upper class, with a sizeable, yet diminishing, poverty class predominantly of minority peoples, and an overwhelmingly large middle class – i.e., without a real working class. I have developed elsewhere the argument that the promotion and extension of homeownership has served both politically and economically as the principal device for coping with an otherwise intractable housing affordability problem – as a mechanism for integrating a large proportion of the working class into the myth of middle class America and also for stimulating the economic growth on which the myth rested (Stone, 1980a; 1980b). Yet, the unfolding of this historical process has not only failed ultimately to solve the affordability problem, as is increasingly apparent, but has also contributed significantly to the broader economic instability and depression of which the housing crisis seems to be only a part; so that there really can be no solution to the housing affordability problem without a solution to the broader political and economic crisis, but at the same time there can be no solution to the broader problems that does not deal with the roots of the housing crisis.

The housing affordability problem arises from an inherent conflict or contradiction between two of the most basic institutions of capitalist society – the labor market and the housing market. Most people have to work for wages or salaries in order to obtain the necessities of life, but despite the real and substantial increase in average or per capita real incomes over the past hundred years due to rising productivity, union organizing, political action, and intensive exploitation of other parts of the world, the inescapable pressure on employers to hold down costs in order to compete and maximize profits means that the labor market essentially exerts a downward pressure on wages, in no way guaranteeing any family that it will have sufficient income to pay for adequate shelter and other necessities.

On the other side, the cost of housing in the market is

determined by the interaction of the costs of land, production, financing, marketing, operation, and, in most instances, repeated resale and refinancing. The cost of housing thus bears no direct relationship to people's incomes, i.e., to their ability to pay, but since housing is a necessity which few people in this country provide directly for themselves by building log cabins or mud huts, the need to be able to purchase housing and also obtain the other necessities of life impels the struggle for higher wages. The housing market thus tends to exert an upward pressure on wages in opposition to the pressures of the labor market. And since housing costs are particularly decisive in determining the standard of living of every household, the conflict between the housing and labor markets is particularly acute and much more profound than the relationship of any other necessity to the labor market.

Although the squeeze between incomes and housing costs is an inescapable fact of life for large numbers of people in our society, it is not a problem which can be ignored, for the limit on incomes tends to undermine the profitability of the housing market and all of its related industries, the upward pressure on wages tends to squeeze the profitability of employers in general, and the affordability squeeze on so many families is a potential source of unrest and political instability. Thus, over the course of this country's history there have been a variety of reactions, responses, and interventions to cope with the housing affordability problem without altering the basic institutions of our economic system. These responses can be grouped into five major historical periods, although the early periods tend to overlap in time because of significant regional and urban-rural differences. I refer to the five periods as the primitive, medieval, classical, baroque, and rococo.

Throughout the history of rural America, there have been tenant farmers whose responses to the squeeze between unstable and often meager farm income and the rent for their land have ranged from starvation and bankruptcy to mass political action and even landlord lynchings and insurrection (Heskin, 1981, pp. 180–1, 186–7). In general, though, these were struggles over the farmers' means of production – land – rather than over shelter. For the most part, whether they were tenant farmers, squatters, or held some form of conditional or freehold title to land, rural Americans have obtained shelter through their own direct labor, sometimes with the aid of their neighbors' labor, and as time has passed with greater proportions of materials purchased rather than hacked out of the forest or soil. Under such circumstances, the conflict between incomes and housing costs was truly primitive, as it was largely not a monetary conflict, but rather a manifestation of the age-old rural struggle for survival – balancing the need to produce food against the time and resources needed to provide adequate shelter. Although for those who were most fortunate the houses which evolved were often marvelous in design and amenity, even today much rural housing in the U.S. remains remarkably primitive.

With the rise of industrial capitalism and the attendant growth of cities in the middle of the nineteenth century, housing as well as human labor became commodities to be bought and sold for money. Relatively few urban residents, apart from the poorest shanty dwellers, built their own housing, and only the well-to-do could afford to buy their own housing. This, then, was the heyday of the urban landlord and housing entrepreneur – the medieval period of housing. Most housing construction, particularly rental housing, was financed with entrepreneurial capital and private borrowing. Mortgage lending institutions (mainly savings banks and savings and loan associations) existed, but were less important than other sources of financing and primarily loaned to people well enough off to have saved some money for a house of their own. In this period, the conflict between incomes and housing costs appeared principally via the squalid and overcrowded living conditions of the rapidly growing urban working class. Within the constraints of low wages, the housing provided was of low quality to begin with, with few if any services and amenities, and packed full of people in order to generate an acceptable return for the landlords.

As long as the flow of immigrants into the cities provided employers with an adequate supply of cheap labor, the conflict between incomes and housing costs posed problems for the system only when tenants organized rent strikes or rioted and, more significantly, when disease and fire threatened both wealthier neighborhoods and the reproduction of an adequate labor force. The resulting codes and ordinances halted new construction of the worst types of tenements, but did not eliminate many that already existed and certainly did not result in new and better quality affordable housing for the poor. Rather, urban building turned more toward housing for the emerging middle class, housing which only gradually filtered down to the poor over succeeding generations, with inevitable decline in the quality of the housing. With this transition, entrepreneurial dominance was gradually replaced by the growing power of institutional mortgage lenders, as the medieval period gave way to the classical.

Emerging out of both the successes and failures of nineteenth-century capitalism, financial institutions provided a way of relieving some of the squeeze between incomes and housing costs by stretching out payment of the initial construction cost. Their ability to channel billions of dollars into housing indeed defined the dominant form that consumption has taken throughout this century, namely debt-financed suburbanization.

In the latter part of the nineteenth century, rapid technological progress and the rise of large corporations led to the growth of a new technical and managerial middle class. These people had enough income to maintain some savings, which they put primarily into savings accounts and life insurance policies. Seeking outlets to invest these rapidly accumulating funds, around the turn of the century the banks and insurance companies began to finance large amounts of housing construction, and over the next three decades institutional mortgage lenders came to dominate the housing industry, largely financing the pre-World War I streetcar suburbs, the first wave of auto suburbs in the 1920s and modern apartments in the central cities.

Between 1900 and 1930 non-farm residential mortgage debt grew from under $3 billion to over $30 billion.[10] This investment contributed significantly to economic growth over the period, but because it was debt financing that rested upon the expectation of future repayment, the mortgage system was very dependent upon continuous economic growth and prosperity. Furthermore, since lenders required a large downpayment and sufficiently large and secure income from each borrower in order to minimize risk, the growth of the mortgage and homeownership markets was still limited by the income/housing cost squeeze. Thus, when housing construction slackened after the mid-1920s, lenders increasingly financed housing speculation and cost inflation, which sustained the illusion of prosperity, but only for a while. The net result was that mortgage debt grew in the 1920s four times faster than the overall economy, i.e., much faster than the ability to repay it. So when the economy collapsed at the end of the decade, the mortgage system was a big part of the debacle. Millions of people lost their homes to foreclosure because they did not have the incomes to pay off their mortgages. Millions lost their savings because the banks had invested in home loans that could not be repaid. Savings deposits failed to grow again until the start of World War II; with no new funds available for investment, private residential construction practically came to a halt and the private housing market nearly ceased functioning.

While the classical period of U.S. housing ended with the Depression, the new institutional framework for housing finance which was erected in the 1930s was still built around the central feature of the classical system – mortgage lending by private financial institutions – reflecting the power these institutions continued to wield and the general philosophical commitment to have the government assist rather than replace private investment. Thus the major and ultimately most profound and pervasive forms of federal intervention in housing were the system of central banking and deposit insurance provided by the Federal Home Loan Bank System, the mortgage insurance programs of the Federal Housing Administration and, a decade later, the mortgage guarantees of the Veterans Administration, and the secondary mortgage market facilities of the Federal National Mortgage Association. All were designed to stimulate and protect private institutional mortgage lending and hence can be seen as a baroque extension, elaboration, and enhancement of the classical form of housing finance.

Strategically, the rebuilt mortgage system was built around the much wider promotion of debt-encumbered homeownership through the creation of the low-downpayment, long-term loan to replace the earlier type of large-downpayment, short-term mortgages which had restricted the market to the relatively well-off groups in the population. The new type of loan was designed to undercut the affordability problem in several ways: economically, by both lessening monthly payments for a given loan and reducing the personal savings needed to buy; politically, by promoting the illusion of ownership through the reality of debt. Furthermore, by making loans more easily available, the effective demand for houses was expected to increase, which in turn would contribute to overall economic growth as well as benefit the construction and lending industries in particular.

Of course it took World War II to restart the economy and generate the savings needed to set the reconstructed mortgage system into operation. Savings which had accumulated during the War, along with housing needs virtually unmet since the start of the Depression, provided the impetus for what indeed became the post-war housing boom, facilitated by federal support for financial institutions to provide the new long-term, low-downpayment loans. The suburban boom produced about 30 million new housing units in two decades, increasing homeownership from about 40 per cent at the end of the War to over 60 per cent by the 1960s. Housing construction accounted for one-third of all private investment and nearly one-half of all public and private construction during this period. And housing debt represented the biggest single component of a vast explosion of private borrowing, as Table 4.3 shows. Yet, despite the success of the new mortgage system in dealing with the housing affordability problem for the majority of Americans and contributing to the post-war prosperity, the edifice contained some inherent flaws and weaknesses that began to emerge in the late 1960s, bringing forth the crisis that only seems to worsen, and with it the transition from the baroque to a truly rococo period of housing finance.

First, even as mortgage lending contributed to expansion it grew much faster than the overall economy, and hence faster than the ability to repay this debt, just as it had during the 1920s. As Table 4.3 shows, between 1946 and 1965 residential mortgage debt grew about three times as fast as GNP and disposable personal income, so that once again the debt that was essential to prosperity was placing an increasingly heavy burden on the future.

Second, while the expansion of mortgage credit contributed immensely to the growth and profitability of the entire housing industry, increasing dependence on credit made the production of new housing and the cost of buying and occupying both new and used housing increasingly sensitive to the supply and cost of mortgage money. No other major industry is as dependent on borrowed funds, and the price of no other major item of consumption as sensitive to interest rates as is housing.

The increased vulnerability of housing to credit conditions has led to ups and downs in housing production as interest rates, the total supply of credit, and housing's share of credit have all varied with the business cycle. Although the business cycle was relatively mild for two decades after World War II, housing production fell an average of 30 per cent during each of the three major periods of restricted mortgage credit that occurred prior to the mid-1960s. Thus, while the mortgage system facilitated large amounts of housing production over this post-war period as a whole, the year-to-year instability left the construction industry permeated with small, labor-intensive firms that could easily enter and leave, but which, for the most part, could never develop factory technology and achieve significant economies of scale. Even more important, because the evolution of the mortgage system has caused housing production to over-react to the business cycle, there arose the danger that a worsening of the cycle could lead not only to wilder swings in housing construction but also to larger economic problems if the inability of buyers to obtain and afford long-term mortgages left developers with houses they could not sell, and thus left lenders with uncollectable construction loans.

TABLE 4.3 *Debt outstanding in the U.S. economy ($ billions)*

	1946	1965	1970	1975	1980
Total debt	$353.2	$1,107.2	$1,600.1	$2,620.4	$4,651.7
U.S. government	228.0	260.6	300.8	446.3	742.8
Federally sponsored housing agencies	0.3	8.7	29.6	81.7	226.6
Other federally sponsored agencies	0.9	6.0	14.0	25.6	47.3
State and local governments	14.9	100.3	144.4	223.8	336.1
Total private debt	109.1	731.6	1,111.6	1,837.3	3,299.5
Residential mortgages	28.3	258.7	357.8	591.4	1,086.8
Commercial mortgages	8.8	55.5	85.2	157.9	256.7
Consumer credit	8.4	89.9	143.1	223.2	385.0
Corporate and foreign bonds	27.7	123.0	202.4	323.4	503.8
Other private credit	36.1	204.6	323.8	546.3	1,067.2
Gross National Product	209.6	688.1	982.4	1,516.3	2,626.5
Disposable personal income	158.6	472.2	685.9	1,084.4	1,822.2
Residential mortgage debt as a per cent of GNP	13.5%	37.6%	36.4%	39.0%	41.4%
Residential mortgage debt as a per cent of disposable personal income	17.8%	54.8%	52.2%	54.4%	59.6%
Residential mortgage interest rate	4.5%*	5.8%	8.5%	9.0%	12.9%

* Approximate.

Sources: Federal Reserve Board, *Flow of Funds Accounts: Assets and Liabilities Outstanding*; U.S. Department of Commerce, *Survey of Current Business*; and Federal Home Loan Board, *Journal*, various issues.

The third major weakness built into the new mortgage system was the financial vulnerability of the so-called thrift institutions – savings and loan associations and mutual savings banks – which have been the mainstays of residential lending. Since they have put nearly all their funds into long-term mortgages, as long as interest rates on these loans were fixed such lenders have received a fairly constant rate of return year after year regardless of what has happened to rates since the loans were made. The thrifts obtained most of the funds they loaned, though, from savings deposits that could be withdrawn with little or no notice. Until the late 1960s, interest rates on savings accounts were generally competitive with other investments and were substantially higher than the rate of inflation, so the imbalance in "borrowing short and lending long" was not yet a problem. Thrift institutions were thus fairly successful at sustaining a steady inflow of funds and using them to support their own growth and a large fraction of the expansion of mortgage credit. In periods of tight money housing funds were restricted primarily because the other major types of lenders – commercial banks and insurance companies – reduced their housing lending; as the major suppliers of housing credit, the thrifts were for a while relatively insulated from the rest of the capital markets and not dramatically affected by economic fluctuations, although their financial structure was inherently flawed.

The fourth major difficulty in the new mortgage system has grown out of the promotion of homeownership and perhaps has more obvious political implications than the other three tensions, as profound as they are. The overwhelming majority of Americans have of course aspired to be homeowners, and for many years the new mortgage system made the dream available to most (though not most of low income or dark complexion) who pursued it, even though this mortgage system saddled people with immense debts. Homeownership became the mark of full citizenship, the symbol of status, almost a civil right to anyone who saved up a little for the downpayment, as well as providing a hedge against inflation and the means to accumulate a little wealth for retirement or one's heirs. Having created the expectation, fostered the hope, promoted the dream, what would be the consequences if the system could no longer deliver the goods?

Housing and the economic crisis

During the 1960s the post-war prosperity began to crumble. Third World insurgency, especially in Southeast Asia, forced the government to increase military spending. Militant social movements plus domestic opposition to the war in Vietnam forced increases in spending for social programs while restricting tax increases. The federal budget thus had a growing deficit in the late 1960s, which had to be financed by borrowing. At the same time, growing competition from Europe and Japan posed an additional economic challenge. These foreign pressures, along with decreasing unemployment and rising wages at home, resulted in a sharp decline in corporate profits in the late 1960s. In response, the corporations began to borrow more money to finance moveouts and mergers which they hoped would restore profits.

The new demands for credit have come on top of the continuing needs of other sectors of the economy, including housing, as Table 4.3 shows. This process has increasingly exposed a basic contradiction in the whole system of debt financing. On the one hand, if the Federal Reserve allows the money supply to increase to meet all the needs for borrowed funds, this contributes to price increases in the economy, since the amount of borrowed money being spent goes up faster than the amount of goods and services being produced. Inflation leads to higher interest rates and more borrowing in anticipation of further price increases. Debt accelerates far ahead of the ability to repay it, leading toward a financial crisis.

On the other hand, if the government tries to restrict the growth of credit to prevent or limit inflation, then some borrowers get squeezed out. Previously accumulated debts eventually have to be paid, and many individuals, businesses, and governments are totally dependent on new loans to pay off the old ones. Without continued access to credit to pay their bills, they may go bankrupt. Since the banks and other creditors have also borrowed heavily to expand their lending and stimulate the economy, a chain of defaults can ensue when they do not get paid. Thus a credit squeeze can bring the financial system to the brink of collapse.

Since the late 1960s the economy has swung more and more violently between the poles of this contradiction. Housing has been at the center of the crisis because of the spread of long-term mortgages and the associated growth of mortgage debt. Since 1966, increased competition for borrowed funds has caused a long-term rise in interest rates on top of ever sharper short-term fluctuations. Periods of tight money have been increasingly severe, with interest rates soaring higher each time and housing credit being ever more drastically curtailed.

As interest rates on savings accounts have become less competitive and even lagged behind the rate of inflation, many depositors have withdrawn savings to invest directly – and more recently indirectly through money market mutual funds – in more profitable instruments offered by commercial banks, governments, and industrial corporations. Thrift institutions have experienced such periods of "disintermediation" four times since 1966, with obvious consequences for their ability to channel savings into residential mortgages and for their ability to survive.

In addition to the problems of thrift institutions, increased corporate and government borrowing has left more diversified lenders with less inclination and ability to finance housing construction whenever credit has been restricted and short-term interest rates have risen. Thus, in the tight money crunch of 1966, housing starts plunged 30 per cent in just six months, to the lowest level since 1946.[11] As the credit supply was allowed to expand again to avoid a more severe financial crisis, housing production recovered in the late 1960s and declined somewhat less severely in the recession of 1969–70 due to some interventions discussed below. Housing then led the credit boom of the early 1970s, as production reached the highest level in history in 1972. But by 1974, when the economy entered what was (until the 1980s) the worst recession since the 1930s the bottom fell out. In 1975 housing starts were more than 50 per cent below the 1972 peak, and the low point was a post-war record below even the 1966 trough. Half a million new homes stood vacant and thousands of apartment buildings were left unfinished as mortgage credit evaporated. Housing production had traditionally led the economy out of a recession, but at the beginning of 1977, nearly a year and a half after the recession had supposedly hit bottom, housing starts were still 30 per cent below what they had been in 1972. By mid-1977, after three and a half years of depression in the housing industry, a new speculative boom finally brought housing production up to an annual rate of about two million units, where it remained until the end of 1978.

As in the past, the expansion of the late 1970s was fueled by the credit expansion policies of the Federal Reserve Board, plus special government efforts in housing finance which prop up the housing industry and use housing as a stimulus to the overall economy. But with inflation accelerating out of control, stimulated in part by the continued availability of high cost credit, toward late 1978 the end of the mini-boom was in sight. Sales of new and existing housing peaked in the fall of 1978; mortgage interest rates passed 10 per cent by the end of the year, signs of overbuilding appeared in some parts of the country, and housing starts dropped about 30 per cent during the first two months of 1979. With the spring of 1979 things picked up a little, and many economists and housing industry forecasters naively and wishfully predicted there would not be a severe housing decline. But with interest rates continuing to rise billions of dollars began to leave thrift institutions as savers sought even greater returns than they could get on newly created high-interest savings certificates. In the fall the Federal

Reserve administered the traditional medicine for an over-heated economy: raising interest rates still higher and severely tightening the money supply. The mortgage industry responded desperately, charging more for mortgages in order to be able to pay higher rates to keep and obtain some funds to lend. Mortgage interest rates passed 12 per cent late in 1979 and reached 16–17 per cent early in 1980, but there was very little mortgage money available even for those borrowers willing and able to pay such rates. New construction plummeted nearly 50 per cent between the fall of 1979 and spring of 1980, dipping again below the one million level. Fears about the impact of the crunch, and the traditional willingness of the Federal Reserve Board to accommodate incumbent presidents in election years, led to an easing of the monetary reins and housing construction took off until the start of 1981, when there was a new administration and a new resolve at the Federal Reserve to control inflation at any cost. Housing production again collapsed, plummeting 50 per cent between winter and fall of 1981, setting another post-war record low of about 850,000 units at an annual rate, and remaining well below the one million level from the summer of 1981 until nearly the middle of 1982, as most commentators ran out of adjectives trying to describe how much worse this depression was than the last worst housing depression.

In addition to its impact on housing production, the crisis has of course also had a devastating effect on the cost of housing. Because of the dependence on credit and the sensitivity of housing costs to interest rates, the cost of shelter reflects a piggy-back effect of rising interest rates on top of rising house prices. Thus between 1970 and 1976, while median family income was rising 47 per cent and the overall Consumer Price Index went up 46 per cent, median sales prices for new houses rose 90 per cent, and the monthly ownership cost for a median-priced new house rose 100 per cent, while the monthly ownership cost for a median-priced existing house rose 65 per cent. Between the end of 1976 and the end of 1981, the median price of a new house rose another 50 per cent, while prices of existing houses rose by over 70 per cent, and mortgage interest rates increased from about 9 per cent at the earlier point to about 16 per cent at the end of 1981; so buyers entering the market had to pay over 200 per cent more for their mortgage payments than did the typical new buyer just five years before. To be sure, first-time homebuyers, who represented 36 per cent of all buyers in 1977, had decreased to under 14 per cent of all buyers in 1981. During the 1950s, about two-thirds of all families could have afforded the typical new house; by 1970 the proportion had declined to one-half, by 1976 to just one-fourth, and by 1981 to less than one-tenth (Frieden and Solomon, 1977; U.S. League of Savings Associations, 1978a, 1978b, 1980, 1982).

Housing has clearly been one of the disaster areas of the past decade. However, the housing sector has not been merely a passive victim of the pervasive crisis. The housing and lending industries, with the aid of the government, have tried to deal with the increasingly weakened and unstable mortgage system, but these attempts have ultimately only exacerbated the difficulties of the overall economy without solving the housing affordability and financing problems. All sorts of new programs, institutions, and techniques have been created, but they truly represent just rococo adornment on the facade of a structure that had flaws from the start and has been decaying from within. No amount of superficial decoration can be expected to prop up an unsound structure; indeed, it only adds more weight, thereby increasing the likelihood of collapse.

The list of additions to the mortgage lending system since the late 1960s is a long one, with new variations appearing almost monthly, and no attempt will be made to describe and evaluate each one. A listing of some of the major elements, though, will serve to indicate the scope of the changes. In the late 1960s and early 1970s the Federal National Mortgage Association was reorganized and privatized, a new federally backed Government National Mortgage Association was created, and a Federal Home

Loan Mortgage Corporation was established, all to create a national money market for housing and to tap new sources of funds for residential mortgages. In addition, private mortgage insurance opened up secondary mortgage markets for raising money and trading mortgages without involvement of government-created agencies, and more recently some private lenders have been issuing mortgage-backed securities without government guarantees. The Federal Home Loan Bank Board has in times of tight money provided huge advances, raised by selling securities in the bond market, to member institutions losing deposits. State and local housing finance and development agencies have raised housing funds by selling tax-exempt bonds; real estate investment trusts have also raised money by using certain tax advantages. In addition to such devices designed to tap the national capital markets and reduce mortgage loan dependence on savings accounts, the thrift institutions themselves have been allowed to try to hold on to savings by issuing various long-term certificates, money market certificates, All-Savers Certificates, and so forth that pay higher rates than traditional passbook savings accounts. There are also alternative mortgage instruments designed to try to protect thrift institutions from interest rate fluctuations and overcome (hopefully only) initial affordability problems of homebuyers, ranging from adjustable rate and variable rate mortgages to graduated payment and shared appreciation mortgages, with a whole alphabet soup of abbreviations for the various types of mortgages to match the alphabet soup of agencies and programs.

The development of these new institutions and devices to raise and allocate mortgage credit has not been entirely successful, as revealed by the production crashes of 1973–5 and 1980–2. They have, however, had two very significant consequences for the overall economy as well as the housing and lending industries.

First, they have increased the total demand for credit in the economy. When the supply of credit has been plentiful, the result has been a more rapid growth in the total amount of debt and a relatively larger share allocated to real estate in general and housing in particular. For example, during the late 1960s, before the new mortgage institutions reached their maturity, the growth of mortgage debt slipped relative to corporate and government borrowing, as Table 4.3 reveals: from 1946 through 1965 residential mortgages accounted for 31 per cent of the total increase in debt; in the following five years the increase in housing debt was only 20 per cent of the total. However, during the boom of the early 1970s, despite the massive increase in corporate and government borrowing, the new institutions enabled housing debt to increase its share to 23 per cent of the total increase in debt. In the late 1970s, even with continued growth of corporate and government borrowing, residential debt accounted for 24 per cent of the total increase in debt in the economy, 34 per cent of the increase in private debt; and residential mortgages plus federally sponsored housing credit accounted for 32 per cent of all public and private borrowing during this period. Indeed, by 1980 over 22 per cent of the total debt (direct plus sponsored) of the federal government was housing-related.

The changes in mortgage financing over the past decade and a half thus gave a tremendous boost to real growth in the economy, but also to the unprecedented inflation and the overblown credit bubble. On the other hand, when monetary policy has sought to contain inflation by reducing the supply of credit, the new mortgage institutions, especially the federally created and federally backed agencies, have only intensified competition for scarce credit, leading to even higher interest rates throughout the system. Higher interest rates not only have added to inflation, but also have led to further withdrawals of savings deposits as savers have pursued the higher returns available elsewhere. Increased withdrawals from thrift institutions have substantially offset the additional housing funds raised through the capital markets and so weakened a number of thrifts that they have been saved only by being absorbed (with federal financial assistance) by larger and stronger financial institutions.

Thus, the attempts of mortgage lenders and others in the housing industry to compete more effectively for funds have not been fully successful, but they have contributed to higher housing costs, higher interest rates generally, and greater concentration in the mortgage industry.

The second major consequence of the new institutions and financing techniques is that residential finance is no longer a relatively separate and insulated component of the credit system. Many investors other than thrift institutions and small savers now have hundreds of billions of dollars tied up with the mortgage system. The stability of the structure of residential debt is thus increasingly vital for the stability of the entire financial structure of American capitalism. But the stability of the housing debt system depends upon continued mortgage payments from people in existing housing and on the ability of prospective buyers to obtain long-term loans for new housing being built with short-term construction loans. The ratio of mortgage debt to disposable personal income climbed from 18 per cent in 1946 to 55 per cent in 1965. Between the mid-1960s and mid-1970s this ratio did not rise, but the ratio does not reflect rising interest rates, so mortgage payments actually grew faster than income even over this period. During the 1960s, the number of mortgage foreclosures per year doubled from about 50,000 to about 100,000, and by 1975 had increased to over 140,000.[12]

In the five years after 1975, residential mortgage debt increased by about $500 billion (see Table 4.3), an increase of nearly 84 per cent. This increase does not even include all the debt that was refinanced by homeowners cashing in on rising property values. With all of the selling and refinancing of existing homes and apartments, probably over $300 billion of the nearly $600 billion in mortgage debt outstanding at the end of 1975 was paid off over the next five years.[13] This means that over 70 per cent of $1.1 trillion in residential mortgage debt at the end of 1980 consisted of loans which had been taken out just since 1975 and at the highest interest rates in history! Mortgage debt thus reached

60 per cent of disposable personal income in 1980. Cou
the immense growth of mortgage debt with the higher-
than-ever interest rates at which it has been borrowed, the
amount of money tenants and homeowners have to lay out
for mortgage payments has more than doubled since 1975,
while disposable income, out of which mortgage payments
(and everything else but personal income taxes) have to be
made, has gone up little more than 50 per cent – suggesting
more starkly than ever the danger for the financial system
posed by the conflict between housing costs and incomes.[14]

A way out?

What then are the prospects, if the problem is as deep and
the dangers as great as I have suggested? The conservative
solution can be called a "managed depression." Conservatives argue correctly that there can be no solution to the
housing crisis without controlling inflation and that federal
bailout of the housing industry will not really solve the
problem but will add to the federal deficit and to inflation.
Their approach therefore consists of continued tight money
and high interest rates on the monetary side; on the fiscal
side they provide tax cuts for large corporations and wealthy
individuals to shield them from austerity, while severely
cutting housing and community development, income maintenance, and social services spending in order to try to offset
the tax cuts and increased military spending.

Despite apparent disagreement at times between the Federal Reserve and the Reagan Administration, the conservative fiscal and monetary policies are basically consistent,
and they can have the effect of bringing down inflation by
imposing high unemployment and redistributing income upward. It is an approach that may be capable of staving off
financial collapse of the economy, but it will never solve the
housing problem. First of all, it leaves the housing industry
more dependent than ever on private credit, since even
federally supported credit activities are being curtailed, yet

it will require virtually permanent credit stringency to not only bring down but also keep down inflation. At the same time, the cuts in housing and other social programs will never reduce the federal budget deficit significantly. The combination of tight money, increased dependence on the market to allocate the scarce credit, and continued federal competition for this credit, will thus leave housing with even fewer resources. Finally, upward redistribution of income is hardly an answer to the affordability problem, for even if inflation is reduced and held down by the conservative policies, any reduction in the growth of housing and other prices will be far exceeded by the reduction in purchasing power imposed by continued high unemployment and social spending cuts.

The conservative approach might appear to some people to be no more than a cynical attempt to protect big business and the wealthy from inevitable depression, while to others – including some who may dislike or disagree with these policies – it may seem like a realistic attempt to avoid cataclysm. Yet ultimately the conservative approach will fail because the high social costs it imposes and the obvious inequity in the distribution of these costs will lead to its political rejection. True conservatives have often had a fairly accurate understanding of the limits of liberal capitalism and have understood what is required economically to keep the system afloat. Their policies involve, though, a degree of social and economic injustice which simply has never been tolerable for very long by the majority of Americans, and thus in the long run the conservative approach will not be fully played out except under a far more authoritarian regime than we yet have.

On the other hand, liberal policies, which have always had and will again have greater political appeal, will lead unwittingly but inevitably to an unmanaged depression – to a genuine financial collapse – with uncertain but potentially terrifying social and political consequences. With the understandable goals of relieving austerity, assuring a little greater equity, and bailing out the gasping housing industry, the liberal approach does involve increased federal spending to maintain most housing and other social programs and to provide bailouts to distressed thrift institutions, builders, and homeowners, while only marginally increasing taxes and slowing the rate of growth of military spending. Thus, despite their declarations of a commitment to cut the federal deficit in order to reduce inflation and credit competition, the fiscal policies being offered by liberals will almost certainly increase the federal deficit.

For example, hundreds of organizations representing and supporting the interests of low-income people, along with their allies in Congress, have been fighting valiantly to prevent tens of billions of dollars in budget cuts which would have the dual effect of drastically raising rents in subsidized housing, as discussed earlier, and reducing or eliminating production of additional subsidized housing. In addition, there have been proposals for single-family homeownership assistance, one component of which would provide homeowners unable to meet their mortgage payments with loans or subsidies for up to two years; the other element, largely designed to bail out the distressed homebuilders (and which passed Congress but was vetoed by President Reagan), would have provided $3 billion to subsidize the mortgage interest rate on purchases of new houses. Furthermore, there are proposals to provide as much as $10 billion in Treasury loans or grants to the depository insurance agencies to pay for mergers or liquidations of distressed thrift institutions. The proposals thus range from "left" liberal emphasis on the needs of the poor, to "right" liberal support for industry, and most are plausible and defensible in their own terms as immediate responses to aspects of the crisis. Yet all accept the existing mortgage and housing markets and simply subsidize them, thereby adding to the overblown credit bubble and federal costs, without touching the sources of the problem. It is easy to defend such proposals as short-term measures, but only if one is unaware of or unwilling to acknowledge how unstable the financial structure is and how such fiscal measures relate to their monetary corollary.

Liberal monetary demands involve, of course, an easing of tight money in order to bring down interest rates and accommodate the credit demands of the federal government without crowding out housing, consumer borrowing, state and local governments, and other businesses. In the very short run, the effect would be a boost to the economy and a reduction in defaults and bankruptcies by individuals and businesses, but soon inflation and speculation would again stretch the credit bubble beyond real growth in the economy, making a crash even more likely than now.

The only sensible and workable alternative then to managed versus unmanaged depression is one which goes beyond the conservative and liberal approaches and instead begins to deal with underlying causes: maldistribution of income; overdependence on credit; and ownership and investment arrangements that encourage speculation (in housing and industry) rather than production, employment, and social well-being. The proposals I am offering here are not long-term measures, but rather steps that can and should be initiated quite quickly. They consist of the following three types of measures for dealing with the overall crisis, each of which will then be discussed more particularly as it relates to housing:

(1)   Cut the federal deficit and begin to redistribute income downward, as follows: cut military spending; repeal the tax cut enacted in 1981; close tax loopholes, including housing-related tax benefits; eliminate the federal income tax for low-income households; and explicitly target housing and economic development subsidies and incentives to entities that engage in productive, non-speculative investment.

(2)   Impose credit control and credit allocation in order to deflate the credit bubble; cut credit for speculation (e.g., in land, existing housing, business

mergers and moveouts, commodities, foreign currency dealings); and assure an adequate supply of low-cost credit for productive investment in housing construction and rehabilitation, rebuilding decaying infrastructure (water and sewer systems, bridges, tunnels, roads, transit systems, power plants, and so forth), and developing job-producing industry.

(3) Control prices through a combination of explicit controls, taxes on speculation, and incentives to transfer housing, land, and enterprises into forms of non-speculative (resident, community, worker, consumer, public) ownership, as detailed in the Achtenberg-Marcuse contribution to this volume.

While the overall fiscal measures I am advocating would help to relieve the pressures on credit and prices and thus contribute to easing the broader economic context of the housing problem, there are also a number of aspects of these proposals that more directly impinge on housing. First of all, a major form of relief for the housing affordability squeeze for low-income households would be to exempt from income taxes (and social security taxes) that income corresponding to the Bureau of Labor Statistics Lower Budget for items other than taxes. For fiscal year 1983 this could be achieved by increasing the personal exemption from the present level of $1,000 to about $3,500 per person.[15] In the long-run, of course, tax credits or a negative income tax at the lowest end would be required to enable poor people to meet their shelter and other needs adequately, but increasing the personal exemption to an average of $3,500 would be an important and immediate response to the shelter poverty problem.

The second area for immediate tax reform affecting housing consists of the housing-related tax expenditures resulting from homeowner and investor deductions. It is estimated that in fiscal year 1982 the homeowner deductions cost the Treasury $35–39 billion and investor deductions cost $3 billion, and that the homeowner benefits will more than double by 1986.[16] This compares with the figure of about $8 billion in direct expenditures for housing subsidy programs in fiscal year 1982. Nearly 75 per cent of the homeowner tax expenditures go to households with incomes over $30,000 a year (U.S Congressional Budget Office, 1981, Table 2, p. 9; Table 5, p. 14), and it is increasingly recognized that these deductions contribute significantly to housing speculation and the demand for mortgage credit by subsidizing high interest rates for high-income people (see the Appendix to Cushing Dolbeare's contribution to this volume for more detailed discussion of this issue). There is thus no sound economic justification for continuing these deductions and much for eliminating them, particularly as part of a tax reform plan that would lower rates for middle-income households while increasing exemptions, as mentioned above, so that homeowners wth incomes under $30,000 a year would not end up paying higher taxes with the elimination of the homeowner deductions. As for the investor deductions, targeting of development subsidies to productive investment would enable responsible developers to build housing without having to rely on selling tax shelters to wealthy investors, while eliminating investor tax deductions would end the tax incentives for the speculative swapping of existing rental housing which is now so profitable but inflationary and unproductive.

Next, there needs to be a change in the way the tax laws treat capital gains in housing, since current laws encourage speculation. Indeed, there is every reason at the very least to treat all capital gains – not just for housing – as ordinary income or perhaps to impose higher taxes on capital gains from speculative as opposed to productive investment. At any rate, while there have been local efforts to control speculation through taxation, utilizing the Internal Revenue Code to control speculation and raise revenue nationally seems like the most efficient and equitable approach. A sliding capital gains tax, with the rate declining sharply with the holding period, and no avoidance of the tax through residential reinvestment, would be a very effective means of discouraging speculation and the attendant rise in occupancy costs. If, for example, the gain on property held less than one year were taxed at 95 per cent and the rate declined by 5 per cent per year through the tenth year, at ten years the rate would be 50 per cent. If the rate dropped 2 per cent per year for the eleventh through thirtieth years, it could then level off at 10 per cent for property held thirty or more years. Long-term owners would thus not be penalized, but speculation would be severely curtailed throughout the country, and at least several billion dollars of additional revenue would be raised each year, and potentially much more if the tax applied as well to investments other than housing.

The proposals for credit control and allocation include a number of micro as well as macro elements. At the macro level, several approaches are possible: one would be to impose high taxes on interest income lenders receive on loans for non-productive or speculative purposes, such as plant relocation, corporate mergers (other than those that save jobs which otherwise might be lost to bankruptcy), or real estate speculation. Alternatively, or in addition, it would be possible through the agencies regulating banks and the securities industry to establish and enforce explicit priority set-asides of credit for productive investment in housing construction and rehabilitation and other purposes suggested above. Such allocation would occur, of course, within the context of a monetary policy designed to reduce the growth of and dependence upon credit throughout the entire economy, in order to retreat from the financial brink and control inflation. This would, of course, along with the other measures, reduce housing speculation and thus the non-productive accumulation of mortgage debt, and would have a significant impact on interest rates, thereby contributing to easing the affordability problem.

For many families, though, even much lower interest rates will not make housing affordable. Mechanisms other than the additional approach of subsidizing private credit will therefore need to be considered over a longer term, such as a publicly capitalized housing bank which could finance low- and moderate-income housing at zero or nominal interest, and direct public construction grants which would make the housing even more affordable than loans. The latter elements would, though, require public expenditures ($10 billion a year would finance about 200,000 new and substantially rehabilitated units), contrasted with credit control and allocation which are necessary initial steps that do not require government spending to help housing.

Troubled thrift institutions should not be merged with other private institutions at public expense, but instead should be folded into a new federal housing bank, which would assume the deposit liabilities and mortgage assets, and would determine which other assets (e.g., securities, buildings) to liquidate. Such a public bank might even continue to operate many of the offices of the former private institutions, accepting deposits and making loans as deposits would justify, but paying slightly lower rates than private institutions (because of greater security and public benefit) and offering mortgages at below market interest rates, but with resale stipulations to restrict speculation.

Finally, at the micro level of the individual homeowner, there is an immediate need to deal with the problem of mortgage default in a way that is more sensitive to the needs of the homeowner than are mortgage lender foreclosure practices, while also serving larger goals of liquidating existing debt and limiting the future growth of housing credit. Lenders holding home mortgages in default and in imminent likelihood of foreclosure ought to be able to sell the mortgages to the federal housing bank, in a procedure similar to that under FHA insurance – but with two important differences. First, the lender should not be assured of receiving the full outstanding principal balance, but at most the market value (which differs from par due to interest rate differences) or even somewhat below market as the cost of having taken the risk of lending. Second, the borrower should be entitled to remain in the home and make payments at an affordable rate – similar to the arrangement under the Home Owners Loan Corporation in the 1930s – but with resale restrictions to prevent future windfalls and speculation. Alternatively and more generously to the homeowner in the short run, the owner might be allowed reduced payments without resale restriction for a finite period of one to two years, at which point if full payment could not be resumed, the owner could voluntarily or, through foreclosure, involuntarily deed the property to a community housing trust; the former owner should then be given a life estate to be able to continue to occupy the premises, at which point the federal housing bank would write down the mortgage to reflect what the former owner (now life tenant) could afford to pay. In this way, financially strapped homeowners would not lose their homes as shelter, but the public interest in reducing speculative resale and attendant mortgage debt would be served.

While the measures discussed so far would have some impact on housing costs by reducing inflation, controlling speculation, removing some housing from the private market, and retiring some outstanding mortgages without refinancing, the primary purpose of these measures is to deal with the dangers of the overall economic crisis. So apart from the defaulting homeowners, who would have immediate cost relief as just described, without other steps most people would only gradually feel the effects on their housing costs, although the tax changes would help the income side of the affordability squeeze for most shelter poor households. Several other steps dealing with housing costs thus comprise the final element of the emergency housing program I am advocating.

The discussion so far has focused almost entirely on the housing system as a whole and to some extent on the problems of homeowners. Yet about a third of all households are renters, and while rents have not on average gone up as fast as typical costs for first-time homebuyers, renters are generally much poorer and a much larger proportion are shelter poor, as discussed earlier. In addition, apart from homeowners facing foreclosure, tenants have far less security of tenure than do homeowners – a problem greatly exacerbated by a vacancy rate of 2 per cent or less in many cities, at least half a million condominium conversions since the late 1970s, plus arson, abandonment and demolition – so that upwards of 2.5 million people are displaced each year, most of whom are tenants and of low income (U.S. Department of Housing and Urban Development, 1981a).

There is thus an immediate need for a national tenants' bill of rights. This should include strong rent control, national in scope but administered locally, to halt all rent increases not justified by documented and legitimate cost increases. Coupled with rent control there must be eviction controls, requiring demonstration of just cause for eviction and not permitting eviction for condominium conversion or luxury rehabilitation. There must also be severe penalties for arson and elimination of the financial incentives for arson, since penalties are often hard to impose due to the difficulties of proving arson. A national bill of rights for tenants should also be a Wagner Act for tenants, legally recognizing the rights of tenants to organize and requiring that landlords bargain collectively with tenant organizations.[17]

Private rental housing is increasingly being recognized as an anachronism, at least by those landlords who are converting to condos, abandoning their buildings, or burning them for the insurance money. To the extent that a national tenants' bill of rights is enacted and enforced, many more landlords would undoubtedly want to bail out, and if conversion and arson are no longer available or profitable other routes must be provided which are not harmful to tenants. Therefore mechanisms must be established – or existing mechanisms more fully utilized – so that private rental housing can be converted into forms of social ownership, such as non-equity or low-equity co-ops, life estate condominiums (i.e., no possibility of speculative resale), ownership by community trusts, or public ownership. In order to achieve such transfer of ownership without increasing rents yet compensating the former owner, it would be necessary first for the new ownership entity to be able to assume any existing mortgages, perhaps with a renegotiated interest rate plus restrictions on pre-sale refinancing or mortgaging at inflated amounts (to pull out equity); second, the departing owner might receive not cash but a mortgage for the agreed upon equity, with the monthly mortgage payment not exceeding the cash flow the former owner realized (unless the old mortgages could be renegotiated at lower rates, in which case the former owner could get more, thus providing an incentive not to make money by taking out big mortgages just before sale).

The private ownership, financing, and disinvestment of rental housing is often quite elaborate and bizarre, so tenant and community groups obviously would need to acquire skill and sophistication in utilizing their bill of rights; but since many already have the skills, and technical resources are available, the most pressing immediate needs are for strong organization and an adequate legal framework. This approach will, not, of course, provide the vital and necessary resources to upgrade the multi-family buildings taken over – that again would require public resources – but it will mean a reduced rate of rent increases, retirement of much outstanding mortgage debt, and greatly increased resident and community control over, responsibility for, and security in multi-family housing at very little cost.

Conclusion

This chapter has had two major purposes. The first has been to present an analysis of the nature and implications of the housing problem in the U.S. – an analysis which reveals both the extent and depth of the housing crisis itself and also the close relationship between the housing problem and the broader and terribly serious problems of the overall economy. The second purpose, growing out of the first, has been to sketch the major elements of an emergency program for dealing immediately with the urgent problems of the broader economy and more particularly with housing.

The proposals which have been presented are not intended to be a comprehensive housing program nor in themselves to provide a long-term solution to the larger problems, but they are offered as absolutely essential and urgent first steps which point toward and contribute to a long-term solution. For the most part the proposals represent institutional changes and reforms, not spending programs, because the analysis suggests that such reforms are more necessary and pressing and because there continues to be widespread and understandable skepticism about the efficacy of spending programs alone. That does not mean that these proposals are incompatible with the efforts to halt and reverse the egregious injustice inherent in and resulting from the cuts in housing and other social programs. It does mean, though, that efforts to resist budget cuts and elimination of social programs must be subordinated to and set into the context of demands for immediate institutional change; otherwise such efforts will end up being counterproductive for the necessary and continuing struggle for social and economic justice.

Notes

1 Extensive discussion of the logic of housing affordability, the procedures used to operationalize the sliding scale, plus comparison with other affordability scales, is contained in Stone, forthcoming, Chapter 3.

2 The most controversial aspect of using the BLS Lower Budgets is whether they provide a reasonable definition of a minimal level of adequacy. The BLS itself has altered its official position on this matter since the budgets were first published in the late 1960s. At the time the Lower Budget was first being developed, the Bureau declared, in U.S. Dept. of Labor, Bureau of Labor Statistics, 1967, p. vii: "The lower-standard budget will represent a minimum of adequacy. . . . The lower-standard budgets are expected to be more appropriate than the moderate budget for use in establishing goals for public assistance and income maintenance programs in the current decade." By contrast, the cover statements accompanying the published sets of family and elderly budgets since the early 1970s

have included such statements as: "The budgets are not intended to represent a minimum of subsistence level of living," or, "The budgets are not intended to represent a minimum level of adequate income or a subsistence level of income."

The change in the official BLS interpretation of the Lower Budgets undoubtedly reflects the retreat by the federal government from a commitment to substantial income redistribution necessary for an income maintenance program with a reasonably adequate minimum support level. As this retreat was associated with the growing economic difficulties of the U.S. since the late 1960s and with the change of administration in 1969, the published disclaimers must be discounted somewhat on political and ideological grounds. At the same time, though, there are some conceptual and methodological problems associated with the BLS Budgets, but no operational alternative has yet been put into place. In 1978 the Bureau began a project to revise the Family Budget Program; an Expert Committee on Family Budget Revisions was established, but its final draft report, *New American Budget Standards*, completed in May, 1980, with the assistance of the Institute for Research on Poverty of the University of Wisconsin-Madison and the Center for the Social Sciences at Columbia University, was never published or acted upon. The analysis summarized here and presented in detail in Stone, forthcoming, has thus been carried out using the BLS Lower Budgets, recognizing certain limitations but hoping that it will contribute to rekindling debate on income distribution and the definition of a minimum adequate standard of living.

The Reagan Administration has decided to eliminate the BLS Family Budget Program beginning in fiscal year 1983; this means that the last published budgets will be for Autumn 1981. Unless and until the program is revived or a new one established, it will be necessary to update the budgets by applying the Consumer Price Index for specific items to the various budget components, in the same way that the BLS itself has updated the budgets.

3 Detailed results on the extent and distribution of shelter poverty from 1970 to 1980, among renters and homeowners, by income and household size, and in comparison the households paying 25 per cent or more of income for shelter, are presented in Stone, forthcoming, Chapter 4.

4 The Housing and Community Development Amendments of 1981, 42 *U.S.C.* 1437a, required that rents in federally subsidized housing be increased to 30 per cent of net income (see n. 5 *infra.* for a discussion of net income definitions as established by statute and regulation, and see the text for alternative possibilities). The Department of Housing and Urban Development published regulations to implement these amendments in the *Federal Register*, May 4,

1982, pp. 19120 and 19128. The regulations require that new tenants pay 30 per cent of net income and that the percentage of net income paid by existing tenants increase from 25 per cent to 30 per cent incrementally over a five-year period; the regulations also require minimum rents of 10 per cent of gross income. Before the regulations could take effect, the House Banking Committee voted to disapprove the regulations, thereby expecting to delay them for ninety days. HUD proceeded to ignore the Committee action and to implement the regulations on August 1, 1982, leading to a lawsuit in Federal District Court in New York City. In October, 1982, the Court denied a motion for a preliminary injunction against HUD; however, this is not the final ruling in the case, and similar suits have been filed in Cleveland, St. Louis, and other cities.

Tables 4.1 and 4.2 include examples of rents before and after these increases for four-person, one-adult families in Section 8 and public housing.

5 For public housing residents, the following deductions are permitted: (1) 5 per cent of the family's gross income (10 per cent if elderly); (2) $300 for each family member residing in the household who is either under 18, or if over 18 is disabled or handicapped or a full-time student; (3) the first $300 of any income of the spouse of the household head; (4) income of any other family member who is under 18 or a full-time student; and (5) medical expenses in excess of 3 per cent of gross income. The Section 8 program permits fewer deductions, limiting them to: (1) $300 for each minor; (2) medical expenses in excess of 3 per cent of gross income; and (3) unusual expenses, such as childcare. Under both programs, net income is defined as gross household income minus these permitted deductions. Rent was then set, prior to the 1982 increases, at 25 per cent of net income (20 per cent for tenants who pay directly for their heat and other utilities), but no less than 5 per cent of gross income in public housing and no less than 15 per cent of gross income in Section 8 (United States Housing Act of 1937, as amended, 42 *U.S.C.* 5301, Sec. 3(1)(D) and Sec. 8(c)).

In order to further cut federal spending for housing subsidies, the Reagan Administration in 1982 proposed elimination of these deductions from income and the inclusion of food stamp benefits as income (Low Income Housing Information Service, 1982, pp. 13, 15). The effect would be even greater increases in subsidized housing rents (as shown in Tables 4.1 and 4.2, under "Alternative Rent," column with deductions of zero). As of the end of 1982 these additional changes had not been adopted.

6 The complete set of computations has been carried out for elderly households of one person and two persons, non-elderly one-adult households of one person to six persons, and non-elderly

two-adult households of two persons to six persons, and with various assumptions about minimum rents.

7   Households receiving federal housing subsidies are mostly under the Section 8, Public Housing, Section 236, Section 221(d)(3) Below Market Interest Rate, Rent Supplement, or Section 202 programs.

The figure of 3.4 million subsidized households is from Philip Abrams, General Deputy Assistant Secretary, U.S. Department of Housing and Urban Development, speaking before the annual meeting of Boston Family Services, June 18, 1982. The figures of 12–15 per cent of needy households have been derived by dividing the 3.4 million figure by the total number of households paying 25 per cent of income or more for shelter and the total number of shelter poor, given above. The actual percentages receiving subsidies are undoubtedly lower, since the number of needy households in 1982 was surely greater than the 1980 figures which have been used for these computations. The $8 billion cost is from *HUD Budget Summaries*, as presented in Low Income Housing Information Service, 1982, Table 1, p. 11, sum of "housing payments" and "public housing operating subsidies."

8   The only detailed computations I have made of the cost of subsidizing all shelter poor households or all households paying 25 per cent or more of their incomes for shelter are based on data in the 1976 Annual Housing Survey. The procedure involved, first, the determination of the number of shelter poor households and the number paying 25 per cent or more, by income, household size, and shelter cost. Then the subsidy cost per household was computed for each income, household size, and shelter cost category. The number of households in each category was then multiplied by the corresponding subsidy cost per household. The result was a total cost of about $30 billion to eliminate shelter poverty in 1976 or about $20 billion to eliminate payments for shelter of 25 per cent or more of income. Since about 21 million households were shelter poor in 1976, the average subsidy per household was about $1,430 per year, or $120 per month; with 22.2 million households paying 25 per cent or more, the average subsidy cost using this standard was about $900 per household per year, or $75 per month. Thus the average subsidy per household to eliminate shelter poverty would be about 60 per cent greater than the average subsidy to eliminate payments of 25 per cent or more.

Between 1976 and 1982 the Consumer Price Index increased by almost exactly 70 per cent, so the average subsidy cost per household in 1982 would be about 70 per cent greater than in 1976, assuming approximately the same distribution of needy households by household size, and assuming that incomes and expenses have both gone up at about the rate of inflation. In fact, the average subsidy cost may have gone up faster than the rate of inflation, since needy households probably have not on average had their incomes go up as fast as inflation; the average subsidy cost per household has therefore been assumed to be 80 per cent greater in 1982 than 1976, which would be $2,575 per year for the shelter poverty standard or $1,620 for the 25 per cent of income or more standard.

In 1980 the number of shelter poor households was about 22 million, and the number paying 25 per cent or more of income for shelter was about 28 million, as indicated above in the text. If the number of households in need of assistance under either definition has increased by 10 per cent between 1980 and 1982, then the cost of eliminating shelter poverty in 1982 would be about $71 billion, and the cost of eliminating payments of 25 per cent or more of income for shelter would be about $50 billion.

The final estimates of cost must then take into account the existing subsidy costs of $8 billion in 1982. Since virtually all existing subsidized households are paying less than 25 per cent of gross income for shelter (even if more than 25 per cent of *net* income, see nn. 4 and 5 *supra*.), the number of households paying 25 per cent or more and the cost of subsidizing them would be over and above the $8 billion spent to subsidize 3.4 million households in 1982; on the other hand, using a 25 per cent of gross income formula rather than the present approach of moving toward 30 per cent of net income might reduce slightly the $8 billion for existing subsidized households. Thus a reasonable approximation to the cost of a subsidy program bringing shelter payments of all households within the 25 per cent of income standard would be about $57 billion in 1982 ($50 billion for additional households plus $7 billion for presently subsidized households).

With the shelter poverty approach, some presently subsidized households (those of low income and large size) are shelter poor and are included in the shelter poverty count of households, but would be entitled to additional subsidy under such an approach; these additional subsidies are included in the $71 billion estimate; at the same time, though, some presently subsidized households (some of small size and moderate income) are not shelter poor and would receive somewhat reduced subsidy under the shelter poverty approach. Some of the existing $8 billion would be reduced using the new affordability standards. Thus, an overall figure of $77 billion ($71 billion plus $8 billion minus an estimated saving of $2 billion), is a reasonable estimate of the cost of eliminating shelter poverty among all households in 1982.

9   Low Income Housing Information Service, 1982, Table A, p. 3, and Table 4, p. 20, derived from *Budget of the United States Government, Fiscal Year 1983, Part 3* and *Special Analysis A*; and U.S. Congressional Budget Office; 1981, Table 1, p. 7.

10   The quantitative data included throughout the rest of this section are from U.S. Bureau of the Census, 1976a; for more detail and page references in this source, see Stone, 1980a and b.

11   Figures on housing starts are published monthly in U.S. Bureau of the Census, *Construction Reports*, Series C20. Mortgage interest rates are published monthly, in the *Federal Home Loan Bank Board Journal,* which also presents sales prices for new and existing homes financed by member institutions of the Federal Home Loan Bank System. Another source on existing home sales prices and volume is National Association of Realtors, "Existing Home Sales," monthly. Also, U.S. Bureau of the Census, *Construction Reports*, Series C25, monthly, presents data on new homes.

12   U.S. Bureau of the Census, 1976b, Table 1287, p. 751. These figures are for non-farm real estate, most but not all of which consists of housing. This particular series has not been published for years after 1975.

13   In the five years from 1976 through 1980, repayments on long-term residential mortgage loans totalled almost exactly $400 billion (U.S. Department of Housing and Urban Development, 1980b, pp. 177–80; 1981b, p. 2).

   While some portion of this $400 billion represents repayments on loans originated during these five years and thus was not part of the $600 billion outstanding at the end of 1975, it is reasonable to conclude that most of the repayments were on loans outstanding at the end of 1975, for several reasons. First of all, the newer the loan and the higher the interest rate, the smaller the fraction of each monthly payment that goes toward repayment of principal; thus monthly payments on loans made after 1975 will on average include much smaller repayments of principal than loans made earlier. Second, the longer a loan is outstanding, the greater likelihood that the loan balance will be repaid through sale of the property or refinancing; the normal life of a long-term mortgage is ten to twelve years, and few are discharged in less than five years. It is therefore likely that the rate of resale and refinancing was substantially higher for mortgages taken out before 1976 than in later years. On the basis of these two factors, probably at least three-quarters of total loan repayments from 1976 through 1980, or more than $300 billion, were on mortgage loans outstanding at the end of 1975.

14   The Mortgage Bankers Association estimated that by the summer of 1982 about 140,000 *home* mortgages were in foreclosure, the highest proportion since they started keeping records thirty years ago, and a rate nearly 66 per cent higher than it had been a year earlier; in addition, more than 5 per cent of all home mortgages were thirty days or more overdue on the monthly payments (Brooks, 1982, p. 68). During the first half of 1982 bank failures reached the highest

level since the start of World War II ("Bank Failure Rate Highest Since 1942," *Boston Globe*, June 17, 1982).

15 Actually, it would be most appropriate to have a larger exemption for the first member of a household and successively smaller deductions for each additional member, to reflect most realistically the cost of supporting households of different sizes.

16 Investor deductions related to housing include expensing of construction period interest and taxes, depreciation on rental housing in excess of straight line, All-Savers Certificates interest exemption from taxes, five-year amortization for rental housing rehabilitation, and exclusion of interest on state and local housing bonds. These deductions are estimated by the Reagan Administration to cost the Treasury $2.7 billion in fiscal year 1982 and $5.3 billion in 1983 (Low Income Housing Information Service, 1982, Table 4, p. 20). Homeowner deductions are estimated by this administration to cost $35.2 billion in fiscal year 1982 and $38.5 billion in 1983 (ibid.), while the Congressional Budget Office estimates the cost to be $39.1 billion in 1982, $47.5 billion in 1983, increasing to $82.5 billion in 1986 (U.S. Congressional Budget Office, 1981, Table 1, p. 7).

17 A local ordinance of this nature was enacted in the late 1970s in Madison, Wisconsin.

5 Mobilize or compromise? The tenants' movement and American politics

John Atlas and Peter Dreier

Tenants, long a sleeping giant in American politics, are beginning to wake up. A new generation of middle-class tenants, seeing the "American Dream" of owning a house slipping away, is joining the urban poor in a growing renters' rights revolt across the country.

With the nationwide rental vacancy rate at its lowest point in three decades, construction of new rental housing almost at a standstill, and rents skyrocketing, tenants are finding themselves with their backs to the wall. They have lost the option to move. With a greater stake in their apartments, America's tenants are proving more willing to fight rent increases, condominium conversions, arbitrary evictions, and unsafe, poorly maintained buildings. Their activism is changing the relative bargaining positions of landlords and tenants. It is adding a new ingredient to the urban political scene. And it is a symptom of the deepening crisis of a political and economic system that relies on the private sector to provide decent, affordable housing.

The theme of this chapter is that the housing crisis is the consequence of a political crisis. Government policy reflects the relative power and influence of different economic and social groups in society. The current crisis is a delayed re-action to a series of government choices made in the immediate post-war period. At that time, the government had an opportunity to satisfy the growing demand for new housing by financing new construction directly, controlling land

and building materials costs, and thus making a decent, affordable home available to all Americans. Instead, it gave in to the real estate/banking lobby, and chose to subsidize private industry to build the needed housing, relying on an expanding economic pie to allow consumers to obtain housing with their rising incomes (Wolfe, 1981). For several decades that policy seemed to work, at least for the top two-thirds of the American population, those who could afford homeownership. But this only postponed the crisis; it didn't solve it.

Since the mid-1970s, when the nation's economic growth began to stagnate, and real incomes stopped their steady rise, the decisions made in the late 1940s have come back to haunt us. The chickens have come home – to *our* homes – to roost. In the past decade, housing prices have escalated dramatically. Whereas two-thirds of all American households could afford to buy a single-family home in the 1950s (using the one-quarter of one's income rule-of-thumb), less than 10 per cent can do so today (Donohue, 1982). Americans who were brought up with the notion that households should spend roughly one-quarter of their incomes for housing are now finding that they must spend 50 per cent or more of their incomes just to keep a roof over their heads.

By relying on the private housing industry to solve the problem, Stone (1978) explains, government policy is on a collision course. Capitalism is based on production of goods for profit. Generally speaking, corporations make the most profit by keeping wages as low as possible. On the other hand, capitalists in the housing market (mortgage lenders, real estate developers, homebuilders, and landlords) charge whatever the market will bear. In other words, the private housing market demands high mortgage payments, land and construction prices, and rents, while the labor market depresses wages and salaries. The result is a conflict between the labor and the housing markets.

Because the United States' global economic and political

power is threatened by both advanced capitalist and Third World challenges, its ability to control a disproportionate share of global resources has eroded. The crunch was inevitable. People are now going deeper and deeper into debt to purchase a home, or increasingly falling behind on their rental obligations; their incomes are no longer keeping pace with housing inflation, as they did during the high-growth years after World War II.

The nation's mainstream housing experts have nothing new to offer to get us out of this crisis. The only way to resolve this tension, without direct government intervention to compete with or replace the private housing industry, is for Americans to live in smaller units at higher prices with fewer services or amenities. In fact, the "neo-conservative" housing experts like George Sternlieb (Norman, 1982) of Rutgers and Anthony Downs (1980) of the Brookings Institution are creating an ideological rationale for lowering the nation's housing standards by claiming that Americans are "over-housed" and should lower their expectations. All they can advise Americans is to tighten their belts, learn to live with less, and pay more for it. Their ideas have filtered into the popular media. *Time* magazine tells readers about "downsizing" their housing dreams (Morrow, 1981). The *Boston Globe* (Richard, 1982), *New York Times* (Husock, 1981; Lindsey, 1981) and *Parade* (Peterson, 1982; Ryan, 1982) feature stories of how Americans are learning to live with smaller (but more costly) homes. Financial columnist Sylvia Porter advises readers: "Downgrade your housing dreams for a while. Share space, rent, consider a mobile home" (Morrow, 1981). Even *Business Week* (1981b) has warned that the nation "has backed away from its longtime commitment to housing as a top national priority. For the next decade, at least, the U.S. is in danger of splitting into a nation of housing haves and have-nots. At best, Americans are going to be paying more for smaller and smaller lower quality dwellings."

Thus, more than three decades later, American society

once again confronts a similar choice, only this time without the promise of an expanding national pie to bail us out of the dilemma. We can continue to rely on the private sector, devising all kinds of tax and other subsidy schemes to bribe banks and builders to provide housing, and falling even deeper into the housing crisis. Or we can find new ways to finance and build housing that rely more directly on public funds, based on the premise that decent housing is a basic right and not a commodity. Experience in some Western European nations, and even some pockets of innovation in the U.S., indicates this can be done.

But it is not enough to devise good policies and programs. There must be a political movement willing to fight for them and win. The present housing crisis is a result of the failure of progressive forces to mobilize a majority for reform. It is a political question, a question of which groups in society will steer the rudder of government policy. Once again, the banking and real estate industries have a stake in the present policy of providing government incentives to the private housing industry. And once again, the poor and the working class – but this time, with the addition of the disenchanted, inflation-pinched middle class – have a stake in more progressive policy. This coalition can no longer go the route of making compromises with builders, bankers, and land speculators, as the progressive coalition did in the 1940s, and as many well-intentioned liberals continue to do today. It is no longer enough to seek a few more rent subsidy funds, a few more mortgage write-downs, and a few more public housing units. That route has been tried and found wanting. So today progressives are confronted with the same choice: *to mobilize or compromise?* If we are not to repeat the mistakes of the past, a broad political constituency must be mobilized to influence and elect government officials around a national commitment to solving the housing crisis by directing public funds into construction of decent, affordable housing for all. Political mobilization is the only route to a real housing solution.

The growing mobilization of tenants during the past decade is a symptom of the housing crisis and a symbol of that new direction. It is showing an increasing number of the nation's sixty million tenants that things will only get better if they organize politically to *expand* their rights and *protect their housing conditions*. On its own, the tenants' movement cannot overhaul American housing policy toward a more comprehensive solution, but it can move part of the way in that direction. Ultimately, we believe, it can form a political coalition with the labor movement, the senior citizens and consumer movements, the women's and environmental movements, and even the peace and human rights movement, to redirect national policy and priorities toward meeting basic human needs rather than wasting them on welfare for the rich, the corporations, and the Pentagon.

The current crisis

The statistics demonstrating the growing housing problems of renters are adequately laid out in the Dolbeare and Achtenberg-Marcuse contributions to this volume. As should be obvious, the situation for renters in America is much worse than for homeowners. The major reason is that homeowners are more affluent than tenants. As Table 5.1 indicates, rates of homeownership increase steadily with income, and most people who can afford to buy a house do so. In 1970, tenants' median household income ($6,300) was 64.9 per cent of homeowners' ($9,700). By 1977, the gap had widened: tenants' median income ($8,800) was only 55 per cent of homeowners' ($16,000). Three years later, it had widened further: tenants' income ($10,600) was only 53.5 per cent of homeowners' ($19,800). This trend reflects two parallel processes. On the one hand, the incomes of tenants – who are concentrated among the minorities, the elderly, and low-wage workers in the secondary labor market – increased more slowly than incomes of homeowners. On the other hand, those tenants at the top of the income scale who could afford to become homeowners, did so, a process Sternlieb and Hughes (1980) call "cream skimming."

This concentration of tenants among the less affluent is pronounced. In 1980, 67.6 per cent of all renters, compared with 37.1 per cent of all homeowners, had household incomes below $15,000. And 89.1 per cent of tenants, but only 63.1 per cent of owners, had incomes below $25,000.

Thus, very few tenants are tenants by choice. They are forced by economic circumstances – and as Table 5.1 indicates, by racial discrimination in the home buying market (Pearce, 1979; Yinger, 1978) – to rent their homes. The nature of the rental housing market is such that tenants must pay a higher portion of their income for lower quality housing (U.S. Department of Labor, 1966). Compared with owning, renting takes a bigger, and less expendable, slice of income, giving tenants less income to pay for other necessities.

TABLE 5.1   *Income, race, and homeownership, in 1980*
(% homeowners)

Income	Households			
	All	White	Black	Hispanic
Less than $3,000	43.7	51.1	26.6	21.0
$ 3,000–$6,999	47.0	52.9	31.1	20.0
$ 7,000–$9,999	53.0	58.1	37.4	24.5
$10,000–$14,999	56.5	59.7	44.3	37.6
$15,000–$19,999	65.5	67.7	52.4	53.5
$20,000–$24,999	74.7	76.7	59.2	62.0
$25,000–$34,999	83.1	84.2	71.0	75.0
$35,000–$49,999	89.5	90.2	80.0	82.6
$50,000–$74,999	92.1	92.4	83.9	92.1
$75,000 and above	92.4	92.7	99.9	73.9
Total	65.5	69.7	43.9	42.4

Source: Calculated by the authors from data presented in U.S. Bureau of the Census, 1981a.

The society-wide desire for homeownership is not simply a matter of cultural preference. It is built into the tax code, as the Appendix to Cushing Dolbeare's chapter in this volume clearly demonstrates. As a result, Hendershott and Shilling (1980) found, these mortgage-related benefits have sharply increased the homeownership rate; at least 4.5 to 5 million fewer households would have been homeowners at the end of 1978 in the absence of these government-induced benefits.

Traditionally, tenants have had few rights that would allow them to improve these conditions. Tenant-landlord law remains exceedingly biased against tenants, still a remnant of its agrarian and feudal origins (Rose, 1973). Except in New Jersey (which has a statewide "just cause" eviction law), in public housing, and in cities with rent control laws, landlords can evict tenants for almost any reason at all, not only failure to pay rent, and they can use the power of the courts to back them up. Besides the right to evict during the term of the lease (for non-payment), landlords can force tenants to move at the end of the lease period for almost any reason whatsoever. (One consequence of the tight rental housing market since the late 1970s has been the decline in the number of landlords who even offer leases. Increasing numbers of renters are tenants "at will.") Homeowners are more secure; mortgage lenders and city officials can take possession of a home (the equivalent of a tenant's eviction) only if the homeowner fails to make payments to the bank or to the tax collectors.

Since the 1970s, in response to tenant protest, a number of states have adopted laws giving tenants more rights and landlords more responsibilities. These include the "implied warranty of habitability" (which guarantees tenants the right to minimum standards of decent housing and that they will not have to pay for "essential services" which they do not receive), and protection against "retaliatory evictions" for complaining to the landlord or local authorities about building maintenance. Other legal reforms deal with security deposits, the right to withhold rents, utility shut-offs, lockouts and seizure of tenants' possessions, standard leases, and housing discrimination (Blumberg and Grow, 1978; Rose, 1973). But because tenant-landlord laws are enacted at the state and local levels, these reforms have not been adopted uniformly; they exist only in areas where tenant activism has been strongest. Many tenants, therefore, are not covered by such laws.

State and municipal building and housing codes provide for minimum standards of health and safety. Although some localities had dealt with this problem earlier, substantial government regulation really began with New York's pioneering Tenement House Act of 1867, which prescribed minimum standards for fireproofing, safety, ventilation, sanitation, and weathertightness of multiple-family housing, and the Tenement House Act of 1901, which created more adequate enforcement mechanisms. Despite scholarly debate on whether such regulations were primarily aimed at protecting slum dwellers or their nearby middle-class neighbors (Lubove, 1962; Marcuse, 1978; Warner, 1972), there is no doubt that these codes have become stronger over the years. But the extreme housing shortage provides landlords with little incentive to obey tenant-landlord laws or housing codes. The rental shortage gives most tenants "no practical alternative but to take what is offered and pay what is asked" (U.S. Department of HUD, et al., 1967). Further, in most cities local housing codes and tenant-landlord laws are not adequately enforced. Municipal inspection departments are understaffed and poorly trained. Many landlords consider a "pay-off" to housing inspectors as a regular cost of doing business to avoid having to maintain buildings up to standards (Greer, 1979; Hartman, 1975). Further, even when landlords are brought to court, many judges are reluctant to put the full force of the law behind landlord violation of tenants' rights or municipal housing codes. Some may fear that enforcement might lead to widespread abandonment, while others have prejudices or political ties to landlords or local government authorities (Carlson, et al., 1965; U.S. Comptroller General, 1972; Fish, 1973;

Greer, 1979; Gribetz and Grad, 1966; Hartman, et al., 1974; Sternlieb, 1966; Sternlieb and Burchell, 1973).

Now: Enter the middle-class. According to *Mortgage Banking* (magazine of the Mortgage Bankers Association of America):

> Households that entered the housing market from 1950 to 1973 experienced little difficulty in making a home purchase. Those entering the market from 1973 to 1978, having virtually the same income after adjustment for inflation, were forced to sacrifice to a considerable degree in order to become homeowners. And many of those entering the market in recent years have effectively been told that there is no room for them in the housing market (Donohue, 1982).

The situation facing tenants has never been rosy, but so long as it was confined to the poor and the near-poor, society did not have to address it as a serious problem – unless, of course, the poor started to riot, as they did in the 1960s. Growing numbers of middle-income households, shut out of the home-buying market, are now facing the powerlessness and frustration that comes with renting. They may not have the same problems as slum-dwellers – such as rats, roaches, and lead paint – but they still face many of the same problems that come with being at the mercy of landlords in a tight housing market. They face escalating rents, the constant threat of eviction, and poorly maintained buildings.

Even the middle-class households who resist renting and decide to buy their own home despite the obstacles find that the "American Dream" isn't what they were promised. To afford a home, they are giving up on many things. They are postponing having children, or having fewer of them. They are living in much smaller homes – including condominiums – than did their parents' generation, without the lawns, or patios, or walk-in closets, or extra bedroom, or numerous appliances they had once expected. They are giving up vacations, movies, and other aspects of the middle-class life-style. They are holding on to their car longer – and not purchasing a second one. Couples are working two, even three, jobs to keep making the payments on their homes. And even so, mortgages in arrears by thirty days or more and the number of foreclosures have both steadily risen, reaching a post-war peak in 1982, according to the Mortgage Bankers Association of America. A growing number of people simply can't make it as homeowners. They will find themselves renters once again (Brooks, 1982; Husock, 1981).

The sleeping giant awakens

Conditions thus appear ripe for the building of a political movement of housing consumers, particularly renters. With the proper leadership, tactics and strategies, tenants could be organized into a relatively powerful movement capable of contending for power and advancing programs that solve the housing crisis.

But there are skeptics. Tenants, they say, are a difficult group to organize politically for a variety of reasons. For one, tenants' organizations have historically been difficult to sustain because of the transient nature of tenancy or because tenants viewed themselves as being on a way-station toward homeownership (Heskin, 1981; Lipsky, 1970; Dreier, 1982a). The difficulty is compounded because to most people housing is a private matter, a refuge for the individual and family from the ravages of the work world. The workplace is a source of drudgery or competition, a continual test of one's worth and self-esteem. Physically as well as psychologically, one returns home to relax, to re-treat, to get away from the pressures of work. People resist coming home after work to fight their landlords or mortgage lenders or to attend a city council meeting. Finally, housing, unlike work, is rarely seen as a collective, or social, activity. The relations of consumption – food, clothing, shelter – are more fragmented than the relations of production. As Weinbaum and Bridges (1976) note, the consumer, unlike the worker, "has no singular and obvious antagonist, but many antagonists: the state, the supermarket, the landlord, etc." Even if one socializes with one's neighbors and fellow tenants, improvements in housing are considered individual matters. In housing, there is a strong "do-it-yourself" ideology. One either improves one's own housing or moves out to bigger, better accommodations.

But times have changed. A number of conditions make the emergence of "tenant consciousness" and tenant organizing more likely. Four factors in particular have made a significant difference in increasing the likelihood of tenant protests in the United States.

The first has been the explosion of grassroots protest during the past decade. The image of the 1970s as a quiet "me decade," a reaction against the noisy protests of the 1960s, is misleading. Not only did many of the civil rights, student, and anti-war activists remain political through the 1970s, but a much broader spectrum of Americans joined the struggle for more rights and freedoms. Throughout the decade, environmental, women's, consumer, senior citizens', human rights, and neighborhood movements emerged, mobilizing millions of Americans around a wide variety of concerns and creating a political climate of what sociologist Daniel Bell (1976) calls "rising entitlements." There was, once again, a climate of protest in the nation, not just among the poor, but among the working and middle classes as well. This momentum carried through into the 1980s, with protest movements against nuclear arms, nuclear power, the dumping of toxic chemicals, and the Reagan Administration's cutbacks of social and welfare programs, consumer and environmental protection, occupational safety, and education. Many of the people who distrusted the radical protesters of the 1960s were among those joining the protests of the 1970s and 1980s.

This growing climate of protest emerged gradually out of changing values. For one thing, the period taught people that "leaders" and "experts" were not always to be trusted, and that they would have to rely on themselves to protect their rights, because the "best and the brightest" often showed little regard for the everyday routines and values of America's vast middle. For example, the urban renewal programs of the 1960s, allegedly set up to "clear" the slums, actually bulldozed stable, working-class neighborhoods (Gans, 1962; Fellman, 1973; Fried, 1973). As Boyte (1980) observes, "The experiences through which people replenish and sustain themselves resemble more and more a kind of "social factory" where they are dominated and exploited as taxpayers and consumers, like they are exploited in the work-place." Infringement on these everyday routines thus became the focal point of protest. Tenant organizations, which deal with a basic necessity within which so much of everyday life goes on, draw a potential strength from this reality – far greater, in some respects, than what can be drawn from the typical exploitation of most consumer–seller relationships. Not surprisingly, women are disproportionately found among the leadership of tenant protest groups (Lawson and Barton, 1980).

The second condition was the increase in long-term tenancies. As the costs of homeownership skyrocketed during the 1970s, many tenants became locked into renting. For an increasing number of families, particularly those of the post-war "baby boom" generation, the American Dream was beyond their reach (Donohue, 1982). An increasing number, including the growing number of single-person, single-parent, and elderly households, would find themselves spending a long time as tenants. Gradually, and unwillingly, they began to think of themselves as long-term, rather than temporary, renters. In addition, even as tenants, they were no longer as transient as tenants once were. When housing choices are abundant, and vacancy rates high, tenants who don't like their apartments vote with their feet: they move (Fredland, 1973; Goodman, 1978; Rossi, 1955). This transiency had always made it difficult to organize tenant groups and to develop stable memberships and leaders. It also led to lower levels of political involvement and less of a stake in community issues. For example, tenants have much lower rates of voter registration and voting than do homeowners (U.S. Bureau of the Census, 1979; Alford and Scoble, 1968). By the mid-1970s, however, tenants had fewer options. The low vacancy rates make it more difficult for tenants to find another apartment and more likely they will stay where they are, even when they are dissatisfied with their apartments. With both traditional options – moving to another apartment or to a single-family home – less available, tenants begin to have a greater stake in the conditions of their apartment and to develop "tenant consciousness."

The third condition was the growing number of tenants living in large buildings or apartment complexes owned by absentee companies. During the 1970s, the economics of apartment ownership and management began to change. Until then, the vast majority of apartment owners were relatively amateur landlords who owned one, or just a few, small apartment buildings. For many, it was not a full-time job, but a sideline to earn extra money. Many lived in their own apartment buildings, knew the tenants on a first-name basis, knew their problems, and might even peg rent levels to their tenants' ability to pay. Such personal, paternalistic relationships between tenants and landlords, although often strained, tended to inhibit tenant activism. It is difficult, in that situation, to see the landlord as an "enemy": he may not have much more money than the tenant. Also, it is hard to organize tenants when only a few of them share the same building or landlord (Gans, 1962; Krohn and Tiller, 1969; Vaughan, 1968).

During the late 1960s and early 1970s there was a boom of suburban garden apartment complexes and of high-rise apartment buildings in cities (Neutze, 1968; Schafer, 1974). One big reason for the growth in large apartment buildings was the urban renewal and federally subsidized apartment programs. Apartments rented by middle-income tenants were part of large buildings and complexes increasingly owned by absentee owners and run by professional property managers. These changes altered the nature of tenant-landlord relations. They became more and more depersonalized. Rent checks were sent to faceless professional management firms rather than handed or mailed to an individual landlord. Absentee owners, who buy apartments for their short-term tax advantages, have less incentive than live-in landlords to make repairs and maintain their buildings. As Roger Starr (1979) has noted, "Locked into a long-term relationship with someone whom he [or she] usually never sees, the tenant cannot truly understand why he [or she] should be asked to pay again and again for something that the landlord already made." A large number of tenants under the same roof, or within the same complex, who have the same landlord, creates the potential for the emergence of a critical mass of tenants who share grievances, form committees, and organize a tenants' group. This depersonalization of tenant–landlord relations and the growing scale of apartment life enhanced the potential for the development of tenant consciousness and activism. From our observations, most tenant activism is found in the large buildings and complexes. This situation is similar to the emergence of industrial unionism, which only occurred when the large absentee-owned factory – with a large number of workers employed by the same company – replaced the small mill where the employees and owner worked side by side.

The fourth condition is the changing role and perception of government and its relationship to the business class. Increasingly, Piven and Cloward argue, the state has become "the main arena of class conflict. Working people who once looked to the marketplace as the arena for action on their economic grievances and aspirations now look more often to the state." (Piven and Cloward, 1982, p. 125). Americans expect the government to protect them from the worst abuses of the private "free market" economy. For the three decades after World War II, the government subsidized the private housing industry with mortgage insurance, roadbuilding programs that opened up the suburbs to new housing development, and tax breaks for homeowners and for rental housing construction. The steady, indeed dramatic increase in homeownership during this period – from roughly 44 per cent of all households in 1940 to about 65 per cent in the early 1970s – in effect "co-opted" the potential for a significant tenants' movement. For those left behind in the rush to the suburbs – the urban poor, the minorities, the elderly – the private housing industry had little to offer. Public housing provided only a minimal safety valve for the poor. After the urban riots of the 1960s, the government increased its rent subsidy and low-income homeownership programs, but these met only a tiny fraction of the overall need.

The new realities of the 1980s, however, make it impossible for the private housing industry and the government to respond in the same way. Affordable housing, like health care, will increasingly come to be seen as a basic right, an "entitlement," that government should make available to all. Obviously, housing consumers will have the most to gain from this, but some sectors of the business community will also be concerned with rising housing costs. Like health care and education, housing is part of the "social wage" – the cost of keeping the labor force able to produce and reproduce itself, so that employers can have a steady workforce. Large corporate employers do not want to pay higher wages simply to permit their workers to put a roof over their heads. Already, in some areas of the country, employers are alarmed because rising housing costs are driving away, or making it difficult to attract, skilled employees (particularly professional-level employees). Some companies are even offering long-term reduced mortgages, or downpayments, to lure potential employees to move (*Business Week*, 1981a; Lindsey, 1981). Most employers, however, do not want to directly subsidize these housing costs.

As the cost of housing continues to skyrocket, some sectors of the business community will call for "cost containment" as they have already done for the skyrocketing costs of health care. Of course, business leaders will resist direct government ownership and production of housing, as they have resisted excluding the private sector from participation in any national health care legislation. But the very call for government to "do something" about housing costs will push politicians into looking for new solutions. In this situation, the housing industry, particularly land speculators and landlords, is especially vulnerable.

Although the housing industry is not an isolated enclave within the overall economy, it is sufficiently distinct from the major manufacturing and service sectors. Indeed, it is this group whose interests have been subordinated when the larger needs of business production were at stake. During both world wars, national rent controls were adopted, promoted by the war-time planners from the corporate world over the objections of the private landlords (Lebowitz, 1981). Other capitalist countries have adopted much stricter controls on housing costs – particularly land, building materials, and financing. As pressure from tenants, home-owners, and segments of the business community mounts, politicians will find it in their political self-interest to jump on the bandwagon to control housing prices. The debate over national housing policy will open up discussion of more public control of housing. In the short-term, though, policies like rent control will meet with more favor from large corporate employers concerned about rising housing costs for their employees. Much as the decades-long struggle for Medicare and Medicaid set the stage for the current round of debates over the structure of health care institutions and the "right" to decent, affordable health care, we can expect a protracted debate over housing, with private real estate interests increasingly on the defensive. These circumstances set the stage for major reforms.

Tactics and strategies

Tenant activism developed steadily during the 1970s and early 1980s. Tenant groups now exist in almost every city and many suburbs. These include building-level, citywide, and several statewide tenant groups. A National Tenants Union (NTU) was formed in 1980 to help coordinate the growing number of tenant activities. In 1975, tenant leaders founded the national magazine *Shelterforce* to report on and encourage tenant activism. The publication has helped to give the movement a sense of identity and coordination, and its editors (along with New Jersey and New York tenant leaders) took the first steps to form the NTU. In addition, many of the grassroots, Alinsky-style community organizations that mushroomed in the 1970s, in low-income and working-class neighborhoods, took on tenant organizing as part of their multi-issue agendas. These groups – such as the Association of Community Organizations for Reform Now (ACORN), Massachusetts Fair Share, and Hartford Areas Rally Together (HART) – had a concern with the problems of older urban neighborhoods; this necessitated some focus on tenant problems. Also, the growing number of activist senior citizen organizations (e.g. the Gray Panthers and National Council of Senior Citizens) around the country made tenant problems one of their priorities, a reflection of the worsening housing situation among older Americans (Cliffe, 1982).

Just as the early stages of the modern labor movement fought immediately for "bread and butter" issues (wages and hours, job security, working conditions), so too does the current tenants' movement focus on defending tenants against skyrocketing rents, arbitrary evictions, unsafe building conditions, and interference with the right to organize. Their tactics include rent strikes, picketing and demonstrations, legal challenges, and electoral politics. The battleground includes tenants' demands for rent control, restriction on condominium conversions, building safety and maintenance, enforcement of housing codes, protection against landlords' "arson-for-profit," greater tenant voice in building management, and greater freedom to organize. The improvements in tenant–landlord law cited earlier – such as the "warranty of habitability" and "retaliatory eviction" protections – now make tenant organizing less risky.

It is possible to offer selective examples that provide some sense of the dynamics and range of tenant activism and landlord–tenant politics.

The success of the New Jersey Tenants Organization (NJTO) – with 80,000 dues-paying members, and an impressive string of electoral victories, plus the toughest tenant–landlord laws in the nation and rent control in more than 100 cities to its credit – serves as a model for the tenant movement around the country. NJTO was formed in 1969, with tenants from the middle-income suburbs near New York City living in large apartment complexes, as well as tenants from the slums of Newark and Passaic (Baar, 1977). From the outset, NJTO developed a three-pronged strategy to build "tenant power" in New Jersey. It combined: (a) direct action tactics (such as rent strikes, demonstrations, picketing and rallies) associated with grass-roots organizing, to keep tenants in motion, heighten solidarity and give them media exposure, thus attracting the attention of politicians; (b) electoral politics, endorsing pro-tenant candidates for local and state elections, who would enact favorable tenants' rights legislation; and (c) litigation to establish protection for tenants engaged in direct action and to strengthen tenant–landlord laws. The organization's leadership recognized that all three were necessary to mobilize tenants and win victories. A strategy that relied too heavily on direct confrontations to win concessions from landlords and political officials would ultimately fail. The problem was that the rent strike, by itself, failed to expand tenants' rights and build stable organizations and grassroots leaders. It did not, for example, lead to any lasting control over rent increases or enforcement of housing codes. Tenants remained subject to arbitrary evictions at the end of their lease or, if they had no lease, on merely a thirty-day notice. Many tenant leaders were harassed and evicted for organizing or even complaining to the building department or other government officials. Thus, NJTO recognized early the importance of developing tenants as a voting bloc and engaging in electoral politics.

The political response to NJTO's early efforts to register tenant voters and engage in election campaigns surprised even NJTO leaders. During the 1970s, NJTO engaged in direct action organizing while also winning court and legislative victories. It won pro-tenant laws on the issues of security deposits, evictions for cause, receivership, public disclosure of apartment ownership, and state income tax credits for tenants. More than one hundred communities passed rent control laws. Tenant leaders were elected or appointed to serve on local rent control boards, watching out for tenant interests and encouraging tenant groups to monitor rent board hearings, formulas for rent increases, condo conversions, and landlords' claims of cost increases. Today there is a powerful and effective group of pro-tenant elected officials in the state legislature. Politicians respect tenants' bloc voting power and return NJTO's endorsement with other favors. For example, in return for tenants' help in electing him as Essex County Executive, the second most powerful office in the state, Peter Shapiro provided funds to establish a Tenant Resource Center, which provides counseling and organizing help, and Pat Morrissey, an NJTO leader, was named to head the Center.

NJTO views election campaigns as organizing tools. At election time, the media and voters pay attention. Campaign workers can knock on doors and talk to people, not only about candidates and personalities, but also about tenant issues. Campaign workers help distribute NJTO literature and thus help promote the organization. An independent poll of New Jersey voters found that NJTO's endorsement gave politicians substantial credibility.

In California, tenants have organized along similar lines. Home prices there skyrocketed in the late 1970s, averaging over $100,000 by 1978, shutting out many middle-income residents from homeownership, while rental vacancies reached record lows. The tenants' movement exploded in 1978, following passage of Proposition 13, the tax-cutting amendment (Dreier, 1979). Throughout the state, tenants expected Proposition 13 to hold down rents; landlords even made such promises. But the anticipated windfall of rent rollbacks did not materialize; in fact, many of California's 3.5 million tenant households received notices of rent *increases* shortly after Proposition 13 passed. This set the stage for a significant tenant backlash. Through the state, tenants who had been hit by increases organized meetings to demand that landlords share their property tax savings with tenants. Newspapers were filled with stories of outraged tenants, embarrassed landlords, and politicians jumping on the bandwagon. As public clamor mounted, some landlords agreed to reduce rents in order to avoid mandatory rollbacks and freezes. But tenant pressure did not subside. And when heavy real estate industry lobbying defeated a statewide bill requiring landlords to pass on their tax savings to tenants, the battle shifted to the local level. Tenant groups began to mobilize in communities across the state, demanding rent control. Experienced tenant leaders began to travel around helping local groups. A statewide organization, the California Housing Action and Information Network (CHAIN), was formed to coordinate local and statewide efforts. By 1981, more than twenty-five California communities, including San Francisco and Los Angeles, had already passed rent control laws and more were considering them.

The tenants' movement has been particularly successful in Santa Monica, a coastal city of 90,000 in Ronald Reagan's backyard. In 1980, the tenants' movement there had passed strong rent and condominium conversion controls, and elected several members to the City Council. A year later, it secured a majority on the Council (its slate included a minister, two union activists, and several tenant activists), and Ruth Yanatta Goldway, the leader of Santa Monicans for Renters Rights, was elected Mayor. Once in office, they enacted a radical program that went beyond tenant problems. This included increased police foot patrols and improved municipal services; increased fees on Shell's underground pipeline, pro-union policies, such as requiring the union label on all city stationery and negotiating a favorable contract with municipal unions; and resolutions opposing U.S. intervention in El Salvador and nuclear proliferation. The City Council named citizen task forces on crime, women's issues and other problems, and appointed progressive activists to such critical positions as city attorney, city manager, and other high-level jobs. The Council also dramatically changed the city's development priorities; for example, it required one developer to build a park, daycare center, and affordable housing units in order to obtain a permit to build a highly profitable hotel complex near the waterfront (Shearer, 1982; *Business Week,* 1981c).

Although the tenants' movement is most advanced in New Jersey and California, similar activities have taken place in cities and suburbs across the country.

New York City is the home of the oldest and one of the most effective citywide tenant groups in the nation, the Metropolitan Council on Housing, started in 1959. In 1976, 86 per cent of the 15,372 tenants in Coop City, a moderate-income housing project in the Bronx, participated in a thirteen-month rent strike, withholding over $25 million in rents (Newfield and DuBrul, 1977). The New York City tenants' movement spilled over to suburban Westchester, Rockland, and Nassau Counties, where several communities passed rent control laws (Lawson, 1980b) and to upstate New York as well. Local tenant groups in New York State formed a statewide New York State Tenants Coalition (recently renamed the New York State Tenants and Neighborhood Coalition) to coordinate activities and work together in Albany.

In Massachusetts, where tenant groups had been active throughout the 1970s in the older industrial cities, a statewide Massachusetts Tenants Organization was formed in 1981, triggering tenant activism in the middle-income suburbs and small towns, primarily around rent increases and condominium conversions. Rising rents spurred tenant activism for rent control in many other communities across the country. Washington, D.C., Boston, and Baltimore, for example, passed rent control laws during the 1970s. (Baltimore's rent control initiative, passed by the voters in 1979, was later overturned by the courts, on the grounds that only the city council, and not the voters, can enact this type of legislation, under Maryland's constitution.) In 1979 and 1980 alone, momentum for rent control existed in cities in at least twenty-six states (National Multi-Housing Council, 1981b).

Another emerging problem, the conversion of rental apartments to expensive condominiums, led to tenant activism in the late 1970s. Some 366,000 units were converted in the U.S. between 1970–9, 71 per cent of which took place in the last three years of that decade. At first concentrated in a few urban areas, by 1980 condo conversions soon spread to most metropolitan areas. Conversions are highly profitable for landlords, developers, and the banks that finance the process, but also result in widespread displacement. Most tenants cannot afford the price of condominiums, but with vacancy rates so low, they have difficulty finding another suitable apartment. As a result, tenant opposition has emerged to delay evictions by requiring a year or more notice, to prohibit evictions altogether, or to require tenant approval before conversions can proceed. By early 1981, some form of tenant protection against condo conversion had been passed in twenty-four states and the District of Columbia (Dreier and Atlas, 1981; National Multi-Housing Council, 1981a; U.S. Department of Housing and Urban Development, 1980a).

While the tenants' movement has primarily been concerned with protecting tenants from rent increases and evictions, and with improving conditions, other issues have emerged as well. In Boston, for example, the Symphony Tenants Organizing Project (STOP) came together to investigate and fight fires that had been sweeping the neighborhood for several years. It began by trying to enforce the housing codes, but soon discovered that many fires were deliberately set by landlords in order to collect the insurance from buildings that had been abandoned or allowed to deteriorate. By generating considerable publicity and pressure around this "arson-for-profit" scheme, STOP got action by law enforcement officials and insurance companies, including the arrest of thirty-three landlords, lawyers, insurance adjusters, public officials, and a state police lieutenant who had been bribed. STOP has continued to organize tenants around rent increases, evictions, and "gentrification."

In many older cities, abandoned housing has triggered tenant activism, including a tactic known as "squatting," in which tenants take over abandoned buildings and simply refuse to move (similar to workers' "sit-down" strikes). This tactic is used primarily by low-income tenants. Owners of these buildings often have not paid property taxes, so many abandoned buildings are owned by the city. Tenants have demanded that the city government allow them to fix these buildings with "sweat equity" and live there permanently. In 1981, ACORN (the Association of Community Organizations for Reform Now) coordinated a campaign along these lines in Philadelphia, Detroit, Boston, and several other cities. In New York City, several programs are designed to turn abandoned properties over to tenant and non-profit community groups (Schur, 1980). In most localities, squatting still meets official resistance, eviction, and penalties.

Some tenant groups have organized as unions, seeking collective bargaining between tenants and landlords. Typically, this strategy is in response to rent increases and poor maintenance. Tenants engage in a rent strike, as well as demonstrations and picketing, to force the landlord to sit down and negotiate with the tenants' group. Tenants hope that the landlord's legal fees, the withheld rents, and public embarrassment (one Boston group spread "wanted" posters, with the landlord's photograph and name on them, throughout the city) will force landlords to bargain. Because tenants risk eviction for such actions, it is not a widely used tactic unless tenants already have achieved laws protecting them from eviction – or have faith in a sympathetic judge. In Chicago, Boston, and elsewhere, tenants have negotiated settlements with landlords, contracts which recognize the tenants' union and through which tenants gain a greater voice over rent increases, maintenance, and other conditions. Yet in no city or state are tenants' collective bargaining rights written into law (although from 1978–81 Madison, Wisconsin had a "Rental Relations Ordinance" that required landlords to bargain in good faith with any legally constituted union of their tenants). Unlike labor unions, which are protected by the National Labor Relations Act, tenants' unions have no automatic right to be recognized when more than half of the tenants (in a building or with the same landlord) vote for a union.

Tenant groups have also organized against involuntary displacement due to "gentrification," when private developers (often with the aid of public subsidies or tax breaks) build an office complex, luxury residential center, hotel or convention center, or other major project. These developments often displace low- and moderate-income tenants – either directly (by tearing down their housing), or indirectly (by "upgrading" the neighborhood, attracting higher-income residents and boosting rent levels, or inducing condo conversions). These anti-displacement efforts, however, involve great difficulties, since typically such developments are seen as "revitalizing" the city, broadening the tax base, improving blighted neighborhoods (LeGates and Hartman, 1981). Tenants have little leverage, other than costly, complex, and drawn-out court battles (usually to deny government subsidies to such projects) or direct action civil disobedience (which can delay projects, but rarely stop them). The principle of revitalizing neighborhoods without displacement requires a direct challenge to free market principles (i.e., controls on land speculation, even public ownership of land). It is only where tenant groups and their allies have more direct influence on government policy – as in Santa Monica, where they control local government – that the pace and direction of local development can be altered to stop displacement due to gentrification.

The discussion so far has focused primarily on tenants in

private housing, but tenants in public housing have also engaged in rent strikes, direct action, and legal and electoral activity to improve living conditions, often gaining concessions from local housing authorities. In the U.S., however, public housing accounts for less than 2 per cent of all housing. Public housing is funded primarily at the federal level, but controlled by local housing authorities. Federal funding priorities thus directly impact public housing tenants, as the Reagan Administration's policy of increasing rents and lowering operating subsidies indicates, but tenants have little influence over national decisions. The National Tenants Organization, formed in 1969, sought to organize public housing tenants at the national level, but exercised only minimal and fleeting influence for a few years (Marcuse, 1971). Local public housing tenant groups have won concessions over project maintenance and tenant in-put in decision-making, but local housing authorities are ultimately dependent on federal funds, and public housing has not been a priority of federal policymakers, in part because of the prejudice against public housing's predominantly low-income and minority group residents.

Tenants in public and subsidized housing share few similar targets with tenants in private housing, thus making joint action unlikely. Public and subsidized housing, for example, is exempt from local rent control laws, often eliminating these tenants as potential allies with private housing tenants. Although these tenants frequently live in large complexes, and share the same landlord (the local housing authority or a private developer with government sponsorship), they rarely form enough of a critical mass in any one locality to constitute an effective political bloc. Two of the largest mobilizations among subsidized housing tenants – the Coop City tenants group in the Bronx and the Tenants First Coalition in Massachusetts – made some short-term gains, but soon fell apart (Brodsky, 1975). Tenants in state-subsidized housing in Massachusetts recently formed a statewide tenants group, as part of the Massachusetts Tenants Organization, to fight for their rights.

To counter the growth of tenant activism, landlords have also developed greater cohesiveness and coordination. Homebuilders and real estate agents have been influential in local, state, and national politics for decades (Checkoway, 1980; Lawson, 1980a; Lilley, 1980; Wolman, 1971). But until recently apartment owners have not. Increasingly, however, they have begun to develop their own networks and organizations. The large apartment owners and developers have taken the lead, but they have consciously sought to include both "mom and pop" landlords, and even homeowners, in their efforts to broaden their appeal as defending "property rights" from government and tenant interference. Landlords have considerable resources at their disposal. Real estate interests are usually the major campaign contributors in local elections (Dreier, 1982b). During initiative campaigns on rent control, for example, landlord groups consistently outspent tenant groups by large margins. By vastly outspending tenant groups, landlords have recently defeated rent control initiatives in Seattle, San Diego, and Oakland (November, 1980), in Minneapolis and San Bernardino (November, 1981), and again in Oakland (November, 1982). Well-organized tenants have, however, been able to defy the landlords despite these odds. In 1980, for example, California's landlords tried to undermine local tenant victories by sponsoring a statewide initiative that would have effectively eliminated local rent control ordinances. With help from their counterparts around the nation, the landlords raised and outspent rent control advocates, $4.9 million to $45,000, with expensive television, radio, billboard, and direct mail campaigns. CHAIN, the tenants' statewide network, coordinated an effective grassroots campaign to overcome these heavy odds and defeated the landlords' initiative, 65 to 35 per cent.

In 1978, the nation's large apartment owners and developers formed the National Rental Housing Council to provide local landlord groups with advice on media campaigns, legal tactics, and research against rent control and other pro-tenant demands. In 1980 it changed its name to the

National Multi-Housing Council (NMHC), reflecting the growing number of condominium developers and converters among the landlords' ranks.

Following the defeat of the anti-rent control initiative in California in June 1980, the NMHC proposed federal legislation that would deny federal housing funds to any city with effective rent controls – a proposal designed to knock the wind out of the tenants' movement's sails. The NMHC proposal was recommended by President Reagan's transition team on urban affairs in 1980 and again by his President's Commission on Housing in 1982 (both panels were heavily dominated by bankers and real estate people; see Hartman, 1983a), and proposed in Congress by Republicans in 1980, 1981 and 1982. It was defeated each time by an unusual combination of activist tenants and conservative legislators who saw it as an unnecessary federal interference in local affairs.

The burgeoning self-consciousness and activism among both tenants and landlords at the local, state, and national levels has made tenant-landlord conflict a significant feature of America's political landscape since the 1970s. Despite the growing momentum of the tenants' movement, the conflict so far has resulted in, at best, a stalemate. Growing numbers of city councils and state legislatures have been forced to consider tenants' rights legislation, and the number of pro-tenant laws continues to increase. But the overall picture is still one dominated by landlords and real estate interests. Most tenants in most communities are still not protected by rent or eviction controls. Even though tenants are often able to defeat landlord-backed proposals, these efforts force tenant groups to devote a great deal of their meager resources to these defensive holding actions.

Future directions

The tenants' movement, still in its infancy, has made significant progress, but has a long way to go. Even at this early stage, it is worth reflecting on just where it might go and how it might get there.

The tenants' movement has its own agenda. For the most part, this is a defensive agenda, seeking to improve tenants' status *vis-à-vis* landlords. This includes, as has been mentioned, such remedies as rent control, restrictions on evictions, improved maintenance, condo conversion regulation, tenant voice in management, fair housing laws against discrimination, limits on speculation and gentrification, more public subsidies for renters, and reducing the risk for tenants who organize. Effective organizing around this agenda is the first goal of all tenant organizing. The tenants' movement is still primarily a local phenomenon, and it is still a minor actor on the larger stage of American politics. The sum of its local activities does not add up to a significant political force at the national level, where major housing policy decisions get made. The tenants' movement can ignore national politics only at its own risk.

Yet even the tenants' own limited agenda raises questions of long-term strategy and program. As strong rent controls and other reforms put the squeeze on speculative profits, more landlords may abandon their properties, convert them to condominiums, or cut back on repairs. And certainly they will be less likely to invest in new rental housing. Real estate groups, of course, argue that the pro-tenant reforms are destroying the nation's housing. This is obviously misleading, since the nation's housing crisis is much bigger than the landlords' declining profits. It has to do with the very nature of housing as a speculative commodity and the inability of Americans to afford housing on their incomes. It raises questions about both the private financing and construction of housing and the overall distribution of wealth and income in our society, issues discussed at length in Emily Achtenberg and Peter Marcuse's contribution to this volume.

But how should the tenants' movement respond to this reality of housing disinvestment? Already, tenant organizations are beginning to take advantage of this situation by advocating housing programs that turn over ownership and/ or control to the residents at prices they can afford. This process should be encouraged. For many tenants, non-profit and cooperative associations, sweat equity, or homesteading programs are the only short-term options, even though they run the risk of leading to a greater financial burden. These options, however, provide valuable political lessons. When cooperative housing is a result of a political struggle – a squatters' action, a rent strike which drives the landlord out of business – those involved begin to develop greater self-confidence in common political action. The process of co-operative ownership and self-management itself helps people to overcome their cynicism and powerlessness. Moreover, tenant ownership and management is an important short-term means of ameliorating the most authoritarian aspects of bureaucratic and private landlord control.

The biggest limitation of this approach is the danger of gaining ownership without control. Most major expense items for existing apartment buildings are not subject to much control by the owners. Mortgage payments may take 40 per cent or more of the rents. Property taxes take about another 15 or 20 per cent, utility bills 10 to 15 per cent, management staff 5 per cent, and insurance 2 to 3 per cent of the rents. In other words, at least three-quarters of the rent goes for costs that are beyond the tenants' control. The remaining costs, which the tenant-owners do control, have to cover the maintenance and repairs. Many buildings have high repair and maintenance costs and are poorly weatherized, since landlords have milked the building without spending money for needed upkeep. Eventually the tenant-owners may reach the point where they must choose between raising rents to cover increased costs, letting the building go into default and possible foreclosure, or seeking a "bail-out" from an outside investor. In short, changing ownership patterns in housing will not put all decision-making power in the hands of tenants.

Thus, tenant groups need to go into such struggles with their eyes wide open. Rent control and other self-help housing reforms are important stepping stones, but they are not the ultimate goal of a desirable housing policy. Their importance is in the process of building a political movement that can move beyond the tenants' immediate agenda. As such, these reforms are a direct extension of a broader economic program of greater economic democracy and public control of major investment decisions. The tenants' movement *raises political consciousness*. Tenant issues, particularly rent control, are powerful weapons in changing people's attitudes about what's right and wrong, and what is possible and impossible regarding private property rights. The underlying assumption of rent control is that landlords do not have a right to make as much profit or charge as much as they want. "What the market will bear" is no longer a fair measure of what is right. This can lead people to work for more democratic control over ownership and investment in housing. The tenants' movement also *builds grassroots organizations and wins victories*. Organization is necessary to develop leaders, to give people an opportunity to develop political skills (chairing meetings, talking to the press, making speeches, lobbying elected officials), and to shift people from being passive spectators to being active, self-confident citizens. It allows them to think, "You *can* fight City Hall." Victories improve people's lives directly and immediately. Rent control, for example, keeps their housing costs down. Anti-eviction laws and controls on condo conversions give people security and stability. These are necessary before tenants can start thinking about long-term solutions to the deeper housing crisis. Like the labor movement before it, the tenants' movement cannot begin promoting wider social goals until it has a stronger political foundation.

The tenants' movement is thus a building-block for a more comprehensive political movement, and in its own way, contributes to that process, without which no housing reform is possible. As Lawrence Goodwyn has written about the populist movement in America:

In their institutions of self-help, populists developed and acted upon a crucial democratic insight. To be encouraged to surmount rigid cultural inheritances and to act with autonomy and self-confidence, individual people need the psychological support of other people. The people need to "see themselves" experimenting in new democratic forms (Goodwyn, 1978).

Thus, while fighting for their own reforms that bring them together in collective action, the tenants' movement cannot isolate itself from the broader struggle for social change. To avoid the *cul-de-sac* of ownership without control of housing, the tenants' movement needs allies who can work for more public control over land, utilities, and finance capital – that is, for a program of greater social ownership and finance of housing (see the Achtenberg and Marcuse chapter in this volume; also Hartman and Stone, 1978). In turn, tenants need to join these allies on a broader progressive agenda of democratic reform, of which housing is only one part.

This requires a coalition strategy. While tenants need to form their own independent city, state, and national organizations, they will also have to enter into coalitions with other progressive groups to win many of their demands. Issues will have to be designed that will bring public housing tenants, federally subsidized tenants, moderate-income private tenants, and moderate-income homeowners together. The tenants' movement potential is limited by its numbers. Many cities, but no states, have renter majorities. In the nation as a whole, tenants comprise less than one-third of all Americans. A political movement that does not broaden its base to address the concerns of a broad majority cannot expect to win a contest for political power in America.

During the past decade, fortunately, the nation witnessed a dramatic upsurge of political activism of all kinds: neighborhood groups, consumer and environmental organizations, welfare rights campaigns, the senior citizens' and women's movements, and peace and disarmament activism. Even the American labor movement has begun to emerge from several decades of conservative leadership and political decline. The massive union-sponsored "Solidarity Day" march in 1981 to protest the Reagan Administration's program would have been unthinkable just a decade earlier.

Although all of these movements have their own immediate goals and agendas, they do have at least one thing in common. They are all under attack by big business, the New Right, and the Reagan Administration. Reagan's election, and subsequent policies of redistributing wealth to the rich, big corporations, and the Pentagon, reflect the relative weakness of each of these movements at the national level. The neo-conservative call for belt-tightening in housing is paralleled in most other areas as well. While each movement goes its separate way, big business and New Right groups band together to support candidates and policies that run roughshod over workers, consumers, the elderly, women, the poor, the environment, and tenants. Only a common strategy that brings these movements and organizations together can hope to overcome the power of big business, because together they represent the majority of Americans.

This strategy of coalition politics is nothing new. It formed the basis of Franklin D. Roosevelt's New Deal, bringing together workers, farmers, minorities, and ethnic groups, and forging a new political force during the Depression. It both shifted political loyalties to the Democratic Party and enfranchised millions of Americans who had not participated in the political system. Since the peak of the New Deal's popularity, however, voting participation has gradually declined (Burnham, 1980). In the 1980 presidential election, only 53 per cent of the potential voters went to the polls. None of the candidates projected a program or a vision that appealed to the alienated, angry population. In most local and Congressional races, the turnout is even smaller. Ironically, the vast majority of non-voters are the very people who have been mobilized by the grassroots movements of the past decade. It is obvious that to be effective these movements have to bring their members and supporters into the electoral system and to elect progressives to public office who can translate their issues into policies. As a coalition these groups have to work together, promoting candidates who support their common goals and issues. Only now, the New Deal program does not go far enough. The nation needs to go as far beyond the New Deal as the New Deal went beyond Hoover. The progressive coalition can no longer afford to make compromises of the type it made following the Depression. It must articulate and work for a program of democratizing major investment decisions (Carnoy and Shearer, 1980). It must recognize, as Starr and Esping-Anderson (1979) note, that the failure of liberalism has not been "excessive government interference in the private sector," but "excessive private interference in government policy." Our current housing crisis is only one example of that truth.

Tenant groups have had some recent experiences in building coalitions around progressive policies. In San Francisco, for example, the city-wide tenant group helped forge a coalition of renters and homeowners called San Franciscans for Affordable Housing. It was made up of thirty-five groups, including labor, seniors', civil rights, women's, gay, and church organizations. The coalition sponsored a comprehensive housing program on the November, 1979 ballot that included a tenants' bill of rights, assistance for low- and moderate-income homeowners (to construct, purchase, and rehabilitate homes), control over speculation, restrictions on condominium conversions, and strict controls on rent increases. Although the initiative lost, that loss came about primarily because the city's governing Board of Supervisors took steps to undercut the initiative by unanimously passing a weaker set of condominium conversion and rent controls (Hartman, 1979).

An even broader coalition was initiated by the New Jersey Tenants Organization. NJTO leaders realized that the tenants' movement there had almost exhausted its single-issue agenda and needed allies to move beyond rent control. In

1981, it brought together the state's major progressive unions, women's group (NOW), senior citizens', civil rights, environmental, and peace organizations to discuss working together in forthcoming elections. Each group had a list of candidates – some to defeat, others to help elect – in the state legislature elections. The groups discovered that despite some differences, there was considerable overlap in their lists of friends and enemies. They joined forces and established the N.J. Public Interest Political Action Committee. It intends to pool resources, money, and volunteers to elect common friends and defeat common enemies. The initial assumption is that any candidates who can gain the support of *all* these groups have a coherent progressive political outlook. But explicit discussion of long-range program and policy is premature, something that will emerge as the coalition wins victories and the groups develop greater confidence in each other's contributions to the collective goals. This is part of the dynamics of movement-building that Goodwyn observed among the populists.

Obviously, it is important to develop a comprehensive program, for housing in particular, and for the larger economy in general. It is important to recognize that housing is not an isolated enclave but part of the larger economy that allocates scarce resources according to political priorities. For the coalition-building strategy to work, tenant and other groups must recognize their mutual interest not only in providing affordable housing, but in dealing with related issues of employment, public health, social welfare, and income distribution. No program of redistributing and democratizing the nation's wealth can hope to work, for example, without a dramatic shift in priorities away from wasteful military spending, so that resources can be directed towards providing for basic social needs and jobs. Similarly, no progressive program will work unless government revenues are collected more progressively and loopholes closed for big business and the wealthy. Finally, a progressive program requires more direct public, consumer, and employee participation in decisions about how resources are to be used and spent. This means, first of all, electing grassroots activists to public office, so that "government" itself becomes a vehicle for popular enthusiasm. Putting limits on campaign contributions from big business and overall campaign spending would certainly help reduce the influence of big corporations on the political system. More directly, however, consumers and employees should be elected to membership on corporations' boards of directors, as Senator Howard Metzenbaum's Corporate Democracy Act proposes, and ultimately exercise greater ownership and control of corporate wealth. One model is Sweden's Meidner Plan, a proposal to establish "wage earner funds" – a system of mutual funds collectively owned by Swedish employees who would gradually come to own the vast majority of shares in Swedish business. Finally, local and national government should have direct ownership and control over basic industries. This includes energy corporations, utilities, and railroads; a national health service; and a public bank that would provide loans on the basis of social priorities.

All this may seem a long way from a local rent strike and other tenant movement concerns, but it is actually a direct extension of the logic of the tenants' movement. The American tenants' movement has made significant gains, although in the context of the nation's housing crisis it has only made a small dent. But crisis creates opportunities, for the tenants' movement, and for other progressive movements as well. The importance of the tenants' movement is its potential for politicizing and mobilizing a great part of America's population around immediate problems, then pointing the way toward larger solutions as part of a broad coalition to democratize American society.

6 Decent housing for all: An agenda

Paul Davidoff

The authors of this book have been asked to think about the major components of a new set of housing programs that might be adopted when an administration is in power which believes in the reduction or eradication of poverty rather than its enlargement. This chapter focuses on three policies that could become part of the 1984 political platform of the Democratic Party and could shape a progressive housing agenda. These policies aim to significantly alter present housing conditions and practices. They are to be viewed as part of a larger national program intended to advance the relative power and economic status of lower-income, female, and minority households. These housing policies should be joined with parallel policies from other subject areas to form a national progressive agenda.

The three policies to be addressed here comprise important parts of, but not a whole, national housing agenda. The first policy discusses entitlement to decent housing and the substantive content of the concept "decent housing." The second policy proposes using housing development resources for job and income improvement for lower-income persons. The third policy concerns both the mobility and stability rights of housing users. The three policies are:

1 To establish for all Americans a *legal entitlement* to decent housing.
2 To employ resources in the development of housing so

as to expand the economic well-being of lower-income households.

3 To establish a legal right not to be removed from a preferred present place of residence, as a corollary to the Constitutionally guaranteed right to travel protecting the right of movement to a preferred new residential location.

Policy 1. Housing as entitlement

The Reagan Administration made it very clear at the outset, in the form of testimony by Budget Director David Stockman, that it did not accept the concept of entitlement. It rejected the idea that citizens were entitled as a matter of right to minimum standards of decency; so it is quite clear that any discussion of entitlement is aimed at a future administration. A progressive administration would establish more firmly than ever the concept that citizens *are* entitled as a matter of right to a set of conditions meeting minimum standards of decency.

Since 1949 this nation has been committed to "a decent home and a suitable living environment for every American family." As has long been known, that commitment is only a promise for millions of citizens. Although progressives have continuously called for the realization of that commitment, seldom has there been a discussion of its substance. What does it mean? When should it take place? And, how should it be enforced? It is important to reflect on these questions, and to do so for pragmatic reasons rather than abstract ones. By giving content to this important national goal, it may become possible to compose a plan for realization of points towards it over a reasonable period of time. By better understanding the constituent parts of the condition of decency in housing and suitability in environment, it may be possible to better define the resources required in order to establish a good and fair set of housing conditions for every American.

As proponents of the right to decent housing for every American, it is incumbent upon us to be able to identify the resources required to achieve the conditions we project for a different time period. (And we should go beyond the present Congressional mandate that speaks only of every "American family": such rights should not be limited to those who hold citizenship, nor to those in traditional families.) The determination of resources required depends on the constituent conditions of decency. Some are structural and more costly to achieve than those which are non-structural. The elimination of discrimination in housing through the full enforcement of fair housing legislation should be considerably less costly to achieve than the establishment of physical conditions required to satisfy code standards. But, if affordability is a part of decency, the costing out of the required production of housing units to achieve this condition becomes an important calculation in determining what it will cost the nation to establish decent housing. Further, if locational choice is to be considered an important aspect of decency in housing, then its achievement must be accounted for in developing a budget for decent housing.

If a decent dwelling unit is one that meets minimum building and housing code standards, then the cost of bringing the nation's housing stock up to standard is computable, given the agreement about the number of occupied and vacant units required. If our concept of decent housing requires a higher standard of construction and maintenance, then the difference between this and code standard must be computed. One useful starting figure is the $55–77 billion a year (in 1982 dollars) calculation Michael Stone arrives at in his contribution to this volume.

It may be easier to clearly define decent housing than to define a suitable living environment. Does environment refer to physical or social conditions? Does it refer to economic opportunities? Is a town with a shut-down steel plant and no available jobs providing a suitable living environment?

Certainly, one attribute of a suitable living environment

would be the existence of popular or democratic control over decisions affecting that environment. Still another important social and psychological consideration affecting suitability is the issue of permanency of residency. Living in perpetual fear of displacement can strongly affect the quality of life in a neighborhood. This pollutes the atmosphere in those neighborhoods. Granted that the congressional authors of the 1949 promise of a suitable environment were not thinking about this type of issue, it is still a quality-of-life issue very much a part of city living in the 1980s.

We who are the advocates of the entitlement principle must develop the rationale for this argument. Why do we conclude that housing should be a right? Safe and sanitary housing is a basic human need. Along with food and clothing, it is essential to survival. Should there be a debate about just what conditions of decency ought to be included within a package of entitlement rights, we might be inclined to place housing right at the very top. It could be argued that access to decent housing is more important than access to decent health care and education. Under a decent administration, it would not be necessary to choose among the three. I raise these choices here for the purpose of assisting housing advocates in considering the range of issues involved in housing rights advocacy.

Certainly, one of the crucial arguments in favor of adopting housing as an entitlement is that it is wrong to impose on any household the necessity of living in indecent shelter. Principles of justice and fairness support this contention. It is clear that from other perspectives of justice and fairness present conditions of housing indecency are not viewed as violations of principles. We are, after all, engaged in a political debate, up to now, and particularly in the days of Reagan and Stockman, we have not been the winners in this debate.

It may be that the contention that decent housing should be understood as a right to which all are entitled must be considered in light of America's relative affluence. One point of view is that there are sufficient resources in the nation to enable all to live decently and to guarantee decent housing for every household. The nation's present economic conditions and allocation of resources, particularly those to the military, are the obstacles to be overcome. (Michael Stone performs a useful function by placing his $55–77 billion figure in the context of our gross national product, our military budget, and current levels of tax expenditures for homeowner deductions.) The progressive argument is that resources applied to meet housing and other social needs are available and, aside from the moral justification for reducing military expenditures, on pragmatic grounds better serve the economy.

Recognizing the difficulties of persuading a majority of legislators and a president that housing should be viewed as an entitlement, progressives should constantly keep in mind that housing is essential to individual well-being. For this reason it must be considered a basic right.

I would like to suggest two other actions that might increase support for the entitlement policy. The first is to demonstrate the benefits to society at large emanating from the elimination of indecency in housing. It could be argued that the increase in housing production would produce jobs and investment opportunities. Further, reducing housing indecency would lead to reduced special dependency and required welfare assistance. This point addresses a larger issue, which is that the maintenance of poverty and racism in our society requires far greater social payment than would be necessary in a situation in which those conditions were eliminated. The high taxes paid to cover the cost of unemployment and social dependency are the price paid for the nation's failure to move towards a full-employment and guaranteed-decent-income society. In one sense what I am saying is obvious. I do think progressives have not made as strong an argument to the public as they might have about the high cost of maintaining indecency. In other words, as strong as is the moral case for establishing decency, the reduction of the tax burdens inherent in social dependency must also be considered.

A second means to an adoption of housing as an entitlement would be the development of a program that would increase standards of decency over time. Such a program might commence with efforts to rapidly eliminate the worst results of housing indecency. Among the greatest tragedies are those that result in deaths from residential fires caused by inadequate wiring, heating, or arson. Congress and state and local legislatures might set a timetable for the reduction of fire-caused deaths resulting from substandard housing conditions and appropriate the required funds to achieve this goal.

Fair housing represents a special issue related to decent housing. Entitlement to decent housing should be free of discrimination which denies housing choice. The Fair Housing Act of 1968 provides the basic legislation, but far stronger enforcement power is required. Racial, ethnic, age, and sex discrimination continue to pollute housing markets. The Reagan Administration and Congress have stopped, for now, attempts to increase government power to enforce the Fair Housing Act. State legislatures and Congress should be called on to act to make the enforcement of fair housing more effective.

In concluding this section on housing entitlement, let me suggest some steps in the process leading to adoption by Congress of legislation guaranteeing to each American household a decent home and a suitable living environment:

1 Housing advocacy agencies must adopt this goal and elucidate its content.
2 We must detail the stages of progress towards this goal and a timetable for their achievement. This entails a description of specific methods, their costs, and a schedule of yearly objectives.
3 We must attempt to have one or both major political parties adopt a platform in 1984 urging movement towards or outright adoption of a commitment to entitlement. At a minimum there should be a clear rejection of the Stockman-Reagan view.

4 We must nominate a presidential candidate who will commit to making entitlement a part of her or his campaign.

5 We must support candidates for lesser office who will back entitlement.

Policy 2. Housing as a form of economic development aimed at reducing poverty

Poor housing in the United States results from lower-income households' lack of sufficient political and economic power to demand and receive decent and affordable housing. Advocates of decent affordable housing often neglect to recognize that the problem at its root is not only housing but inadequate income resulting from a maldistribution of income and wealth in the United States. The long-term goal is to eliminate the need to house or subsidize the poor – to eradicate the condition of being poor, to eliminate poverty.

The main proposition directed here at housing advocates needs to be directed at all advocates who seek to improve the living condition of the poor in any of the functional or service areas, but who fail to work equally as hard for a more equitable distribution of income and wealth.

One means for bringing about a more redistributive approach to the housing field, and it would be true in other areas, is to consider ways in which programs may be inclusive *of* the poor as well as being *for* the poor or some other group. The notion of any inclusion policy was first applied to suburban zoning issues. More recently, it has been carried over to neighborhood and city programs. Here I want to suggest how it might affect national housing policy.

In fighting exclusionary zoning, inclusionary remedies were developed. They mandated that specific action be taken to include housing for the poor in developments built under a zoning code. The concept was then applied to city revitalization efforts where it was seen that the gentrification process was excluding the poor by displacing them.

In work carried out under a contract with the New York State Division of Housing and Community Renewal, the Metropolitan Action Institute has been developing a program of inclusionary revitalization. This program seeks to demonstrate an alternative to the revitalization displacement syndrome. Seeing the advent of new investment as a propitious occasion to bring job and wealth opportunities to residents who are poor, Metropolitan Action is working to provide them with both jobs and ownership of enterprises.

Inclusionary revitalization argues for enabling local residents to be a strong part of their neighborhood's rebuilding; it rejects the commonly accepted notion that a neighborhood must be revitalized at the expense of its lower-income residents. It does not reject the movement of higher-income groups into a neighborhood; instead, it welcomes them, provided that there is no displacement. Many neighborhoods in New York have so much abandoned housing and vacant land that it is possible to create a plan for mixed-income revitalization. Such a plan is now being proposed by a coalition of low-income organizations in New York's Lower East Side. They propose this as an alternative to that which they see Mayor Koch promoting – the gradual takeover of the neighborhood by higher-income populations.

The goal of inclusionary revitalization is not only to enable the poor to remain, but for them to prosper as new investment comes to their neighborhood. They should find decent jobs. Because many low-income residents cannot work, due either to age or family responsibilities, it is necessary also to consider benefits other than jobs that can flow to these residents.

This work at the local level has suggested certain principles for national housing policy. Traditionally, national housing legislation has identified the contribution that housing can make to the national economy. For example, in the 1949 Housing Act not only did Congress make its promise of decent housing, it also stated in its Declaration of National Housing Policy:

> The Congress further declares that such production is necessary to enable the housing industry to make its full contribution towards an economy of maximum employment, production, and purchasing power.

Congress has directed that funds be employed to provide housing for the poor or housing subsidies. It has assumed that the traditional free enterprise economy would be responsible for the construction of such housing. But if we look to national housing development as a means to foster the economic development of lower-income populations – that is, if lower-income populations were seen to be not only beneficiaries of housing units, but as potential producers and employees in the process of providing housing – then a far greater benefit would flow from national housing action. All of this assumes that some day the nation will return to its senses and commit resources to the construction of housing, resources other than those expended by enabling tax deductions to be taken for mortgage interest payments and those expended for tax credits related to housing partnerships.

The next national housing act should have these inclusionary goals. The act should make it a national objective to create jobs in construction, administration, and management of housing under its programs, including a large number of lower-income persons. These persons should be afforded opportunities at higher as well as lower levels of work. In addition, to the extent feasible, the production of goods supplied to producers of housing should be from companies owned totally or in part by workers. Moreover, special training programs should be established so that community-based organizations can undertake ownership and management of enterprises benefiting from the act. Companies and banks benefiting from contracts under the act would be expected to hire a significant portion of lower-income persons or contribute a significant sum for the benefit of lower-income communities. The federal government would provide incentives to those industries that were required to undertake this type of affirmative action.

In sum, it is not enough to build for the poor. If building is done by the poor, then in time there will be fewer poor for whom to build.

Policy 3. The right to remain and the right to move

A major function of housing is to provide location. A dwelling unit is located in space. It provides residence at a particular place. While that place may be a chance location for some, for most the place is crucial due to its access to job opportunity, transportation, environment, education, health, or some other good. Housing's locational value may be almost as important as its shelter function.

Except for Native Americans and slaves, America has offered a favored location. Its history is one characterized by great mobility. People emigrated to this nation and, once here, migrated to places of opportunity. The Sun Belt is the latest in the favored locations.

In the 1970s, a cadre of housing advocates turned their attention to expanding housing locational choice. They saw the denial of housing opportunities in the suburbs as being both a violation of an individual's right to move to a place of choice, and a restriction on the ability of the nation to combat poverty. The latter point related to the growing number of jobs in the suburbs and the possibility that a suburban residential location could afford access to these jobs.

The movement to expand the opportunities for lower-income and minority households enabling them to reside in suburbs has not won the universal acclaim of housing advocates. For many, the action in the suburbs represented an encroachment on resources sought to improve living conditions within cities. A part of the discordance found in the housing movement on this issue can be blamed on the scarcity of public housing funds. There is also concern that if the suburbs were opened, the battle to save inner-city communities would be dissipated through the loss of energetic residents who would leave the city for the suburbs. This conflict between advocates concerned about housing rights for the poor and minorities has hampered the development of a stronger coalition of forces. It is essential to the building of a strong movement that there be a resolution of the conflict.

Grounds for the resolution were considered at an April, 1980 conference of the National Low Income Housing Coalition. At the time of the meeting, HUD was sponsoring a Regional Housing Mobility Program aiming to enlarge housing choice of Section 8 Certificate recipients. Strong opposition had developed on the part of inner-city groups fearing their own displacement through gentrification processes. On the other hand, suburban open housing advocates had sought HUD's assistance in such a regional mobility program for a decade. The tentative agreement achieved at that conference was along these lines: first, support for the right of individuals to move to any place of their choice without being deterred by private or public acts of discrimination; and, second, scrapping of HUD's Regional Housing Mobility Program (later ordered by the Reagan Administration, but for different reasons) and the establishment of a program which emphasized the right of households to remain in place and not to be confronted by displacement resulting from development programs supported by HUD or other public agencies.

Since that 1980 meeting, increasing concern has developed in the ranks of housing advocates about the socially destructive effects of residential displacement of lower-income and minority households resulting from the increasing pace of revitalization of city neighborhoods. As one who has and is participating in efforts to expand housing opportunities in the suburbs, I find it increasingly important that efforts to battle housing exclusion focus on the problems of displacement in the cities. In both cities and suburbs the poor and the minorities confront denial of housing opportunities. In the suburbs, the denial takes the form of zoning and other public acts preventing lower-income households from acquiring units. In cities, the injury is inflicted by casting households from their dwellings. In one situation households cannot get in; in the other they cannot remain.

Though far from won, the battle against suburban exclusion has gained some notable legal victories. Perhaps the most important is that arising from the case of *So. Burlington County NAACP v. Township of Mt. Laurel* (67 NJ 151, 336 A2d [1975]) where the New Jersey Supreme Court struck down exclusionary zoning as violative of equal protection and due process guarantees contained in the New Jersey Constitution. In that case and others in New Jersey and elsewhere, courts have determined that suburban townships have obligations to provide a variety of housing for the population. *Mt. Laurel* specifically required the township to provide for a fair share of the region's need for low- and moderate-income housing.

The battle against exclusionary zoning in the suburbs has led to the development of what are termed "inclusionary" remedies. These are zoning and other devices employed to assure that a certain proportion of private housing development will be set aside for low- and moderate-income households. Many of these techniques are described in *Housing Choice* (Suburban Action Institute, nd [1979]).

In another New Jersey case involving a lawsuit against the exclusionary zoning practices of the town of Mahwah, the plaintiffs have sought a ruling from the State Supreme Court requiring towns to have inclusionary provisions in their ordinances in order to meet the *Mt. Laurel* ruling stating that a share of a region's need for housing for low- and moderate-income households be met. In January, 1983, the New Jersey Supreme Court unanimously upheld and strengthened the *Mt. Laurel* ruling, outlawing exclusionary zoning. The court said that housing is a state function and that every locality must act affirmatively to create the opportunity for housing to be constructed for lower-income people. In New Jersey, and in other states that adopt the

Mt. Laurel theory, a major roadblock to creating decent housing in suitable living environments has been removed. The court recognized that its decision does not build housing, but that it can stop the unfair prohibition of housing development.

It is important to observe that even President Reagan's Commission on Housing has found that zoning has been abused through exclusionary devices. The Commission found:

> Exclusionary zoning can have socially discriminatory effects, preventing the construction of multifamily or other housing projects that could be built for occupancy by moderate-income households. Growth controls should be justified by a vital and pressing governmental interest (U.S. President's Commission on Housing, 1982, p. xxxiv).

The work to stop residential displacement has not advanced as far as has the battle against exclusionary zoning. Advocates are searching for a legal argument by which to protect the right of tenants to remain in place. I want to suggest a possible legal handle on which to develop an effective argument. The legal argument is this: the right to remain in place is a part of the right to move. The U.S. Supreme Court has recognized the primacy of mobility in this nation and has found implicit in the Constitution the right to travel. This doctrine has a long history in the Supreme Court. The leading case on this is *Shapiro v. Thompson*, 394 U.S. 618 (1969), in which the Court stated: "This court long ago recognized that the nature of our Federal union and our constitutional concepts of personal liberty unite to require that our citizens be free to travel throughout the length and breadth of our land uninhibited by statutes, rules or regulations which unreasonably burden or restrict this movement." That right is much more than the right to take a trip. It is the right to find protection from the laws throughout the nation and the right to move from place to place without being forced to remain against one's will in one part of the nation. The right to travel is a means for assuring the possibility of economic and social mobility. It enables citizens to place themselves where there appears to be opportunity.

I think it is not illogical to consider that in certain circumstances stability of place is important for purposes of achieving economic or social mobility. Moreover, remaining in place may be necessary in order to maintain contact with an important community and to continue friendships. Further, for certain individuals the pain of giving up a dwelling may be extremely severe. In addition, it can probably be found that the disruption of life caused by involuntary displacement falls disproportionately on lower-income and minority households, perhaps to the extent that discrimination can be surmised.

The right to remain in place, as with most other freedoms, has limits. Within the current legal and economic system, a tenant has certain obligations in regard to payment of rent and care of the leased unit. The right to reside in place does depend on the ability to pay rent and does require that one not destroy the rented premises.

The right to reside in place is not fully acknowledged as a right, let alone as a part of the Constitutionally protected right to travel. In proposing that it be so considered, I am suggesting that in the first instance we who have this concept seek to give it substance and to build support for it as a moral imperative. Building the foundations for social approval of the doctrine can lead to its political development as legislation. Perhaps only after the idea has gained some positive, legal sanction will it be possible for it to receive the respect accorded to mobility under the right to travel.

Independent of whether it makes sense to tie stability of residence to the right to travel, much thought needs to be given to the issue of preventing unjust displacement. Assuming that a tenant pays rent and maintains the premises decently, should a landlord have a right to displace him/her? Under what circumstances? If a decent (and that has to be defined) alternative dwelling is found by the landlord within the community, should the landlord have the right to displace the tenant?

In developing legal support to protect tenants against displacement, another way of stating the right to reside in place is to refer to it as a right not to be unreasonably removed from occupancy. Thus, one should not be removed for arbitrary or discriminatory reasons. Nor should one be removed if all the preconditions of occupancy continue to be met. However, a different issue arises around the right of the landlord to earn a higher return on investment. Is that an arbitrary reason? Most likely not. But what if it can be shown that the present rate of return is reasonable? Then the landlord's ability to remove the tenant should be restricted.

Finally, it should be noted that the issue of displacement arises at this time precisely because the nation's trickle-down theory of urban development makes it necessary to push around the poor so that the wealthy can pay the taxes required to provide the welfare the displaced resident requires. What we need is a new urban program that gives highest priority to those who have the greatest needs. (Some aspects of a new program are presented in the previous section.) Such a program would not displace involuntarily. It would afford the option to move to improved living quarters for those who choose to do so. Even the best system might require some displacement. In such a case, there would be relocation to a place of choice and compensation for lost community as well as for moving.

The word inclusion may be carrying more weight than is necessary, but it is a useful word to convey a sense of social equity, a sense of embracing all. An inclusive society would have room for all; it would not exclude or displace. A good society, be it public or private, must account for all of its citizens. It cannot choose to make outcast or poor certain segments who, because of their race, sex, age, or other characteristics, are deemed less worthy. An inclusive society must be democratic and thus enable all to participate in it fully.

7 Towards the decommodification of housing: A political analysis and a progressive program

*Emily Paradise Achtenberg and Peter Marcuse**

The housing problem

"Americans today are the best-housed people in history," the President's Commission on Housing assures us (U.S. President's Commission on Housing, 1982, p. xvii). Indeed, the current economic wisdom is that Americans are over-housed and that too many of the nation's resources are devoted to housing at the expense of productive business investment (Downs, 1980; Sternlieb and Hughes, 1980, pp. 3, 89). For the good of the economy as a whole, we are told, we should build fewer new homes, tighten our belts, and learn to pay more for less.

Yet, while most Americans have improved the physical aspects of their shelter in the post-war period, their housing problems have increased in other ways. Especially over the past decade, it has become more and more difficult to find – and keep – housing that is affordable, well-maintained, secure, and located in a supportive neighborhood of choice. For the poor, minorities, and female-headed households, the housing problem has reached crisis proportions. And while those who are worst off are disproportionately tenants, the impact of the housing crisis today is increasingly

* An earlier version of this chapter, "Housing and Neighborhoods," was presented at the founding conference of the Planners Network, Washington, D.C., May 8–10, 1981.

shared by low- and moderate-income homeowners.
A few statistics illustrate the dimensions of the problem:

Availability: Over the past decade, the supply of available housing has decreased relative to need. For homeowners, who now constitute approximately two-thirds of all U.S. households, the vacancy rate has remained low and relatively stable at 1.2–1.4 per cent. For renters, the vacancy rate in 1980 was 5.1 per cent, down from 6.6 per cent in 1970 (5 per cent is the generally accepted minimum rate required to support normal household mobility (U.S. Bureau of the Census, 1982b, Table A–1)). Available rental vacancies are considerably fewer in the central cities, where the supply of apartments is being depleted through condominium conversion, changes of land use, arson, and abandonment. Virtually no new apartments are being built today, and a recent governmental report aptly characterized rental housing as an "endangered species" (U.S. Comptroller General, 1979).

In general, not enough new units are being produced to replace those that have been lost and to accommodate our growing population, even by official government standards. The ten-year National Housing Goal of 26 million new and rehabilitated units, established in 1968, was not achieved; by 1978, only 21.5 million units had been built, including just 2.7 million of 6 million targeted subsidized units, a shortfall of 55 per cent (Stone, 1980a). Annual housing starts numbered less than 1 million in 1982 – the lowest rate in post-war history – compared to 2.38 million in 1972. Not surprisingly, the government has now officially abandoned the embarrassing task of establishing national housing production goals (U.S. President's Commission on Housing, 1982, p. xxxv).

Affordability: The decline in housing affordability over the past decade is the most significant measure of the current housing crisis. For renters, housing costs are increasing almost twice as fast as incomes: between 1970 and 1980, median rents rose 123 per cent while median renter incomes rose only 67 per cent (U.S. Bureau of the Census, 1982b, Table A-2). Looked at another way, in 1970, 40 per cent of all renter households paid at least 25 per cent of their incomes for housing (the old rule of thumb for what families could afford), and 25 per cent paid at least 35 per cent. But in 1980, the proportion of renters paying 25 per cent or more of their incomes had increased to 53 per cent, and 34 per cent paid more than 35 per cent. An astonishing 20 per cent of all renter households – one in five – devoted at least one-half of their incomes to housing, leaving little for other necessities (U.S. Bureau of the Census, 1972; and 1982b, Table A–2).

One aspect of the government's response to this problem has been to increase the housing affordability *standard*. Not long ago, a rent-to-income ratio of 20 per cent was considered appropriate. Today, the official criterion of affordability (and the rate to be charged in federally-subsidized housing, based on recent legislative amendments) is 30 per cent. Apart from its arbitrary nature, this simplistic approach fails to recognize that two families having different income levels and different non-housing budgetary needs – e.g., for food and medical care – can afford to spend quite different amounts for housing, relative to income. With a more complex income-dependent affordability standard, a typical family of four would require an income of about $17,000 in order to spend 25 per cent of it for housing. (For a more complete discussion of this concept and its implications, see Michael Stone's chapter in this volume.)

The government now claims that the statistical decline in rental housing affordability is largely attributable to housing quality improvements, especially with the shift of higher-income renters to homeownership (leaving a disproportionate share of the rental stock to the poor). However, even the cost of a "constant-quality" rental unit has risen faster than renter incomes in the last decade (U.S. President's Commission on Housing, 1982, p. 10).

While the disparity between renter and homeowner incomes has increased significantly (the median income of renters is now about half that of homeowners, as compared to two-thirds in 1970), homeowners too have experienced growing housing affordability problems. Between 1970 and 1980, the median sales price for existing homes virtually tripled, from $23,400 to $64,600 (U.S. Congressional Budget Office, 1981).[1] Median monthly housing costs rose 112 per cent for homeowners in mortgaged units, who represent two-thirds of all homeowners. But median homeowner incomes rose by only 104 per cent (U.S. Bureau of the Census, 1982c and nd). While the affordability gap for higher-income homeowners was to some extent offset by the rising value of income tax deductions for mortgage interest and property taxes, on a cash flow basis many homeowners' resources were increasingly strained. Finally, with the rising cost of homeownership today, fewer and fewer renters can afford to buy. In 1981, first-time homebuyers represented only 13.5 per cent of the sales market, as compared to 36 per cent in 1977 (U.S. League of Savings Associations, 1982).

Quality: Today, neighborhood conditions are the most serious problem of housing quality. In 1979, 73 per cent of all renters and 62 per cent of all homeowners found their neighborhoods to be deficient in one or more respects (e.g., excessive noise, litter, or crime, streets needing repair or lighting). Forty-five per cent of all renters and 50 per cent of homeowners were dissatisfied with public transportation, schools, police protection, or other neighborhood services (U.S. Bureau of the Census, 1982a, Tables A–2, A–3).

But even as to individual units (despite improvements in the standard measures of crowding, plumbing facilities, and dilapidation), the level of maintenance and services is a persistent problem. In 1979, 24 per cent of renters and 19 per cent of homeowners had insufficient heat in some form (ibid., Table A–2).² Thirty-two per cent of all rental units and 10 per cent of all owner-occupied homes were considered by their occupants to be in fair or poor condition (ibid). The problem of neglected maintenance followed by housing abandonment is a growing one in many large cities; New York City alone loses 30,000 units a year for this reason (Marcuse, 1979a, p. 70; Stegman, 1982, p. 181).

Security: The involuntary displacement of families from their homes and neighborhoods is an aspect of the housing problem which has received growing national recognition. According to recent government estimates, 600,000–850,000 households, or 1.7–2.4 million persons, are forced to move each year because of private market activity. Over 40 per cent of these moves are attributable to increased housing costs, with sale of the building accounting for another 23 per cent (U.S. Department of Housing and Urban Development, 1981a, pp. 25–6).

Homelessness – the ultimate outcome of housing insecurity and unavailability – has become a significant phenomenon in many cities; recent estimates for New York City indicate a population of at least 35,000 homeless persons (Baxter and Hopper, 1981, p. 171). And while tenants are most vulnerable to being forced out of their homes, homeowners are also increasingly threatened by mortgage foreclosures and eviction. Residential mortgage delinquencies are now at a thirty-year high, with an estimated 140,000 homes in the process of foreclosure (Brooks, 1982).

Inequality: While the housing crisis affects a growing proportion of our population, it is consistently worse for some than for others. For example, 72 per cent of all households earning less than $10,000 pay 25 per cent or more of their incomes for housing, while only 3 per cent of those with incomes of $50,000 or more pay this much (U.S. Bureau of the Census, 1981, Table A–1). Ten per cent of female-headed households live in housing that is officially rated as inadequate, as compared to 7.5 per cent of all households (U.S. President's Commission on Housing, 1982, p. 9). Among homeowners, 63 per cent of black and 58 per cent of Hispanic households are dissatisfied with neighborhood services, as compared to 49 per cent of all households (U.S. Bureau of the Census, 1982a , Tables A–2, A–3, A–6, A–9). Low-income, minority, and female-headed households are more likely than others to be displaced even though their housing options are more limited (U.S. Department of Housing and Urban Development, 1981a, p. 38).

Oppression: Finally, the housing problems faced by disadvantaged groups have broader social consequences. Housing, after all, is much more than shelter: it provides social status, access to jobs, education and other services, a framework for the conduct of household work, and a way of structuring economic, social, and political relationships. Racial segregation in housing, which is severe and getting worse in many areas (Taeuber, 1975), limits educational and employment opportunities for minorities even as it forces them to pay more (relative to income) for declining services. Housing design and locational patterns reinforce the traditional division of labor within the male-dominant family, foster unpaid work in the home, and restrict opportunities for female labor-force participation (Saegert, 1981; Rothblatt et al., 1979). In this way, the housing crisis today expresses and perpetuates the economic and social divisions that exist within the society as a whole.

Causes of the problem

But why is the housing problem so bad, and why is it getting worse? There are many contributing factors, but the principal reason is that housing in our society is produced, financed, owned, operated, and sold in ways designed to serve the interests of private capital. Housing – a necessity of life – is treated not as a social good but as a commodity.

Government policies affecting housing, which supposedly serve the common good, systematically operate to reinforce the profitability of the housing sector and of the business community as a whole. Such improvement in housing as has occurred historically has only come about when it has served the interests of private capital, or when pressures from below (both political and economic) have forced it to occur.

The private housing sector and private capital

In the most immediate sense, the supply, cost, quality, location, and use patterns of housing in our society reflect the market activities of the private housing sector, which is itself comprised of multiple interests. These include real estate developers, builders, materials producers, mortgage lenders and other providers of housing credit, investors, speculators, landlords, and homeowners. While each of these "actors" makes money from housing in a different way, they share a common interest in housing as a profitable commodity. (Homeowners, of course, have a contradictory relationship to their housing as both shelter and investment, a matter of significance for this analysis.)

For housing consumers, the consequences are manifold. First, the high and rising cost of housing in the marketplace reflects, in part, profits made during the initial production or development stage. Land and construction loan interest (including profits to speculators and private lenders) are by far the most rapidly rising elements of housing production costs (U.S. President's Commission on Housing, 1982, p. 181). Further, most materials used in the construction of housing are produced by giant corporations with few incentives for cost control.

Once a house or apartment building is completed, its cost to the consumer also reflects the speculative gain generally made by each successive owner who trades it for profit in the marketplace (housing is perhaps the only common commodity whose market value increases with age). And since virtually every real estate purchase is financed with borrowed funds, added to that is the cost of mortgage interest, which has skyrocketed in recent years. For tenants and homeowners alike, mortgage payments – reflecting both the market price of housing and the interest on the permanent loan – constitute the single largest element of monthly housing costs (40–65 per cent). Other significant cost elements are the property tax – a regressive tax on real estate as a form of private wealth – and utilities, with their substantial profit component.

The quest for profits also limits the production of housing because the privately controlled resources required for its production are allocated to housing only when it is profitable for developers, land speculators, materials producers, and mortgage lenders to do so. For example, at the peak of economic booms when business is expanding, commercial banks traditionally cut back on housing loans in favor of more profitable, short-term lending to government and corporate borrowers. And savings and loans, which are legally required to make their funds available to housing, have less money to lend because their depositors seek more profitable investment outlets elsewhere. Similarly, scarce urban land is available for housing only when housing is its "highest and best" (most profitable) use; and even basic construction materials are diverted from the housing sector when they can be sold more profitably elsewhere. The result is an extremely cyclical pattern of housing construction, which has significantly inhibited the productive capacity of the housing industry (ibid, pp. xxi, 182; Solomon, 1981, p. 200).

In addition, because housing is adequately maintained only when it yields a profit, real estate owners and lenders "disinvest" from poor or "high-risk" neighborhoods through undermaintenance, tax delinquency, arson, abandonment, and redlining, accompanied by the withdrawal of public services (Marcuse, 1979b; 1981). At the same time, housing capital and credit are reinvested in the speculative purchase and refinancing of existing buildings in profitable "upscale" neighborhoods, without adding to the housing stock or improving its quality. Finally, discriminatory practices persist in the housing market, in part because they benefit certain segments of the housing industry. For example, blockbusting tactics enable real estate speculators to buy cheap and sell dear, while mortgage lenders can convert their old loans to higher-yield investments in both the newly segregated block and re-segregated white neighborhoods (U.S. Commission on Civil Rights, 1975).

At the same time, the private housing sector operates within the broader context of an economic, social, and political system which serves the interests of private capital (business) more generally (Offe, 1975). The way in which the organization of production and the relationship between different economic and social groups interacts with the commodity nature of housing and is in turn reinforced by the private housing system is basic to understanding – and addressing – the root causes of our housing problems.

For example, as noted above, the cyclical nature of economic activity in our profit-oriented system shapes the flow of capital and credit to the housing sector and structures opportunities for profit in housing development, finance, and ownership. Thus, while housing is crowded out on the upswing of the business cycle, it has traditionally led the way out of recession as business demand slackens. In turn, this counter-cyclical pattern of housing activity has played an important role in stabilizing the economy, and in restoring conditions for more profitable business growth (Solomon, 1981). In recent years, however, fluctuations in both the housing and business cycles have tended to be more extreme and mutually reinforcing. This has led to a period of prolonged "stagflation" which has significantly intensified the housing crisis and the problems of the economy as a whole.

At the same time, the unequal distribution of income and wealth created by our profit-motivated production system leaves many people with jobs and incomes that are inadequate to meet the rising cost of housing, while others are quite well-off. The movement of business capital in recent years from manufacturing to the more profitable service sector (and from Frostbelt to Sunbelt) has exacerbated these disparities, through the transformation of both the labor market and the housing market. Thus, in some cities, plants shut down, blue-collar workers lose jobs, real estate owners and lenders disinvest, and the housing market collapses. In others, well-paid technicians, managers, and professionals attracted by revitalized service industries compete with low-paid workers for scarce housing, creating profitable opportunities for real estate speculation and gentrification. The net result is a loss of affordable housing at both ends, while communities and cities are transformed to meet the changing requirements of profit-oriented production.

Similarly, racism and sexism in the society as a whole help to structure patterns of housing use which serve the interests of capital at the expense of disadvantaged groups. Racial discrimination in employment makes housing less available to and affordable by minorities, while discriminatory housing practices foster the creation of segregated, disenfranchised communities that either become ripe targets for profitable business redevelopment or are abandoned by the public as well as by the private sector. Housing options for female-headed households are similarly restricted by women's inferior employment status. At the same time, housing design and development patterns isolate and tie women to the home and increase profit opportunities, not just for the real estate industry, but also for the producers of a vast array of household consumption goods. Finally, the social and economic inequalities perpetuated by the housing market reinforce stratification within the labor market which supports the profitability of business and the tractability of labor in general.

The role of government

While government policies have led to some improvements in housing, they have not solved the housing problem. Indeed, in some respects they have operated to intensify the housing problem, especially for low-income and minority groups. In any case, government actions affecting housing have not stemmed primarily from a benevolent desire to assist the ill-housed, but have tended to serve two major functions.[3]

Accumulation: Enhancing opportunities for private profit, both within the housing sector and, more importantly, for the business community as a whole. This includes actions taken to assure that the minimal housing requirements of the workforce are met in a manner consistent with the needs of profit-oriented production. It also includes housing-related measures geared to promoting more profitable economic growth – for example, by stimulating housing production to restart the economy in a recession, or by choking off housing credit to curb inflation.

Legitimation: Preserving "social peace" against the threat of disruption (real or perceived) from disaffected social groups, through measures that stabilize and reinforce the existing social and economic order. These include housing concessions granted in order to integrate subordinate groups within the dominant system, as well as the use of housing for purposes of repression, oppression, and exploitation.

Particular housing policies may serve both of these functions, and will reflect the political, economic, and social situation (and balance of forces) at a given time. Neither the business community nor the government acts monolithically in relation to housing; even within the housing sector, different interests may have conflicting needs for government support (e.g., mortgage lenders want to raise interest rates, developers want to lower them). Moreover, the requirements of the housing industry may be incompatible with those of business or of the economy as a whole at certain times, as during inflationary periods when continued housing expansion cannot be supported. In general, the government acts to mediate or manage these conflicts – as well as those resulting from the political pressures exerted by organized housing consumers – in ways that best support the accumulation and legitimation needs of the system as a whole.

These patterns are illustrated by the history of federal efforts to promote homeownership in the post-war period. After World War II, the pent-up need for housing, coupled with war-induced prosperity and the increased productive capacity of the economy, stimulated a huge housing construction boom. With expanded federal mortgage insurance and tax incentives for homeownership, the suburban single-family tract house became the vehicle for this explosive growth, supported by the development of federally assisted infrastructure and highways.

While the post-war homeownership boom helped many Americans to improve their living standards, it also provided vast new outlets for profitable investment by real estate developers, mortgage lenders, and other segments of the housing industry. The creation of new demand not just for housing but for a wide variety of household consumption goods was profitable for business as a whole. And with long-term mortgages (and other forms of household credit), consumer buying power could be expanded without creating new pressures on business for higher wages.

At the same time, federal promotion of homeownership gave working families an economic and social "stake in the system," at the price of reduced mobility (and hence more limited bargaining power with employers). It provided housing consumers with the illusion of control but the reality of burdensome long-term debt. And it channeled their legitimate shelter needs into concerns with investment risk and profitability. Federal homeownership policies also fostered racial exclusion, reinforced the oppression of women, and increased the housing problems of the poor by eroding the central city tax base.

In recent years, the growing problems of the economy and of the housing industry have significantly altered the functions of homeownership. Unprecedented inflation (fueled in part by the tremendous increase in residential mortgage debt) and the lack of new housing construction have driven up the value of existing homes and encouraged the use of homeownership as an investment vehicle, especially by those in upper-income tax brackets. Today, the same tax incentives that fostered the growth of the suburbs are stimulating housing speculation and displacement of the poor from the inner city, as affluent condo converters bid up the price of scarce housing resources (Goetze, 1981; *Boston Globe*, 1982).

While buying a home has now become a privilege reserved for the wealthy, the supposed benefits of homeownership for many others are gradually being undermined. With today's variable-rate mortgages, rising property tax bills, and credit shortages for housing, few moderate-income homeowners can count on stability of costs or liquidity for their investments. And a growing number who live a paycheck or two ahead of the bank risk the loss of their equities – as well as their homes – to foreclosure, as the recession and unemployment continue.

Public housing – the only government program that has over the long run directly addressed the housing needs of the poor – was originally designed for other purposes. The earliest government-sponsored projects were built to ease housing shortages for munitions and defense workers during World War I, thereby aiding the U.S. war production effort. The National Housing Act of 1937 was primarily a public works program, intended to stimulate the depressed economy and to stem the tide of social unrest by providing jobs for temporarily unemployed city workers. After World War II, more public housing was built to appease the discontent of returning veterans. Locally, public housing often pro-

vided a vehicle through which politicians could dis
patronage.

In the 1950s, as government slum clearance uprooted the
poor from central cities and the upwardly mobile left the
projects for the suburbs, public housing was increasingly
occupied by lower-income households and in many large
cities by minorities. Political pressures generated by the
ghetto rebellions and by the civil rights and welfare rights
movements of the 1960s led to significant reforms, including
rent reductions, liberalized admission criteria, and protection against arbitrary eviction. Ultimately, many large projects became the "housing of last resort" for those left
behind by the restructured economy (primarily elderly and
female-headed households on fixed incomes).

Today, public housing suffers from official neglect,
chronic underfunding and undermaintenance, and often inefficient and bureaucratic management. It has become an
oppressive device for stigmatizing the poor, for maintaining
racial and class divisions, and for discrediting the concept
of public enterprise in our society. Together with the other
lower-income housing production programs of the 1960s and
1970s – which provided lucrative tax shelter benefits and
direct subsidies to the private housing and mortgage lending
industries – public housing has met only a fraction of the
existing need. And as the programs for providing lower-
income housing have become increasingly dependent on the
system of private housing development, finance, and ownership, their costs have risen dramatically. Today the direct
subsidy cost for a new unit of Section 8 housing is estimated
at $4000–5500 per year (U.S. Department of Housing and
Urban Development, 1982).

As for neighborhood policies, the federal role is well
known. Urban renewal enhanced opportunities for profit in
the development of prime inner-city real estate while fos-
tering business and institutional expansion. In the process,
at least one million lower-income and minority households
were uprooted and their communities destroyed (Gans,
1982, pp. 385–6).

In the 1960s, with the growing threat of social disorder in the cities, outright "slum clearance" efforts were replaced with more muted attempts at housing rehabilitation and ultimately with the neighborhood-oriented Model Cities and Community Action programs of the Great Society. Then in the mid-1970s, as the problems of the economy worsened and the protest of the poor seemed to weaken, Community Development Block Grants provided the vehicle through which funds for neighborhood programs could be drastically cut, in exchange for increased local political control over resource allocation. Currently, block grants provide little more than a limited form of revenue-sharing to offset the impact of local "fiscal crisis" cutbacks, and an arena in which local neighborhood groups are pitted against one another in the battle for diminishing resources.

Finally, the overall pattern of federal housing and neighborhood subsidies in the post-war period has been highly regressive, reinforcing the unequal distribution of income and wealth. Direct federal budget outlays for housing and community development, currently totaling about $14 billion, have barely kept up with inflation. But housing-related tax expenditures (revenues lost through homeowner and investor tax deductions) have more than doubled since 1979 and are expected to approach $44 billion in 1983 (Low Income Housing Information Service, 1982, p. 20). Not included in this 1983 total is the loss of billions from accelerated depreciation of commercial and residential real estate, now the standard method for writing off the value of rental property (U.S. Office of Management and Budget, 1982, p. 7). These hidden subsidies primarily benefit those in the top 10 per cent of the income distribution. (For a more detailed discussion of tax expenditures for housing, see the Appendix to Cushing Dolbeare's chapter in this volume.)

Today, federal policies affecting housing and neighborhoods are part of an explicit government strategy to bolster corporate profits at a time when business is increasingly threatened by a deteriorating economy. The overall approach is one of income redistribution directly to business through tax cuts, deregulation, and other measures, combined with reduced social spending to offset the tax cuts and continued credit restrictions to curb inflation.

In support of this effort, all federal assistance for housing production and even federally supported housing credit activities will be drastically curtailed or eliminated. Limited demand-side subsidies are replacing existing production-oriented subsidies for assisted housing, assuring that the publicly aided stock will shrink as units are lost through deterioration, demolition, and private resale (facilitated by government policy as discussed in greater detail in Florence Roisman's chapter in this volume). Housing vouchers as presently proposed may aid private landlords but are unlikely to increase the housing supply or add to its quality. At the same time, continued credit stringency and reduced federal involvement in housing finance will diminish housing's share of resources in the economy as a whole.

These measures, coupled with the impact of continued high unemployment and income maintenance cutbacks on consumer purchasing power, are guaranteed to make the housing crisis even worse, especially for the poor and increasingly for middle-income households also. But while it is tempting to view the current situation as a regressive departure from the mainstream of post-war housing policy, our analysis suggests that the basic accumulation and legitimation functions served by government have not changed. Rather, the underlying balance of economic, social, and political forces has shifted as the limits of post-war prosperity have been reached.

As long as the expanding economy provided room to increase living standards and sustain business growth at the same time, improvement in housing was possible. But today, as major U.S. corporations are increasingly threatened by foreign competition, Third World resistance to U.S. exploitation, and uncontrolled inflation, business wants a larger share of the shrinking economic pie. Housing can be easily targeted for attack – precisely because of the wasteful way it has been produced, financed, and owned in our society.

Indeed, some segments of the housing industry will suffer as public and private resources are reallocated to bolster the profitability of more powerful corporate interests. Others – such as developers and investors who can shift their resources into downtown office, commercial, and retail construction or the luxury rehabilitation and conversion of well-located inner-city housing (aided by substantial tax incentives) – will continue to prosper. But housing consumers – especially lower-income and minority households – will pay the real price, in the form of reduced housing options, less stability, and higher costs. Moreover, the fundamental problems of the U.S. economy and the squeeze on corporate profits which are the root of today's housing crisis are likely to continue well beyond the (hopefully short-lived) Reagan Administration. What is at stake politically is how the economy (including the housing sector) will be restructured in the long run to respond to these conditions, and in whose interest the restructuring will occur.

The limits of housing and neighborhood struggles

A significant factor in the housing and neighborhood gains of the post-war period, to the extent that they have been achieved, has been the role of popular struggle. During the Depression, the threat of massive unrest around issues of housing and job security led to moratoria on mortgage foreclosures, the enactment of the public housing program, and a variety of federal supports for homeownership. In the 1960s, housing again became a direct political issue largely through black-led tenant protests linked to the civil rights and welfare rights movements.

These efforts achieved some gains of considerable importance for the poor. For example, massive rent strikes in St. Louis, Newark, and elsewhere led to major reforms in the public housing program. Local urban renewal struggles in white ethnic as well as minority communities forced significant concessions in the form of replacement housing,

ing (e.g., as to rents, condition, occupancy terms, evictions, demolition, resale), and for measures to curb the speculative buying and selling of private homes. Housing already in the public sector should also be preserved, upgraded, and re-oriented in the direction of social ownership, with increased control by residents in place of centralized, bureaucratic control (see Florence Roisman's contribution to this volume for detailed steps on how to do this).

In the long run, as much housing as possible should be converted away from ownership for profit. Social ownership can take a variety of forms, including direct ownership by government or non-profit entities, collective ownership by resident-controlled corporations or neighborhood councils, non-equity or limited-equity cooperatives, or non-specula-tive resident ownership of single-family homes. What mat-ters is not the precise legal ownership structure, but that the housing has the attributes described above and is perma-nently removed from the speculative market. Residents of socially owned housing would pay rent based on true ability-to-pay, resulting in rent-free housing for many (or equivalent income support). And residents would have the right to permanent occupancy as long as they comply with reasonable tenure obligations (including non-interference with the rights of others).

Social production:
Upgrade and expand the housing supply, and increase social control over the housing production process (including hous-ing design, development, construction, and materials pro-duction). To provide an adequate supply of housing, the existing housing stock (ownership and rental) should be upgraded as rapidly as possible to appropriate standards of safety, liveability, space, and energy-efficiency. In addition, the rate of new housing construction should be increased to meet the needs of newly formed households, to replace lost or unrepairable units, to reduce overcrowding, and to facil-itate adequate mobility and choice.

Certainly in the foreseeable future most aspects of hous-

relocation benefits, and resident participation. These efforts also helped to launch the new subsidized housing production and neighborhood programs of the Great Society.

Despite their successes, the housing and neighborhood struggles of the 1960s remained fragmented along tenure and racial lines, and were limited in focus to particular issues or targets. They failed to broaden their concerns beyond local demands or generalized calls for "social justice" or "community control." Nor did they come to grips with the systemic nature of the housing crisis. As a result, when the worsening problems of the economy in the early 1970s made further concessions more difficult, the protest movement (in housing and other areas) all but collapsed. Thus the stage was set for President Nixon's 1973–4 freeze on subsidized housing, the defunding of "categorical grant" programs, the urban "fiscal crisis," and the beginning of the ideological attack on housing standards.

The 1970s saw the growth of a geographically widespread neighborhood movement, involving primarily homeowners, and dealing with a range of economic issues. With a more diverse agenda than the 1960s protest movements, these groups won significant legislative and regulatory reforms, including nationally mandated disclosure requirements for mortgage lenders aimed at stemming the tide of neighbor-hood disinvestment. But the neighborhood movement has been unable to respond effectively to the problems of sky-rocketing mortgage interest rates and scarce housing credit, which have made it impossible to improve housing and still keep it affordable.

At the same time, there has been a recent revival of tenant activism around the issues of high rents and condo-minium conversions in revitalizing areas. But while rent control has helped to mitigate the skyrocketing cost of hous-ing to consumers, it has not addressed the problems of housing deterioration and abandonment. Very strict rent control (were it ever enacted) might even exacerbate these problems. Moreover, rent control in today's inflationary economy does not suffice to make housing affordable, especially for lower-income households.

Now that the political counter-attack on housing is in full force and housing and economic conditions are worsening, there is an opportunity to develop a broad-based progressive housing movement which can unite low- and moderate-income tenants and homeowners around their common interest in decent, affordable housing and adequate neighborhoods. The growing elusiveness of homeownership for the vast majority of tenants and the decreasing ability of low- and moderate-income homeowners to benefit from their housing as an investment makes tenure distinctions less important, while increasing neighborhood problems create a basis for common action. Moreover, the traditional housing solutions of subsidies and tax incentives for the rich, combined with federal credit manipulations, seem less and less workable even to those who view them as in general desirable. Needed is a program that can alter the terms of existing public debate on housing, that challenges the commodity nature of housing and its role in our economic and social system, and that demonstrates how people's legitimate housing needs can be met through an alternative approach.

A program for housing decommodification[4]

General principles

As shown in the previous sections, the problems of housing availability, affordability, quality, security, inequality, and oppression are rooted in the commodity treatment of housing and in the general relationship between housing and private capital in our society. Racism and sexism, primarily linked to the needs of capital, significantly influence the nature of our housing problems. The dominance of capital in relation to housing is expressed in the organization of

housing ownership, production, and finance; in the use a disposition of land; in neighborhood development and s vice patterns; in the particular housing problem of minori and women; and in the allocation of resources both to a within the housing sector.

The following program has as its primary goal:

> To provide every person with housing that is affordable, adequate in size and of decent quality, secure in tenure, and located in a supportive neighborhood of choice, with recognition of the special housing problems confronting oppressed groups (especially minorities and women).

The program calls for decommodification in the very br est sense, not only in the way that housing is directly duced, financed, owned, and disposed of, but also regard to housing resource allocation, decision-making, use patterns generally. This broad scope reflects the that in a profit-oriented economy even where housin partially or totally removed from the commodity marke may be far from decent, affordable, or secure (squa settlements, company housing, and public housing are a examples). Thus, the objective, broadly stated, is to the role of profit from decisions affecting housing, su tuting instead the basic principle of socially determ need.

Social ownership:
Control the speculative private ownership of housing expand the amount of housing under public, collective, munity, or resident ownership that is operated solely resident benefit and subject to resident control, with resal profit prohibited. An essential first step in the decomn fication of housing is to eliminate the cost of specul ownership and the arbitrary control that profit-orie owners have. In the short run, this suggests the nee increasingly strict regulation of privately owned rental h

ing production will continue to be performed by the private sector – but in order to meet these goals at reduced cost, the production process must be increasingly subject to public control. Government subsidies and financing assistance can be conditioned on the provision of social benefits (such as job creation for lower-income and minority residents, or the allocation of development profits for community use), with the housing thus produced ultimately transferred to the public or to resident groups for social ownership. The long-term goal is to move towards social ownership of the materials production industries, an increasingly strong public and community development sector, and perhaps a growing role for worker-controlled and public construction companies.

Public financing:
Reduce the dependence of housing production, ownership, and improvement on private mortgage credit, and increase public control of housing finance capital. Our analysis (and the experience of Western European countries) shows that even with social ownership and production, as long as housing remains dependent on private mortgage credit, it will continue to be expensive to society and in short supply. To address this problem in the short run, regulatory measures should be devised to allocate more private credit to housing, and alternative public sources of housing credit should be developed (such as state housing banks and public pension funds). In the long run, housing production and rehabilitation should increasingly be financed through direct government spending – in much the way we build military facilities – with direct grants to public and community developers for the production of socially owned housing. This housing would be permanently debt-free, with no mortgages or bonds to repay. At the same time, as a growing portion of the existing stock is converted to social ownership, the mortgage debt on these properties could be paid off (over time) and permanently eliminated.

Social control of land:
Control speculative private use and disposition of land, and preserve and expand the supply of land under public control and ownership. Land is a scarce public resource, given value by public action and having pervasive influence over community life. Its control is an indispensable element in planning for society's housing (and other) needs, and its rising cost is a significant deterrent to housing development. To reduce land costs and ensure an adequate supply of developable land for housing, increased public control over the private use and disposition of land is needed, through a variety of regulatory, tax, and planning measures. The existing supply of socially owned land should be preserved and expanded through such measures as government and community land-banking, moving towards broad social ownership of land suitable for housing use and progressive land-use planning.

Resident control of neighborhoods:
Limit the adverse impact of profit-oriented development and service patterns on lower-income and minority neighborhoods, and increase control by residents over neighborhood decisions, on a non-exclusionary basis. Increased residential security and improved living conditions for lower-income and minority residents will require a reorientation of neighborhood development and service patterns to reflect social and community needs rather than profit considerations. At a minimum, this means that any private development activity (especially if publicly assisted) should be regulated to minimize its adverse impact on lower-income and minority neighborhoods (impacts such as direct or indirect housing or job loss). While private developers should be held accountable for these social costs, the public benefits of private development activity should also be maximized, e.g., by providing jobs, housing, community facilities, or services for lower-income and minority residents in conjunction with such activity.

Similarly, public planning for the design and delivery of

public services should be responsive to community (and especially to user) needs. In order to achieve this type of accountability, the residents of lower-income and minority neighborhoods should be increasingly involved in development and service decisions. Neighborhood control does not need to be increased for the rich, the powerful, and the entrenched, who already control not only their communities but most decisions in the society at large. It is, however, a progressive force in those communities whose residents do not have access to privileges and power, and whose ability to manage their own destinies is limited, rather than buttressed, by the power of capital. Resident control in any neighborhood should operate within a basic non-exclusionary framework, and should not be misused to exclude or deny access or opportunity.

Affirmative action and housing choice:
Eliminate the discriminatory, exclusionary, and oppressive uses of housing, especially in relation to racial minorities and women; and provide housing in forms and locations that address the special situation of oppressed groups including the right to remain in place or to move to other neighborhoods of choice. Special steps must be taken to address (and redress) the particular housing problems confronting oppressed groups in our society. These include increased, affirmative efforts to control and ultimately eliminate the pervasive forms of discrimination and exclusion that presently exist in the housing market. Housing resources must also be targeted for the revitalization of existing minority communities, in order to protect and affirm the right of minority residents to enhance their social and political cohesiveness by remaining in place if they choose to do so. At the same time, the right of mobility for minority residents must be expanded by providing increased housing options in other neighborhoods of choice, without diminishing the prior commitment to neighborhood revitalization. Affirmative efforts are also needed to develop housing of appro-

priate size, type, and design to free women from domestic oppression and exploitation.

Equitable resource allocation:
Allocate available resources for housing and neighborhoods based on need; and provide adequate resources through the public sector, raising the necessary funds through progressive means. Resources currently available for housing and neighborhoods (from the private as well as the public sector) should be increasingly targeted for purposes that benefit lower-income and minority households. In the long run, in order to provide decent, affordable housing and viable neighborhoods, the level of resources allocated to housing and the role of the public sector must be substantially increased. A major shift in public spending priorities (most notably away from military spending) as well as increased taxes on corporate and individual wealth and profits would be required in order to generate the needed revenues in a progressive way. At the same time, a progressive, non-speculative approach to housing production, finance, and ownership would make it possible to use these increased resources with much greater cost-effectiveness.

Strategic implications

What are the strategic implications of a program for housing decommodification in the U.S. today, given current political and economic conditions?

Certainly, the experience of other modern Western industrial societies suggests that many of these proposals can be quite compatible with a private market economy, at least under some historical circumstances. Strict rent controls, for instance, have appeared as a feature of the private housing market in virtually every Western European country since World War II, in some cases since World War I. England and West Germany both have more than 30 per cent of their housing stock outside the private, profit-oriented sector, under government or non-profit ownership. Significant construction has been done by the public sector in England; controls over land use in France are virtually all-inclusive in key development areas. The share of the public budget allocated to housing is from two to five times higher in Western Europe than in the U.S., and even residential investment as a percentage of GNP is considerably higher (6.4 per cent in West Germany and 7 per cent in France, as compared to 4.4 per cent in the U.S., between 1970–8; U.N., Economic Commission for Europe, various years).

Yet in the U.S. context today, any major effort to reduce opportunities for private profit in housing development, ownership, and finance, and the tax reforms and income redistribution required to accomplish it, may well require far-reaching political and economic change. The pursuit of a progressive housing program is likely to challenge deep-seated ideological buttresses to the established system. In the context of the current capital accumulation crisis, the stakes (on both sides) are even higher. A program for housing decommodification can therefore become a critical element in the development of a broad-based movement for increased social control over investment and production in the society as a whole. For this reason, the program should not be viewed primarily as a legislative platform (although legislation may be based on it), but as a *political* program strategically linked to organizing efforts for progressive change.

Thus, progressive housing strategies should address immediate organizing (as well as housing) needs and should be relevant to ongoing organizing agendas. But they should also help to reveal the systemic nature of the housing crisis, and the possibility of an alternative approach. Finally, progressive housing strategies should help to unite diverse constituencies within the housing sector (such as lower-income tenants and homeowners) and should offer the potential for promoting coalitions between organized housing consumers and other progressive groups. Some examples are suggested below.

Social ownership: One possible application of the program would involve the broadening of local tenant organizing efforts into more affirmative struggles for social ownership. Campaigns for increasingly strict control of rents, evictions, ownership conversion, speculation, and occupancy conditions in private rental housing could be coupled with the development of programs for public takeover of buildings in non-compliance with this regulatory scheme, as a first step towards social ownership. The burgeoning squatters' movement in cities that have already acquired a substantial inventory of abandoned, tax-title buildings could go beyond its current focus on individual "self-help" and homeownership to provide new models of non-speculative public, community, and collective ownership (or ownership by individual residents with appropriate equity and resale controls). Block grant, Urban Development Action Grant (UDAG), rental assistance, or other funds could be targeted to these properties for rehabilitation and operating subsidies.

Relatedly, tenants in privately owned, federally subsidized housing that is in various stages of mortgage default, assignment, or foreclosure could demand a write-down (or long-term deferral) of the properties' outstanding mortgage debt and conversion of the housing to social ownership. This is contrary to HUD's current policy of remortgaging and/or selling these properties to the highest bidder, often without subsidies. Rehabilitation could be financed debt-free by tapping the FHA mortgage insurance funds (financed in turn by mortgagor contributions and off-budget Treasury appropriations), and available rental assistance subsidies could also be provided. In this way, a growing portion of the existing private rental stock could be converted to permanently debt-free social housing that is relatively affordable and in good condition.

At the same time, any effort to increase social ownership should involve major local and national campaigns to defend existing public housing, by organizing against rent increases, maintenance and service cutbacks, and plans for private resale or demolition. These efforts should be coupled with affirmative programs for a rent policy based on true ability to pay, adequate and permanent operating subsidies, modernization funds, and increased resident control of management.

Neighborhood control: In the neighborhoods, anti-displacement activities involving both tenants and homeowners can be broadened to address the need for social control over private investment decisions. Thus, local groups can demand that developers of downtown office buildings, or institutions expanding into lower-income neighborhoods, provide a specified number of jobs and/or housing units for lower-income and minority residents, to compensate for the direct or indirect social cost of such ventures. The same concept of "inclusionary development," discussed in greater detail in Paul Davidoff's chapter in this volume, is applicable where the developer receives public benefits (such as zoning variances, property tax breaks, UDAG grants, or even building permits). A portion of the development profits, tax increment, UDAG loan pay-backs, equity syndication proceeds, or other revenues generated by these ventures could also be allocated directly to public entities or community-based groups to finance neighborhood projects, housing, or services in the impact area.

Campaigns to restore public services and jobs for public employees can be linked with demands for higher or additional taxes on new hotels, offices, and shopping centers, or on the profits of condominium conversion or real estate speculation. Finally, neighborhood groups can demand compensation (reparations) from business to offset the adverse impact of plant closings or new development on their communities (e.g., in the form of emergency housing assistance funds or grants for the production of new, lower-income housing). These strategies offer the potential for alliances with progressive workplace organizations, or with groups opposing public service cutbacks.

Resource allocation: Finally, efforts to oppose federal budget cuts for housing can be tied to demands for a re-allocation of government spending priorities, elimination of regressive housing tax expenditures, and large-scale progressive tax reform. And alternative programs for housing production, finance, and ownership can be devised to show how the increased funds might be used in a progressive way. For example, the elimination of 100 B–1 bombers from the military budget would generate $28 billion for the construction of over 500,000 new housing units through direct government spending for (debt-free) social ownership. The elimination of housing-related tax expenditures for high-income investors and homeowners with incomes over $50,000 could provide about $15 billion for rental assistance to tenants in socially owned housing, to reduce shelter costs to more affordable levels. An additional 10 per cent tax on corporate after-tax profits could add another $12 billion for neighborhood improvements (more than three times existing outlays for the entire Community Development Block Grant program). These campaigns should, of course, be linked with the efforts of other progressive groups to restore social spending and oppose U.S. militarism, at home and abroad.

In these ways, hopefully, programs and strategies to challenge the commodity nature of housing and solve our housing problems can become part of the solution to the problems of our economy and society as a whole.

Notes

1 The median value of all homes – as opposed to the median price of all homes sold in a given year – rose at an even higher rate from 1970 to 1980 (see Cushing Dolbeare's chapter in this volume).
2 Excludes units with only fireplaces, stoves, portable heaters, or room heaters without flue or vent.
3 The terms adopted in the text stem from an extensive literature (and debate) about the role of the state, which has been very fruitful in

many areas. (For a more detailed discussion of their application, see Marcuse, 1978 and 1980.)

4 We gratefully acknowledge the prior work of Chester Hartman and Michael Stone (Hartman and Stone, 1980), and of the Boston Urban Analysis Group (Louise Elving, Kathy Gannett, John Grady, Marie Kennedy, Kathy McAfee, and Michael Stone) in which co-author Emily Achtenberg participated, in conceptualizing many ideas developed in this program.

Appendix: Housing action resources

The consolidated References which follow this Appendix offer a guide to important background readings and data sources that underlie the analyses and proposals put forth by the contributors to this volume. For readers interested as well in activist organizations working for progressive housing reform, the following listing is offered:

ASSOCIATION OF COMMUNITY ORGANIZATIONS FOR REFORM NOW (most commonly known by the acronym ACORN), 413 8th Street S.E., Washington, D.C. 20003, 202/547–9292. A neighborhood-based organization of low- and moderate-income people with chapters in twenty-six states. Their major housing activity has been a squatters' campaign, seizing abandoned buildings in a dozen cities to dramatize the housing crisis. They also have worked on homesteading, public housing, and mortgage foreclosure issues. Publishes the quarterly newspaper *USA* and (irregularly) *The Organizer*.

CENTER FOR COMMUNITY CHANGE, 1000 Wisconsin Avenue N.W., Washington, D.C. 20007, 202/338–6310. Provides technical assistance, monitoring functions, and publications on a variety of community development and housing issues.

CENTER FOR METROPOLITAN ACTION (formerly Suburban Action Institute and Metropolitan Action Institute), Queens College, Flushing, New York 11367, 212/544–6166. An advocacy planning and research organization which works to expand metropolitan housing and job opportunities for lower-income and minority households and against displacement in cities. Also engages in litigation against restrictive zoning practices. Publishes the monthly newsletter *Inclusion*.

CITIZEN ACTION, 1501 Euclid Avenue, No. 500, Cleveland, Ohio 44115, 216/861–5200. A national federation of ten statewide multi-issue groups (Massachusetts Fair Share, Virginia Action, Connecticut Citizen Action Group, Ohio Public Interest Campaign, Oregon Fair Share, etc.). Its member groups organize campaigns on "redlining," displacement, foreclosure, neighborhood crime, arson, and related issues. Publishes the quarterly *Citizen Action News*.

COALITION FOR THE HOMELESS, 105 E. 22nd Street, New York City, New York 10010, 212/460–8110. National advocacy group for the homeless, representing forty local and regional groups. Assists in litigation, establishment of care facilities, and publicity around the issue of homelessness. Publishes the bi-monthly newsletter *Safety Network*.

CONFERENCE ON ALTERNATIVE STATE AND LOCAL POLICIES, 2000 Florida Avenue N.W., Washington, D.C. 20009, 202/387–6030. Provides resources to progressive state and local officials; publishes useful studies and reports, including many dealing with housing.

HOUSING ASSISTANCE COUNCIL, 1025 Vermont Avenue N.W., No. 606, Washington, D.C. 20005, 202/842–8600. Provides technical assistance to local non-profit organizations and public agencies to develop low-income housing; has a revolving seed money loan fund for rural housing development; undertakes research on rural housing; publishes analyses of rural housing issues, including the bi-weekly *HAC News.*

INSTITUTE FOR COMMUNITY ECONOMICS, 151 Montague City Road, Greenfield, Massachusetts 01301, 413/ 774–5933. Provides technical, financial, and construction assistance to community land trusts and other community development efforts.

LOW INCOME HOUSING INFORMATION SERVICE, 323 8th Street N.E., Washington, D.C. 20002, 202/544–2544. Formed to educate the public and low-income housing groups about low-income housing needs, programs, proposals, legislation, and administrative actions. Publishes the *Low Income Housing Round-Up* (twice monthly when Congress is in session, monthly during recesses) and occasional *Special Memoranda.*

NATIONAL ASSOCIATION OF HOUSING COOPER-ATIVES, 2501 M Street N.W., No. 451, Washington, D.C. 20037, 202/887–0706. An organization of housing cooperatives, regional cooperative housing associations, non-profit and public organizations, and cooperative professionals. Publishes a bi-monthly newsletter.

NATIONAL COMMITTEE AGAINST DISCRIMINA-TION IN HOUSING, 1425 H Street N.W., No. 410, Washington, D.C. 20005, 202/783–8150. A fair housing advocacy organization, with over seventy affiliates. Has a litigation program, carries out research into extent and causes of housing discrimination, provides technical assistance to state and local public and private fair housing organizations. Publishes bi-monthly *Trends in Housing.*

NATIONAL HOUSING LAW PROJECT, 1950 Addison Street, Berkeley, California 94704, 415/548–9400. A Legal Services national support center. Publishes many handbooks and the bi-monthly *Housing Law Bulletin.*

NATIONAL LOW INCOME HOUSING COALITION, 323 8th Street N.E., Washington, D.C. 20002, 202/544–2544. The principal national lobbying group for low-income housing legislation. Membership embraces a wide range of consumer and producer groups.

NATIONAL PEOPLE'S ACTION, 954 W. Washington Boulevard, Chicago, Illinois 60607, 312/243–3038. A grass-roots organization that mobilizes people around a variety of housing-related (and other) issues, including mortgage and insurance "redlining" and lending practices generally, heating oil and natural gas prices, HUD policies, and misuse of Community Development Block Grant funds.

NATIONAL RURAL HOUSING COALITION, 1016 16th Street. N.W., No. 8G, Washington, D.C. 20036, 202/775–0046. Advocates for decent housing for rural Americans; provides information on rural housing and community development programs to members of Congress and the public. Publishes a bi-weekly *Legislative Update.*

NATIONAL TENANTS ORGANIZATION, P.O. Box 208, Parksville, New York 12768, 914/292–6264. An organization primarily of local public housing and subsidized private housing tenant groups that works for tenants' rights and progressive reform in national, state, and local housing legislation and program administration.

NATIONAL TENANTS UNION, 380 Main Street, East Orange, New Jersey 07018, 201/678–6778. Holds annual conventions and functions on local, state, regional, and national levels to coordinate actions of local tenant organizations. Publishes the quarterly *NTU News.*

NATIONAL TRAINING AND INFORMATION CENTER, 954 W. Washington Boulevard, Chicago, Illinois 60607, 312/243–3035. Carries out research and provides technical assistance on housing issues. Part of a national urban neighborhood investment program with Aetna Life and Casualty in nine neighborhoods in six cities. Publishes *Disclosure*, a newspaper appearing nine times a year.

PLANNERS NETWORK, 1901 Que Street N.W., Washington, D.C. 20009, 202/234–9382. A national organization of progressive urban and rural planners, organizers, and academics. Publishes a bi-monthly *Newsletter*, containing useful resources and references, and carries out housing-related research and advocacy projects.

RURAL AMERICA, 1900 M Street N.W., No. 320, Washington, D.C. 20036, 202/659–2800. A national membership organization (founded as the Rural Housing Alliance) for rural and small town people. Involved in self-help, farmworker, and low-income housing. Manages revolving loan fund for low-income rural housing development. Publishes handbooks on self-help and cooperative housing. Midwest (Iowa) office involved in fighting farm foreclosures. Publishes the bi-monthly *ruralamerica*.

SHELTERFORCE, 380 Main Street, East Orange, New Jersey 07018, 201/678–5353. A national housing resource center dealing with landlord-tenant law, housing policy, organizing strategies, and legal developments. Provides resources to local housing groups, including training and videotapes. Publishes the quarterly newspaper *Shelterforce*.

References

Abrams, Philip (1983), "Comment on 'Housing Allowances: A Critical Look,' " *Journal of Urban Affairs*, 5, 2, Spring.

Alford, Robert and Scoble, H. M. (1968), "Sources of Local Political Involvement," *American Political Science Review*, 62, pp. 1192–1206.

Andreassi, Michael W., MacRae, C. Duncan, and Rosenbaum, David I. (1980), *Metropolitan Housing and the Income Tax: Stack Algorithm Sensitivity Analysis*, February, Washington, D.C., Urban Institute.

Atlas, John and Dreier, Peter (1980), "The Housing Crisis and the Tenants' Revolt," *Social Policy*, 10, 4, January-February, pp. 13–24.

Baar, Kenneth K. (1977), "Rent Control in the 1970's: The Case of the New Jersey Tenants' Movement," *Hastings Law Journal*, 28, pp. 631–83.

Baxter, Ellen and Hopper, Kim (1981), *Private Lives, Public Spaces*, New York, Community Service Society.

Bell, Daniel (1976), *The Cultural Contradictions of Capitalism*, New York, Basic Books.

Blumberg, Richard and Grow, James R. (1978), *The Rights of Tenants*, New York, Avon Books.

Borgos, Seth (forthcoming), "Squatting in the United States: A Review of Recent History," in forthcoming collection cited in note 2 to Hartman chapter of this volume.

Boston Globe (1982), "Condominium Buyers the Economic Elite," June 20.

Bourdon, E. Richard (1980), "Condominium Conversions: Possible Changes in Federal Tax Laws to Discourage Conversions and Assist Rental Housing," Congressional Research Service, Report No. 80–71 E., April.

Boyte, Harry (1980), *The Backyard Revolution*, Philadelphia, Pa., Temple University Press.

Brodsky, Barry (1975), "Tenants First: FHA Tenants Organize in Massachusetts," *Radical America*, 9, March-April, pp. 37–48.

Brooks, Andree (1982), "Foreclosing on a Dream," *New York Times Magazine*, September 12.

Bureau of National Affairs (1983), *Housing and Development Reporter*, 10, 42, March 14.

Burnham, Walter Dean (1980), "The Appearance and Disappearance of the American Voter," in Richard Rose (ed.), *Political Participation*, London, Sage.

Business Week (1981a), "America's New Immobile Society," July 27.

Business Week (1981b), "Housing's Storm: The Squeeze on Builders, Lenders and Buyers," September 7.

Business Week (1981c), "A Radical City Council Has Business Fuming," October 26.

Carlson, Richard, Landfield, Richard, and Loken, James (1965), "Enforcement of Municipal Housing Codes," *Harvard Law Review*, 78.

Carnoy, Martin and Shearer, Derek (1980), *Economic Democracy*, White Plains, N.Y., M. E. Sharpe.

Carron, Andrew (1982), *The Plight of the Thrift Industry*, Washington, D.C., The Brookings Institution.

Checkoway, Barry (1980), "Large Builders, Federal Housing Programmes, and Postwar Suburbanization," *International Journal of Urban and Regional Research*, 4, pp. 21–45.

Cliffe, Chip (1982), "Seniors and Tenants: Decent Housing for Everyone," *Shelterforce,* 7, pp. 8–9.

Clymer, Adam (1983), "Spending in Congressional Races in '82 Was a Record $314 Million," *New York Times*, January 11.

Cummings, Judith (1982), "Increase in Homeless People Tests U.S. Cities' Will to Cope," *New York Times*, May 3.

Donohue, Joseph J. (1982), "Interest Rate Pressure on the First-Time Homebuyer: The Affordability Question," *Mortgage Banking*, 42, May, pp. 10–17.

Downs, Anthony (1980), "Too Much Capital for Housing?", *The Brookings Bulletin,* 17, Summer, pp. 1–5.

Dreier, Peter (1979), "The Politics of Rent Control," *Working Papers*, 6, April, pp. 55–63.

Dreier, Peter (1982a), "The Housing Crisis: Dreams and Nightmares," *The Nation* August 21, pp. 141–4.

Dreier, Peter (1982b), " 'Rent-a-Politician' Exposed," *Shelterforce*, 7, pp. 3–4.

Dreier, Peter and Atlas, John (1981), "Condomania," *The Progressive*, March, pp. 19–22.

Fellman, Gordon (1973), *The Deceived Majority*, New Brunswick, N.J., Transaction Books.

Fish, John (1973), *Black Power/White Control*, Princeton University Press.

Fredland, Daniel R. (1974), *Residential Mobility and Home Purchase*, Lexington, Mass., Lexington Books.

Fried, Marc (1973), *The World of the Urban Working Class*, Cambridge, Mass., Harvard University Press.

Frieden, Bernard J. and Solomon, Arthur P. (1977), *The Nation's Housing: 1975 to 1985*, Cambridge, Mass., Joint Center for Urban Studies.

Gans, Herbert (1962), *The Urban Villagers*, Glencoe, Ill., Free Press.

Gans, Herbert (1982), *The Urban Villagers* (rev. ed.), New York, Free Press.

Goetze, Rolf (1981), "The Housing Bubble," *Working Papers*, January-February, pp. 44–52.

Goodman, John L. (1978), *Urban Residential Mobility: Places, People and Policy*, Washington, D.C., Urban Institute.

Goodwyn, Lawrence (1978), *The Populist Movement: A Short History of the Agrarian Revolt in America*, New York, Oxford University Press.

Grad, Frank (1968), *Legal Remedies for Housing Code Violations*, Research Report No. 14 to the National Commission on Urban Problems, Washington, D.C., U.S. Government Printing Office.

Greer, Edward (1979), *Big Steel*, New York, Monthly Review Press.

Gribetz, Judah and Grad, Frank (1966), "Housing Code Enforcement: Sanctions and Remedies," *Columbia Law Review*, 66, pp. 1254–90.

Gulino, Denis (1983), "Mortgage Delinquency Rate Surges," *Washington Post*, March 29.

References

..., Chester (1975), *Housing and Social Policy*, Englewood Cliffs, N.J., Prentice-Hall.

Hartman, Chester (1979), "Landlord Money Defeats Rent Control in San Francisco," *Shelterforce*, 5, Fall, p. 3.

Hartman, Chester (1982a), "Housing," in Alan Gartner, Colin Greer, and Frank Riessman (eds.), *What Reagan Is Doing to Us*, New York, Harper & Row, pp. 141–61.

Hartman, Chester (1982b), "Housing Allowances: A Bad Idea Whose Time Has Come," *Working Papers*, November-December, pp. 55–8.

Hartman, Chester (1983a), review of *The Report of the President's Commission on Housing, Journal of the American Planning Association*, Winter, pp. 92–4.

Hartman, Chester (1983b), "Housing Allowances: A Critical Look," *Journal of Urban Affairs*, 5, 1, Winter, pp. 41–55.

Hartman, Chester (1983c), "Rejoinder" (to "Comment on 'Housing Allowances: A Critical Look,' " by Philip Abrams), *Journal of Urban Affairs*, 5, 2, Spring.

Hartman, Chester (forthcoming), "The Right to Stay Put," in Charles Geisler and Frank Popper (eds.), *Land Reform, American Style*, Totowa, N. J., Littlefield, Adams.

Hartman, Chester, Keating, Dennis, and LeGates, Richard (1982), *Displacement: How to Fight It*, Berkeley, Ca., National Housing Law Project.

Hartman, Chester, Kessler, Robert, and LeGates, Richard (1974), "Municipal Housing Code Enforcement and Low Income Tenants," *Journal of the American Institute of Planners*, 40, pp. 90–104.

Hartman, Chester and Stone, Michael E. (1978), "Housing: A Radical Alternative," in Marcus Raskin (ed.), *The Federal Budget and Social Reconstruction*, New Brunswick, N.J., Transaction Books, pp. 205–48.

Hartman, Chester and Stone, Michael E. (1980), "A Socialist Housing Program for the United States," in Pierre Clavel, John Forester, and William W. Goldsmith (eds.), *Urban and Regional Planning in an Age of Austerity*, Elmsford, N.Y., Pergamon, pp. 219–41.

Hellmuth, William F. (1977), "Homeowner Preferences," in Joseph A. Pechman, *Comprehensive Income Taxation*, Washington, D.C., Brookings Institution.

Hendershott, Patric and Shilling, James (1980), "The Economics of Tenure Choice: 1955–1979," Working Paper No. 243, Cambridge, Mass., National Bureau of Economic Research.

Herman, Robin (1981), "City Planning to Expand Use of Armories to House Homeless," *New York Times*, December 1.

Heskin, Allan David (1981), "The History of Tenants in the United States: Struggle and Ideology," *International Journal of Urban and Regional Research, Housing: Special Issue*, 5, 2, pp. 178–204.

Hombs, Mary Ellen and Snyder, Mitch (1982), *Homelessness in America: A Forced March to Nowhere*, Washington, D.C., Community for Creative Non-Violence.

Husock, Howard (1981), "The High Cost of Starting Out," *New York Times Magazine*, June 7.

Jobs With Peace (nd [1983]), *Housing & Jobs: A Blueprint for Survival*, Boston, Jobs With Peace.

Krohn, Roger and Tiller, Ralph (1969), "Landlord-Tenant Relations in a Declining Montreal Neighborhood," *Sociological Review Monographs*, 14, pp. 5–32.

Lawson, Ronald (1980a), "The Political Face of the Real Estate Industry in New York City," *New York Affairs*, 6, April, pp. 88–109.

Lawson, Ronald (1980b), "Tenant Mobilization in New York," *Social Policy*, 10, March, pp. 30–40.

Lawson, Ronald and Barton, Stephen E. (1980), "Sex Roles in Social Movements: A Case Study of the Tenant Movement in New York City," *Signs*, 6, Winter, pp. 230–47.

Lebowitz, Neil H. (1981), " 'Above Party, Class or Creed': Rent Control in the United States, 1940–47," *Journal of Urban History*, 7, pp. 439–70.

LeGates, Richard and Hartman, Chester (1981), "Displacement," *Clearinghouse Review*, 15, July, pp. 207–49.

Lilley, William III (1980), "The Homebuilders' Lobby," in Jon Pynoos, Robert Schafer and Chester Hartman (eds.), New York, Aldine, pp. 30–48; first published as "Washington Pressures/Homebuilders' Lobbying Skills Result in Successes, 'Good Guy Image,' " *National Journal*, February 27, 1971, pp. 431–45.

Lindsey, Robert (1981), "Housing Costs Are Turning Off Flow of Americans to California," *New York Times*, December 31.

Lipsky, Michael (1970), *Protest in City Politics*, Chicago, Rand McNally.

Low Income Housing Information Service (1982), "The Reagan Budget and Low Income Housing," Special Memorandum No. 15, February 15.

Low Income Housing Information Service (1983), "The 1984 Reagan Budget and Low Income Housing," Special Memorandum No. 18, February.

Lubove, Roy (1962), *The Progressives and the Slums*, University of Pittsburgh Press.

Marcuse, Peter (1971), "Goals and Limitations: The Rise of Tenant Organizations," *The Nation*, July 19, pp. 50–3.

Marcuse, Peter (1978), "The Myth of the Benevolent State," *Social Policy*, 8, January-February, pp. 21–6.

Marcuse, Peter (1979a), *Rental Housing in the City of New York, Supply and Condition, 1975–78*, New York City Department of Housing Preservation and Development.

Marcuse, Peter (1979b), "The Deceptive Consensus on Redlining," *Journal of the American Planning Association*, 45, 4, October, pp. 549–56.

Marcuse, Peter (1980), *The Determinants of Housing Policy*, Papers in Planning 22, New York, Columbia University, Graduate School of Architecture and Planning.

Marcuse, Peter (1981), *Housing Abandonment: Does Rent Control Make a Difference?*, Washington, D.C., Conference on Alternative State and Local Policies.

Marcuse, Peter (1982), "Determinants of State Housing Policies: West Germany and the United States," in Norman S. and Susan Fainstein (eds.) *Urban Policy Under Capitalism*, Beverly Hills, Ca., Sage, pp. 83–118.

Mariano, Ann (1983), "Home Foreclosures Jump Sharply," *Washington Post*, February 24.

Morrow, Lance (1981), "Downsizing the American Dream," *Time*, October 5.

National Commission on Urban Problems (1969), *Housing Code Standards: Three Critical Studies*, Research Report No. 19, Washington, D.C., U.S. Government Printing Office.

National Housing Law Project (1981), *HUD Housing Programs: Tenants' Rights,* Berkeley, Ca., National Housing Law Project.

National Housing Law Project (1982), *FmHA Housing Programs: Tenants' and Purchasers' Rights*, Berkeley, Ca., National Housing Law Project.

National Multi-Housing Council (1981a), "The Rent Law and

Legislative Activities Affecting Condominium and Cooperative Housing," Washington, D.C., National Multi-Housing Council.

National Multi-Housing Council (1981b), "The Spread of Rent Control," Washington, D.C., National Multi-Housing Council.

Neutze, Max (1968), *The Suburban Apartment Boom*, Baltimore, Md., Johns Hopkins University Press.

Newfield, Jack and DuBrul, Paul (1977), *The Abuse of Power*, New York, Viking.

New York Times (1981), "Pact Requires City to Shelter Homeless Men," August 27.

New York Times (1983a), "Farmers Are Dispersed by Gas in Sale Protest" (Springfield, Colorado), January 5.

New York Times (1983b), "Equality in Shelters," February 9.

New York Times (1983c), "Sheriff Turns to Court to Stop Foreclosures" (Youngstown, Ohio), February 27.

Norman, Michael (1982), "Interview with George Sternlieb on Rental Housing," *New York Times*, April 4.

Offe, Claus (1975), "The Theory of the Capitalist State and the Problem of Policy Formation," in Leon N. Lindberg (ed.), *Stress and Contradiction in Modern Capitalism: Public Policy and the Theory of the State*, Lexington, Mass., Lexington Books, pp. 125–44.

Pearce, Diana (1979), "Gatekeepers and Housekeepers: Institutional Patterns in Racial Steering," *Social Problems*, 26, pp. 323–42.

Peterson, George (1977). "Federal Tax Policy and Urban Development," Testimony before Subcommittee on the City of the House Banking Committee, June 16.

Peterson, Norma (1982), "Is the Rebellion Over? Adult Children – by the Thousands – Are Moving Home Again," *Parade*, January 31.

Piven, Frances Fox and Cloward, Richard (1982), *The New Class War*, New York, Pantheon.

Richard, Ray (1982), "Adult Children Returning Home to Live," *Boston Globe*, April 23.

Robbins, William (1983), "Pittsburgh Homeowners Given a Reprieve in a Rising Flood of Foreclosures," *New York Times*, January 9.

Rose, Jerome (1973), *Landlords and Tenants*, New Brunswick, N.J., Transaction Books.

Rossi, Peter (1955), *Why Families Move*, Glencoe, Ill., Free Press.

Rothblatt, Donald, Garr, Daniel J., and Sprague, Jo (1979), *The Suburban Environment and Women*, New York, Praeger.

Rousseau, Ann Marie (1981), *Shopping Bag Ladies*, New York, Pilgrim Press.

Rule, Sheila (1983a), "New York is Facing a Lawsuit on Care of Homeless Families," *New York Times*, March 31.

Rule, Sheila (1983b), "Meeting Housing Needs for Homeless Families," *New York Times*, April 1.

Rule, Sheila (1983c), "17,000 Families in Public Housing Double Up Illegally, City Believes," *New York Times*, April 21.

Ryan, Bill (1982), "Our Incredible Shrinking Houses: What They Have Been Doing to Our Homes to Save Space, Energy and Dollars," *Parade*, March 28.

Saegert, Susan (1981), "Masculine Cities and Feminine Suburbs: Polarized Ideas, Contradictory Realities," in Catherine Stimson et al. (eds.), *Women and the American City*, University of Chicago Press, pp. 93–108.

Schafer, Robert (1974), *The Suburbanization of Multifamily Housing*, Lexington, Mass., Lexington Books.

Schur, Robert (1980), "Growing Lemons in the Bronx," *Working Papers*, 8, July-August, pp. 42–51.

Shearer, Derek (1982), "How Progressives Won in Santa Monica," *Social Policy*, 12, pp. 7–14.

Shribman, David (1983), "How the Bankers Lobby on Withholding Issue," *New York Times*, April 8.

Solomon, Arthur P. (1981), "Flawed Analyses of Market Trends Fuel Assaults on Housing Expenditures," *Journal of Housing*, April, pp. 194–200.

Starr, Paul and Esping-Anderson, Gosta (1979), "Passive Intervention," *Working Papers*, 7, July-August.

Starr, Roger (1979), "An End to Rental Housing?", *The Public Interest*, Fall, pp. 25–38.

Stegman, Michael (1982), *The Dynamics of Rental Housing in New York City*, New York City Department of Housing Preservation and Development.

Sternlieb, George (1966), *The Tenement Landlord*, New Brunswick, N.J., Rutgers University Press.

Sternlieb, George and Burchell, Robert (1973), *Residential Abandonment: The Tenement Landlord Revisited*, New Brunswick, N.J., Rutgers University, Center for Urban Policy Research.

Sternlieb, George and Hughes, James W. (1980), *America's Hous-*

ing: Prospects and Problems, New Brunswick, N.J., Rutgers University, Center for Urban Policy Research.

Stone, Michael E. (1978), "Housing, Mortgage Lending, and the Contradictions of Capitalism," in William Tabb and Larry Sawers (eds.), *Marxism and the Metropolis*, New York, Oxford University Press, pp. 179–207.

Stone, Michael E. (1980a), "The Housing Problem in the United States: Origins and Prospects," *Socialist Review*, 52, July-August, pp. 65–119.

Stone, Michael E. (1980b), "Housing and the American Economy: A Marxist Analysis," in Pierre Clavel, John Forester, and William Goldsmith (eds.), *Urban and Regional Planning in an Age of Austerity*, Elmsford, N.Y., Pergamon, pp. 81–108.

Stone, Michael E. (forthcoming), *Shelter Poverty: New Ideas on Housing Affordability*, Albany, State University of New York Press.

Stone, Michael E. and Achtenberg, Emily (1977), "Hostage: Housing and the Massachusetts Fiscal Crisis," Boston, Mass., Boston Community School.

Struyk, Raymond J., Tuccillo, John A., and Zais, James P. (1982), "Housing and Community Development," in John L. Palmer and Isabel V. Sawhill (eds.), *The Reagan Experiment*, Washington, D.C., Urban Institute Press, pp. 393–417.

Suburban Action Institute (nd [1979]), *Housing Choice: A Handbook for Suburban Officials, Non-Profit Organizations, Community Groups, and Consumers*, New York, Suburban Action Institute.

Taeuber, Karl (1975), "Racial Segregation: The Persisting Dilemma," *Annals of the American Academy of Political and Social Science*, 87.

Teeley, Sandra Evans (1981), "Home Mortgage Default Rate at Record High," *Washington Post*, December 14.

United Nations, Economic Commission for Europe (various years), *Annual Bulletins of Housing and Building Statistics for Europe*, Geneva.

U.S. Bureau of the Census (1972), *Census of Housing: 1970, Metropolitan Housing Characteristics, U.S. and Regions*, Report HC(2)-1, Washington, D.C., U.S. Government Printing Office.

U.S. Bureau of the Census (1976a), *Historical Statistics of the United States, Colonial Times to 1970*, Bicentennial Edition, Washington, D.C., U.S. Government Printing Office.

U.S. Bureau of the Census (1976b), *Statistical Abstract of the United States: 1976,* Washington, D.C., U.S. Government Printing Office.

U.S. Bureau of the Census (1979), *Voting and Registration in the Election of November 1978,* Washington, D.C., U.S. Government Printing Office.

U.S. Bureau of the Census (1981a), *Current Housing Reports, Annual Housing Survey: 1980, Part C, Financial Characteristics of the Housing Inventory, U.S. and Regions,* Series H 150–80, Washington, D.C., U.S. Government Printing Office.

U.S. Bureau of the Census (1981b), *Current Population Reports,* Series P–60, No. 134, Washington, D.C., U.S. Government Printing Office.

U.S. Bureau of the Census (1981c), *Statistical Abstract of the United States,* Washington, D.C., U.S. Government Printing Office.

U.S. Bureau of the Census (1982a), *Current Housing Reports, Annual Housing Survey: 1979, Part B, Indicators of Housing and Neighborhood Quality by Financial Characteristics, U.S. and Regions,* Series H 150–79, Washington, D.C., U.S. Government Printing Office.

U.S. Bureau of the Census (1982b), *Current Housing Reports, Annual Housing Survey: 1980, Part A, General Housing Characteristics, U.S. and Regions,* Series H 150–80, Washington, D.C., U.S. Government Printing Office.

U.S. Bureau of the Census (1982c), *Census of Population and Housing, Supplementary Report: Provisional Estimates of Social, Economic, and Housing Characteristics for States and Selected SMSA's,* PHC 80–S1–1, Washington, D.C., U.S. Government Printing Office.

U.S. Bureau of the Census (1983a), *Housing Starts,* Construction Reports, Series C20–83–2, February, Washington, D.C., U.S. Government Printing Office.

U.S. Bureau of the Census (1983b), *Characteristics of New Housing: 1982,* Construction Reports, Series C25, Washington, D.C., U.S. Government Printing Office.

U.S. Bureau of the Census (nd), "1980 Census Shows an Increase in Nation's Housing Costs," news release.

U.S. Commission on Civil Rights (1975), *Twenty Years After Brown: Equal Opportunity in Housing,* Washington, D.C., U.S. Government Printing Office.

U.S. Comptroller General, General Accounting Office (1972), *Enforcement of Housing Codes*, Report to the U.S. Congress, Washington, D.C., U.S. Government Printing Office.

U.S. Comptroller General, General Accounting Office (1979), *Rental Housing, A National Problem That Needs Immediate Attention*, Report to the U.S. Congress, CED–80–11, Washington, D.C., U.S. Government Printing Office.

U.S. Congressional Budget Office (1981), *The Tax Treatment of Homeownership: Issues and Options*, Washington, D.C., U.S. Government Printing Office.

U.S. Department of Housing and Urban Development (1980a), *The Conversion of Rental Housing to Condominiums and Co-operatives* (3 vols.), Washington, D.C., U.S. Government Printing Office.

U.S. Department of Housing and Urban Development (1980b), *The Supply of Mortgage Credit: 1970–79*, Washington, D.C., U.S. Government Printing Office.

U.S. Department of Housing and Urban Development (1981a), Office of Policy Development and Research, *Residential Displacement – An Update*, Report to the U.S. Congress, Washington, D.C., U.S. Government Printing Office.

U.S. Department of Housing and Urban Development (1981b), "Survey of Mortgage Lending Activity 1980", news release, March 20, HUD No. 81–65, Washington, D.C., U.S. Government Printing Office.

U.S. Department of Housing and Urban Development (1982), Office of Policy Development and Research, *Recent Evidence on the Cost of Housing Subsidy Programs*, October, Washington, D.C., U.S. Government Printing Office.

U.S. Department of Housing and Urban Development, U.S. Department of Justice, and the Office of Economic Opportunity (1967), *Tenants' Rights: Legal Tools for Better Housing*. Report on a National Conference on Legal Rights of Tenants, Washington, D.C., U.S. Government Printing Office..

U.S. Department of Labor, Bureau of Labor Statistics (1966), *Differences in the Characteristics of Rental Housing Occupied by Families in Three Income Ranges Paying Approximately the Same in Six Cities*, Washington, D.C., U.S. Government Printing Office.

U.S. Department of Labor, Bureau of Labor Statistics (1967), *City Worker's Family Budget for a Moderate Standard of Living*,

Autumn 1966, Bulletin 1570-1, Washington, D.C., U.S. Government Printing Office.

U.S. Department of Labor, Bureau of Labor Statistics (1982), "The Employment Situation: November, 1982," Release No. 82-454, December 3.

U.S. House of Representatives, Subcommittee on Housing and Community Development (1982), "Homelessness in America," Series No. 97-100, Hearings, December 15, Washington, D.C., U.S. Government Printing Office..

U.S. League of Savings Associations (1978a), *Homeownership: Realizing the American Dream*, Chicago, U.S. League of Savings Associations.

U.S. League of Savings Associations (1978b). *Homeownership: Affording the Single-Family Home*, Chicago, U.S. League of Savings Associations.

U.S. League of Savings Associations (1980), *Homeownership: Coping with Inflation,* Chicago, U.S. League of Savings Associations.

U.S. League of Savings Associations (1982), *Homeownership: The American Dream Adrift*, Chicago, U.S. League of Savings Associations.

U.S. Office of Management and Budget (1982), "Special Analysis G: Tax Expenditures," Washington, D.C., U.S. Government Printing Office.

U.S. President's Commission on Housing (1982), *Report of the President's Commission on Housing*, Washington, D.C., U.S. Government Printing Office.

Urban Planning Aid (1973), *Less Rent, More Control: A Tenant's Guide to Rent Control in Masssachusetts*, Cambridge, Mass., Urban Planning Aid.

Vaughan, Ted R. (1968), "Landlord-Tenant Relations in a Low-Income Area," *Social Problems,* 16, Fall, pp. 208-18.

Warner, Sam Bass (1972), *The Urban Wilderness*, New York, Harper & Row.

Washington Post (1983a), "Va. Foreclosure Halted: FmHA Faces Lawsuit," March 26.

Washington Post (1983b), "Jake Garn Makes a Lot from Speeches," May 8.

Weinbaum, Batya and Bridges, Amy (1976), "The Other Side of the Paycheck," *Monthly Review*, 28, July-August, pp. 88-103.

Williams, Joan (1981), "It's High Time to Get Homeowners' Deductions Under Control," *Tax Notes*, May 4, pp. 963–70.

Williams, Winston (1981), "Mortgage Defaults Increase," *New York Times*, October 20.

Winerip, Michael (1983), "Married Couples Squeezing Into Parents' Homes," *New York Times*, February 24.

Wolfe, Alan (1981), *America's Impasse*, New York, Pantheon.

Wolman, Harold (1971), *Politics of Federal Housing*, New York, Dodd, Mead.

Yinger, John (1978), "The Black-White Price Differential in Housing," *Land Economics*, 54, pp. 187–206.

Zais, James, Struyk, Raymond, and Thibodeau, Thomas (1982), *Housing Assistance for Older Americans*, Washington, D.C., Urban Institute Press.